A Hiking Guide to Cedar Mesa

SOUTHEAST UTAH

Pueblo III granary site

A Hiking Guide to Cedar Mesa

SOUTHEAST UTAH

Peter Francis Tassoni

The University of Utah Press

Salt Lake City

LIBRARY OF CONGRESS CATALOGING-IN-PUBLICATION DATA
Tassoni, Peter Francis, 1966-
    A hiking guide to Cedar Mesa : southeast Utah / Peter Francis Tassoni.
        p. cm.
Includes bibliographical references (p.).
    ISBN-13: 978-0-87480-680-9   ISBN-10: 0-87480-680-1
    1. Hiking—Utah—Grand Gulch Plateau—Guidebooks. 2. Utah—Grand
Gulch Plateau—Guidebooks. I. Title.
    GV199.42.U82 G728 2001
    917.92'52—dc21   00-013105

For David Brower

For all that he has accomplished in his remarkable life. May his passions not be abandoned by my X generation, but may they inspire every person, and together, may we all promote wilderness values for humanity and planet alike.

Warning!

The Canyon and surface systems of Cedar Mesa are dynamic, evolving landforms subject to equally dynamic weather. Expect changes and hazards. Ultimately your safety depends on your own judgment. Base your choices on experience, personal knowledge, a realistic assessment of your abilities, and the prevailing conditions. The information contained herein is not a substitute for your best judgment. **If you have any doubt as to your ability to hike any of the routes described in this book, do not attempt them.**

Neither the University of Utah Press nor the author is responsible for personal injury, damage to property, or violation of the law in connection with the use of this guidebook.

Any error, omissions or incorrect information contained herein are solely the responsibility of the author. Corrections for future editions are welcome.

Please send all comments and corrections to Peter Francis Tassoni, c/o The University of Utah Press, 1795 E. South Campus Drive, Suite 101, Salt Lake City, UT 84112-9402.

Contents

Maps

Preface

Who do I think I am, advertising the archaeological wonders of the Cedar Mesa area to tourists, backpackers, vandals, and looters? By what authority do I choose which sites will be visited and those that will not? Further, is a guidebook a subtle form of control? And will the promotion of the wilderness experience on Cedar Mesa contribute to its ultimate demise?

I have spent 120 days over three years field researching the contents of this book. I have been touched by this landscape and would prefer to keep its teachings and secrets to myself, but I cannot. The experience of the desert should be available to everyone with the motivation to encounter it.

There are people who discovered this land a week or a year or ten years before me who believe Cedar Mesa is their secret and now that they are aboard, the ladder should be pulled up. But the secret has been out since the Wetherills first found the wonderful artifacts left by the ancient Puebloans and shipped them to museums around the world beginning in the 1890s. Today one can find Global Positioning System coordinates to archaeological sites and petroglyph panels in four-wheel-drive magazine feature articles.

Cedar Mesa has suffered many intentional and unintentional abuses. Sightseers, day hikers, and backpackers are indeed loving it to death. Guidebook or not, more visitors are coming each year. It is my hope that this guide will promote a heightened awareness of the area's sensitive natural and cultural wonders while emphasizing each individual's responsibility to minimize the negative impacts of visitation.

It is also my hope that this book will add to the voices calling for Cedar Mesa's preservation and protection beyond what is currently in place. The increase in visitation here, and across the Colorado Plateau, speaks of a growing human need for wilderness. It needs to be there when we seek solitude in a special place. And while I do not offer this work without a good deal of consideration, I am certain that it cannot destroy Cedar Mesa.

After experiencing these remarkable archaeological sites abandoned by an ancient people, the intricate sculpture of eroded sandstone walls, and the deep silence of a desert sojourn, Cedar Mesa's visitors may become more open to life's larger meanings and less obsessed with the mundane. It is possible that the isolation and renewal of a wilderness experience can change people for the better. I hope so.

Please come with me. But please do so with respect, responsibility, and wisdom so that those who come after you will have the same privilege.

Elk Ridge highlands.

Introduction

CEDAR MESA SANDSTONE FORMS CONVOLUTED CLIFFS WITH ARCHES, natural bridges, hoodoos, spires, hat rocks, ledges, and alcoves. The Ancestral Puebloan culture flowered in this area for more than a millennium and left a legacy of stone tools; woven artifacts; ceremonial, storage, and habitation structures; irrigation and road projects; and rock art panels. Cedar Mesa is an unparalleled outdoor museum of geological features and Ancestral Puebloan culture.

I hiked extensively in the Cedar Mesa area, collecting Global Positioning System (GPS) waypoints and recording the things I saw. Later, I verified my coordinates against U.S. Geological Survey (USGS) 7.5-minute topographical maps and screened out the Bureau of Land Management class 2 and class 3 cultural sites. Then I put everything into a readable format. I consider this book a survey of recreational opportunities available in the Cedar Mesa area, not a comprehensive treatise.

Unlike nearby developed recreation areas such as Mesa Verde, Hovenweep, Chaco Canyon, and Natural Bridges, Cedar Mesa is a primitive area that requires much from those who explore it. Visitors have a responsibility to know, understand, and practice "Leave No Trace" and "Tread Lightly" ethics and skills in this delicate environment. Our treatment of this inspiring landscape will be our legacy.

Crucial to any enjoyable desert adventure is the liberal use of common sense. Please take the time to read the following sections before attempting any of the routes described herein. This guidebook does not teach judgment; it contains information to help individual readers make better decisions. Each reader ultimately controls his or her own actions. The desert is just an objective witness to our choices and their consequences. Have fun. Be careful.

Essentials for Desert Travel

2 quarts to 2 gallons of water per person per day depending on weather conditions
Appropriate topographical map(s) and compass

Toilet paper, resealable plastic bag, evaporate hand sanitizer, and
  plastic trowel
First-aid kit sufficient for your party's size
Signal mirror and pocketknife
Food
Sweater or jacket
Rain gear
Hat with a wide brim, long-sleeved shirt, sunglasses, and sunscreen
Footwear appropriate for the terrain

Ancestral Puebloan Culture

The Ancestral Puebloan culture existed in the Cedar Mesa area for
thirteen centuries and then seemingly disappeared. Today it is widely
accepted that the modern Pueblo peoples—the Hopi of northwestern
Arizona, the towns of Zuni, Acoma, and Laguna, and the communities
along the Rio Grande—are descendants of the prehistoric South-
westerners. Whether their abandonment of much of the area around
A.D. 1300 was precipitated by drought and ecological ruin or by social,
political, or religious influences remains unanswered.

The Ancestral Puebloans depended on a balance between arable soils,
an adequate growing season, and sufficient moisture to nurture crops
and sustain a domestic water supply. In many cases their abandoned
structures, artifacts, rock art, and burials indicate that they planned to
return, but they never did.

Characteristic differences in architecture, ceramics, basketry, tools,
and rock art have allowed archaeologists to construct various
chronologies for Ancestral Puebloan culture. The spiritual concepts,
however, are inferred from historic Puebloan cultures. I have provided a
brief summary, but research into the Ancestral Puebloan culture is far
too extensive for proper treatment here. Interested readers should
consult the "Suggested Reading" section.

Pecos Classification of Northern Southwest Prehistory

6500 B.C.–A.D. 1, Archaic

Subsistence on wild foods and game animals; high mobility; seasonal
cave shelters and open-hearth sites; projectile spearpoints and atlatls.

A.D. 1–450, Basketmaker II

Cultivation of corn, beans, and squash in floodplains; use of grinding slabs (metates); presence of domesticated dogs; shallow pithouses and slab-lined sandstone cists for food storage and burials; introduction of compound darts, coiled baskets, and twined bags; no pottery.

A.D. 450–750, Basketmaker III

Increased cultivation of plants; use of troughed metates and two-handed manos; domesticated turkeys; small villages with deep pithouses; use of surface storage pits, cists, and rooms with jacal-style walls; use of bow and arrow; production of plain Gray and Black-on-White ceramic wares.

A.D. 750–900, Pueblo I

Extensive cultivation of corn, squash, beans, and cotton; loom weaving; masonry techniques; habitation in large villages and unit-pueblos with Great Kivas; plain and neck-banded Gray pottery, Black-on-White and Black-on-Red ceramic wares.

A.D. 900–1150, Pueblo II

Population aggregation into unit-pueblos with Great Kivas; masonry; water control and road systems; twilled ring baskets; Corrugated Gray wares; elaborate Black-on-White ceramic wares.

A.D. 1150–1300, Pueblo III

Use of flat metates; large surface pueblos/cliff dwellings with high kiva-to-room ratios, towers, and tri-walls in defensive positions; peak of artistic and technical quality of Black-on-White, Red, and Orange wares; abandonment around A.D. 1300.

A.D. 1300–1600, Pueblo IV

Large plaza-oriented pueblos with low kiva-to-room ratios; kiva wall murals; kachina cult widespread; introduction of plain utility pottery with higher ratio of Red, Orange, and Yellow wares to older Black-on-White style.

Within the 58,000-square-mile San Juan River basin are several thousand individual archaeological sites. The maximum population

Pueblo III habitation site

estimated for Ancestral Puebloan culture was close to 40,000. Why these
people abandoned their settlements remains enigmatic, but perhaps
there is a lesson to us about the fragility of the desert landscape.

The BLM has documented 1700 Ancestral Puebloan sites in the 650
square miles of Cedar Mesa. Most of the structures date to the Pueblo
II–III periods, while the rock art panels contain images from the Late
Archaic as well as recent Navajo and Hopi figures. The Ancestral
Puebloan peoples frequently built over previous structures, hence a
Pueblo III site might still contain earlier elements. Interestingly, the
Cedar Mesa area seems to have been the western frontier for the
Northern San Juan population, which peaked during the Basketmaker II
and Pueblo III periods.

Identifying sites correctly requires detailed knowledge of
architectural techniques (material attributes, relative scale, spatial
orientation, and design features) and ceramic wares (clays, temper,
firing atmosphere, color of slip, pigment mediums, and design styles).
Provided here are only brief summaries.

The Northern San Juan region is characterized by classic cliff villages
(such as those found in Mesa Verde National Park), surface towers,
plumb walls, structures built over irregularities such as boulders, a
standardized kiva design, smoothed masonry with chinking stones, and

Black-on-White ceramic wares. Structures more often associated with the Kayenta region are also found on Comb Ridge and include rough, chipped masonry with uneven edges and copious amounts of mortar, uneven floors, noncircular kivas, and rooms with three masonry walls and a jacal entrance wall, with an attached low wall containing the deflector stone behind the door.

— Basketmaker II sites are usually identified by lithic scatters and grinding slabs but are devoid of ceramic wares or structures.

— Basketmaker III sites are usually in open places with no visible structures and contain plain Gray wares and trough metates.

— Pueblo I sites contain jacal-wall construction, and the structures are usually arranged in an arc around a proto-kiva. These sites also contain neck-banded Gray ceramic wares and Black-on-White wares.

—Pueblo II sites contain rough-surfaced masonry in adobe mortar and elaborate masonry kivas, D-shaped towers, and water-control structures. Corrugated, Gray, Black-on-White, and Red wares are all present.

— Pueblo III sites contain "dimpled" masonry stones (from being pecked smooth) set side by side, two wide, and evenly spaced, with square corners and chinking stones in the mortar layer. Ceramics include inverted-lip Corrugated wares and broad, bold geometric designs on the Black-on-White ware.

Following are a few generalizations about possible room functions. These characteristics can be seen with binoculars and don't require one to step through the site.

— Granaries tend to be smaller than other structures and contain no smoke-blackening on the interior walls. They have natural flooring and small rectangular doors. The outer wall surfaces may be finished, but the interior walls are still rough.

— Habitation structures are larger, with fire pits and flattened floors with adobe or stone flagging. These structures usually have a T-shaped or rectangular door, and interior walls are blackened from smoke.

— General storage structures have finished interior wall surfaces, natural floors and no smoke-blackening.

— Kivas are circular subterranean structures with a low bench along the inner wall's circumference and six pilasters. A kiva also has a fire pit, deflector stone, ventilation shaft, and a sipapu. The roof contains limbs for support.

Architecture

One significant aspect of Ancestral Puebloan sites is their distinctive utilitarian architecture. The early Basketmaker II pithouse shelters were set partially belowground and built up with timber, branches, and mud. The floor was excavated about a foot into the ground, and sandstone slabs were set upright to line the sides of the roughly circular pit. The walls were built up by cribbing horizontal logs and forming a dome-shaped roof with upright wall poles leaned against a central vertical post. The shelter was weatherproofed by plastering smaller sticks, bark, and mud over the logs.

In the Basketmaker III stage, the Ancestral Puebloan peoples built larger structures by supporting the roof and sidewalls of the pithouses with four upright posts set into the floor. Four horizontal logs were set on top of these posts, forming a square on which the roof timbers rested. Then sloping poles—footed either on the ground surface or on a very shallow ledge called a banquette—were leaned against the roof timbers to constitute the walls. The structures were weatherproofed with successive layers of sticks laid at right angles to the timbers and sealed with juniper bark and brush mixed in the mud and earth plastering. This gave the completed pithouse the general appearance from outside of a flat-topped earthen mound.

Entry to the pithouse was gained either through a ladder in the ceiling smoke-hole or a ground-level antechamber. Inside the pithouse was a clay-lined fire pit, with a stone slab or a set of poles plastered with mud positioned between the fire pit and the antechamber passageway to deflect drafts of air away from the fire. Low partitions, or wing walls, of either stone slabs or wood poles and mud created food preparation areas and storage bins. The earliest known kivas, with their distinctive sipapus, date to Basketmaker III. Also found in historic kivas, sipapus represent the place where Pueblo people emerged from the underworld.

Pueblo I pithouses were almost totally subterranean with slightly domed roofs to shed water. These pithouses retained the four-post roof support, wing walls, central fire pit, ash pit, deflector, ventilator tunnel, and north–south orientation of those in the Basketmaker phase.

During the Pueblo II phase, Ancestral Puebloan peoples began using six masonry pilasters instead of four, and the area around the kiva was filled with earth to create a level work area on the kiva's top. Stone masonry lining replaced the clay-plastered earth sides of earlier pithouses by A.D. 1100.

In the Pueblo III phase, the interior alignment of the fire pit, deflector, and ventilator on a north–south axis remained standard. However, new kiva features included sophisticated murals painted on the interior walls, loom anchors, wall pegs set in pilaster faces, horizontal pole shelves placed between pilasters, small storage niches built into the masonry facing, stone-lined fire pits, and stone anvils set in the floor.

Ceramics and Basketry

Archaeologists speculate that the pottery-making process spread northward out of central Mexico to the Hohokam and Mogollon cultures around A.D. 250. The Ancestral Puebloan peoples were producing pottery by the Basketmaker III phase, around A.D. 500. The distinctive gray and white coloring, produced by firing the vessels in the reduced-oxygen environment of a smothered fire, became a hallmark of Ancestral Puebloan culture. Potters frequently decorated ceramics with geometric designs executed in black paint against a white background but also adorned them with intricate combinations of figures. The painted uncorrugated wares were used for eating and drinking, while the unpainted corrugated wares were employed for cooking and storage.

Ceramic production was not easy. It required the potter to find a source of suitable clay, collect it, clean it, moisten it, and temper it with sand or crushed rock. The potter would then roll ropes of moist clay into coiled sidewalls, smear and scrape the side wall surfaces, dry the vessels in the shade to prevent cracking, and decorate them with paints before finally firing the pottery in either a shallow stone-lined pit covered with wood or dung, or on a mound of burning dung covered by sandstone or sherds. Paint pigments were derived from organic substances such as boiled beeweed or inorganic mineral substances such as iron-oxide powder. The black versus white color balance, the symmetry, and the overall patterning attest to the presence of numerous talented artists among the Ancestral Puebloan peoples. Black-on-White ceramics are associated primarily with the Mesa Verde region (or Northern San Juan) while the Black-on-Red pottery is found mainly in the Kayenta region.

Intact pottery no longer exists at Cedar Mesa sites because of scientific removal, decay, looting, and vandalism. Besides the many excellent books with photographs of Ancestral Puebloan artifacts, several museums in the Four Corners region display wonderful specimens of Ancestral Puebloan ceramic and basketry workmanship. Two of the best are the Anasazi Heritage Museum in Dolores, Colorado, and the Edge of the Cedars Museum in Blanding, Utah.

Baskets were produced and used by all Ancestral Puebloan people. A utilitarian bowl basket was made by plaiting (over one, under one) or twilling (over two, under two) a mat with split yucca leaves and

Anthropomorphic pictographs

attaching it to a willow ring before tying off the cut ends. Ornamental basketry was made by coiling reed and grass bundles and then fixing these coils together with closely set stitches of rabbitbrush and sumac bark. Different colored stitches produced designs of both geometric and natural figures. The Ancestral Puebloan peoples produced trays, bowls, globular containers with no necks, conical burden baskets, and sandals in this manner.

Rock Art

Unfortunately, the oral traditions that accompanied the Ancestral Puebloan rock art are unknown to us, but it is possible to make a few generalizations.

Humanlike figures are called anthropomorphs, animal-like figures are zoomorphs, and figures that are neither human nor animal are labeled abstract. Late Archaic rock art suggests esoteric ritual functions, but Basketmaker II rock art has stronger domestic contexts and interactive connotations. Common figures in Pueblo I–III rock art include anthropomorphs, hands, lizards, birds, game animals, corn, spirals, concentric circles, stepped figures, frets, triangles, and kokopellis (hump-backed fluteplayers). There are patterned abrasions on dwelling walls from tool manufacture and sharpening that also may have had symbolic meaning.

Basketmaker II rock art, compared to the earliest nomadic Archaic style, used smaller anthropomorphs, embellished with more details of ornament and costume, and overall seem less ethereal and forbidding in appearance. During Basketmaker III, Ancestral Puebloan peoples

Anthropomorphic and geometric petroglyphs

introduced birds, animals, and hunting scenes. Pueblo I rock art contains even smaller anthropomorphs with longer necks, triangular bodies that lack arms and legs, human and animal stick figures, handprints, and the earliest kokopelli figures. The Pueblo II phase had fewer anthropomorphic images relative to animal subjects, with an increase in the numbers and variety of birds and quadruped figures, and more representational realism. Pictographs become more popular during the Pueblo III stage with an emphasis on handprints and anthropomorphs, while the petroglyph figures include corn, spirals, concentric circles, animals, and kokopellis.

Most pictographs are monochromatic and were painted with ochre, red, brown, green, blue, and white organic paints that were applied to a cleaned surface with fingers or a brush in a linear application or by using a spattering or smearing technique. Most pictographs are found near dwelling sites and may contain possible shamanic attributes more elaborate and larger in scale than pottery decorations from the same period. Many of the panels are unframed, making it difficult to separate the individual symbolism of the figures from the organizational structure of the whole panel. Even pictographs protected from the elements are not as durable as petroglyphs, which were pecked into rock surfaces in a labor-intensive process. Many petroglyph panels are located along travel routes and are remote from dwelling sites. Some petroglyph sites have extensive post-creation oxidation over the rock art.

Spiritual Concepts

The traditions of the historic Pueblo Indians speak of an upward migration of the ancestors through different levels of the spirit world inside the earth before reaching the surface through the "sipap." The spirits and kachinas accompanied the ancestors into the surface world to guide and teach them. The Puebloan peoples believe they are no more unique or important than any of the other life forms inhabiting their world.

The Ancestral Puebloan peoples probably practiced animism, in which animals and inanimate objects of nature all had souls and, as spirits, could do good and evil things. Their burial methods indicate belief in an afterlife, evidenced by the position of the body and the inclusion of food and water vessels, tools, clothing, and jewelry in the grave. Ancestral Puebloan rituals probably focused on those things necessary for the preservation of life, such as water and crop fertility, and were probably practiced in the pithouses during the Basketmaker phases by family units before community rituals expanded into the kin-kivas and Great Kivas of the Pueblo phases.

Ancestral Puebloan peoples were keen observers of celestial patterns, which they may have used to track the changing seasons and determine the best time for planting crops and other important events. It is believed that the Ancestral Puebloan culture was an egalitarian society organized through ritual knowledge, similar to historic Puebloan societies.

Early Archaeological Expeditions

The January 1891 expedition of Charles McCloyd and Charles Cary Graham into Grand Gulch netted many artifacts to exhibit and sell back in Durango, Colorado. McCloyd and Graham returned to Grand Gulch in the winter of 1892–93. Their success piqued the interest of Mesa Verde discoverer Richard Wetherill and his younger brothers John, Al, Winslow, and Clayton, who mounted the Hyde Exploring Expedition into Grand Gulch in the winter of 1893–94. Many of the artifacts collected by McCloyd and Wetherill found homes in the American Museum of Natural History and the Museum of the American Indian, both in New York City, and the Field Museum of Natural History in Chicago.

Archaeological expeditions to Cedar Mesa included the Illustrated American Exploring Expedition led by Moorehead in 1892, the San Juan Exploring Expeditions led by Charles Lang in 1894–95 and 1898–99, the Whitmore Exploring Expedition led by Wetherill in the winter of 1896–97, an expedition led by T. M. Prudden in 1894–1902, and the Cartier Expeditions led by Nels Nelson and John Wetherill in the 1920s. These early expeditions were organized and carried out principally by local ranchers and amateur archaeologists.

More recently, various academic and BLM-sponsored expeditions have re-excavated many Cedar Mesa archaeological sites. Among them was the 1986 Wetherill-Grand Gulch project, the results of which were published in a book by Fred Blackburn titled *Cowboys and Cave Dwellers: Basketmaker Archaeology in Utah's Grand Gulch.*

Settlement History

When Spanish explorers first visited the Colorado Plateau in the sixteenth century, they found the Navajo Indians occupying Cedar Mesa. Explorers, fur traders, miners, and misfits traveled the San Juan River basin before 1879, but the first organized settlement by white people was the Mormon community established at Bluff on April 6, 1880, by way of the famous Hole-in-the-Rock Trail from Escalante, Utah. It took the 230 pioneers all winter to etch out a trail in the slickrock wilderness and cross the Colorado and San Juan Rivers. Farming was a precarious proposition on the flats of the drought- and flood-prone San Juan River basin, and many settlers relocated to the high country north of Bluff to establish the towns of Monticello in 1887 and Blanding in 1905.

Early cattlemen, including brothers Al and Jim Scorup did well in the rough country, but the desert forage gave out quickly. The rangeland is now degraded and unable to sustain large numbers of livestock although eight grazing allotments remain. Mining has been intermittent, with a brief gold rush along the San Juan River in the 1890s, oil exploration in the early 1900s, and uranium extraction in the 1950s. In 1992, ninety oil and gas leases and ten mining claims were still active. Traditional tribal firewood and pine nut gathering continues on the mesa tops of Cedar Mesa.

Today, tourism plays an important role in the economy of southeastern Utah. Natural Bridges, Rainbow Bridge, and Hovenweep National Monuments, Glen Canyon National Recreation Area, Canyonlands National Park, Grand Gulch Primitive Area, Lake Powell, Monument Valley, and Valley of the Gods attract the most traffic. Other economic activities include rafting trips on the San Juan River and film production.

Conservation

The BLM began stabilizing some of the larger archaeological sites in the Grand Gulch area in 1964 after Secretary of Interior Stewart Udall designated 32,847 acres of the drainage as the Grand Gulch Primitive Area to protect its archaeological and scenic values. This designation, however, is merely an administrative title; the area still has no congressionally mandated permanent protection, although revised grazing agreements finalized in 1970 did remove cattle from Grand Gulch.

Decreasing budgets in the late 1970s slowed the BLM's archaeological documentation efforts as staff positions were eliminated, but 1700 sites have been recorded on the Grand Gulch Plateau, ranging from sites of the Paleo-Indian culture of 11,000 years ago to more recent prehistoric and historic occupations. The Hopi, Navajo, Ute, and Zuni consider many of these sites sacred and still use them for ceremonies and rituals.

In 1991, the BLM recommended wilderness designation for 204,090 acres within the Bullet Canyon, Sheiks Flat, Pine Canyon, Slickhorn Canyon, Fish Creek Canyon, Road Canyon, and Mule Canyon Wilderness Study Areas (WSAs), but Congress has not acted on the recommendation. By 1998, the San Juan–Anasazi complex, which contains Grand Gulch Plateau, had grown to 551,040 acres, of which 210,190 acres are included in BLM WSAs. Cedar Mesa encompasses 152,870 acres or 240 square miles, including the current 37,850 acres of the Grand Gulch Primitive Area.

In 1999, the BLM published its reinventory of lands appropriate for wilderness designation within the San Juan–Anasazi complex, a total of 143,000 acres. The sections include Harmony Flat (10,600 acres), Grand Gulch (55,890 acres), Fish and Owl (31,610 acres), Road Canyon (17,000 acres), Comb Ridge (14,800 acres), and the San Juan River (14,700 acres). The Utah Citizens Proposal for wilderness designation for the same area totals 302,400 acres. It includes Arch and Mule Canyons (15,300 acres), Comb Ridge (15,000 acres), Fish and Owl (59,000), Grand Gulch (139,800), Road Canyon (60,100), and the San Juan River (13,200).

In 1995, almost eight thousand visitors signed registers in Cedar Mesa locations, with 70 percent from outside Utah. Actual visitation is probably 30 to 100 percent higher and rising each year. In 1999, the BLM began a permit system to control the numbers of backpackers and provide revenue for the resource area's maintenance.

The 1993 BLM *Grand Gulch Plateau Cultural and Recreational Area Management Plan* identified five issues affecting the Cedar Mesa area: (1) protecting cultural and archaeological resources from impacts associated with recreational use; (2) developing more comprehensive resource monitoring and resource protection strategies; (3) addressing consequences of expanding visitation on recreation opportunities;

(4) increasing visitor services, facilities, and safety; and (5) expanding visitor education, resource interpretation kiosks, and public involvement in resource management. Impacts from tourism, wilderness designation, and degradation of the plateau's grazing areas remain volatile issues.

BLM volunteers and seasonal rangers placed sixty-four carbonite WSA signs in new "camping or wood cutting" road intrusions along the Grand Gulch access corridors in 1998. In 1999, twenty-five intrusions along the Slickhorn Canyon access corridor were created in October alone, with seven intrusions along the Fish and Owl access corridor. Recreational users searching for new ruin sites or remote camping sites are responsible for most of these intrusions. The BLM is to be commended for its efforts to keep roads properly signed and intrusions properly blocked. Volunteer labor hours totaled 2260 in 1999. That equates to 43.5 hours of work for every week of the year. People are passionate about preserving this area.

A June 1998 Southern Utah Wilderness Alliance (SUWA) fact sheet on Utah wilderness lists an estimate of 11,000 unrecorded sites in the San Juan–Anasazi complex with a concentration of archaeological sites in this region of several hundred per square mile. This is perhaps the highest density of prehistoric sites in the United States. SUWA argues that accessible archaeological sites (those nearest roads) are routinely looted by pothunters, and chaining projects in which heavy bulldozers are used to create cattle-feed areas destroy numerous surface sites. Wilderness designation would limit such destruction of sites by nonrecreational users.

Support Utah's Citizens Proposal to designate 9.8 million acres as wilderness by contacting your congressional representatives directly to voice your concerns and preferences. SUWA and Friends of Cedar Mesa can provide more information.

Geology

Cedar Mesa is part of the Monument Upwarp anticline that starts near Kayenta, Arizona, and extends ninety miles north to the confluence of the Green and Colorado Rivers in Canyonlands National Park. Lake Powell covers the western flank, and the Comb Ridge monocline forms the eastern margin. Cedar Mesa is composed of sedimentary rock layers.

The Monument Upwarp anticline rose 60 million to 70 million years ago during the Laramide orogeny. From Salvation Knoll, the laccoliths of the Abajo Mountains can be seen to the north, the Ute Mountains to the east, the Carrizo Mountains to the southeast, and the solitary Navajo Mountain to the southwest. These were emplaced 28 million to 53 million years ago. The Mule Ear and Alhambra Rock diatremes of intrusive material (seen to the south from Muley Point Overlook and the Goosenecks of the San Juan River State Park) formed 30 million years ago.

The sedimentary rock layers of Cedar Mesa were formed by the relentless effects of gravity, the melt-freeze cycle, and winds and moving water conveying debris down from the highlands and depositing them in lowland areas. The length of the transport, the duration of the deposition, and the deposition environment itself determined the final sedimentary structures of the formation. The Honaker Trail Formation limestone is the calcium carbonate sludge of dead invertebrates deposited on the floor of a shallow marine sea. The Halgaito Shale is marine mud from estuary environments. The beach sand deposits of the Kayenta Formation are parallel-stratification deposits, while the dune sand deposits of the Cedar Mesa, Wingate, and Navajo Formations are cross-stratification deposits. Sandstone and limestone layers tend to have high-angle walls or cliffs, while shale formations have low-angle walls or slopes.

Three basic types of folds describe the various forces applied to rock layers of Cedar Mesa: anticlines are arched or up-folded layers of rock, synclines are down-folded or trough-shaped layers, and monoclines are steplike vertical bends in otherwise horizontal layers. All of these folds can range from several yards to hundreds of miles in length.

Mechanical and chemical erosion is a continuing process. Alcoves, arches, buttes, canyons, fins, meanders, natural bridges, pinnacles, and spires are slowly being created and destroyed. Arches are formed from seeping moisture dissolving the cement between grains of sand in narrow fins of sandstone, combined with frost wedging (water expansion when frozen), wind erosion, and gravity. Running water carves natural bridges. Arches are usually found high on walls near the skyline, while natural bridges are located near the bottom of water channels. A rincon occurs in abandoned meanders where the water has cut a new channel through the wall, isolating an island wall relic.

Geology also determines the soil qualities and the plant communities growing in them. Cedar Mesa is in the Upper Sonoran Zone, dominated by piñon pine, juniper, sage, greasewood, saltbrush, and rabbitbrush. Cedar Mesa also contains two unique habitats: hanging gardens and potholes. The microbiology surrounding these perennial and inter-mittent water sources is uniquely adapted and frequently endemic to these specific sites; adversity creates adaptation. But these sites are extremely sensitive to human impacts. The riparian environments of Cedar Mesa are also important wildlife habitats and plant communities that are frequently scarred by human intrusions.

The Ancestral Puebloan peoples used the naturally occurring chert beds in the Honaker Trail Formation for much of their tool kit. Chert, jasper, flint, chalcedony, agate, and hornstone are rocks composed primarily of microcrystalline quartz with different chemical impurities affecting their color and cleavage strengths. Chert is ideal for making stone tools because it is prone to conchoidal fracturing that creates sharp edges when flaked into a point or cutter. Manos, hammers, and petroglyph pecking tools were often metamorphic rocks smoothed round by river action after being weathered out from the nearby laccolith mountains.

Desert varnish is created by the slow oxidation process that stains the sandstone walls in the Cedar Mesa area with rich colors and interesting striations. Surface minerals that accumulate along rainfall and snowmelt water routes oxidize after evaporation removes most of the water. Most of the present desert varnish was formed in a wetter climate during the recent geological past. The most prevalent colors and mineral combinations are blue-black (manganese oxide), red (iron oxide), and yellow (limonite iron, oxygen, and hydrogen). The petrified wood found in Cedar Mesa was created when the silicates in the volcanic ash and river mud of the Chinle Formation were able to impregnate the wood cells and fossilize the structure.

Roadside Geology

Utah State Highway 95 east of Lake Powell was built atop Cedar Mesa Sandstone. The highway crests the Monument Upwarp near milepost 97. All the strata dip steeply eastward, and the Moenkopi and Chinle Formations are visible in Comb Wash, while the Wingate Sandstone, Kayenta Formation, and Navajo Sandstone comprise Comb Ridge. Near milepost 118 the highway climbs onto a tableland surfaced with Dakota Sandstone, which extends to Blanding.

Utah State Highway 163, north of Mexican Hat is built on the limestone of the Honaker Trail Formation. Highway 163 tops out on the Limestone Ridge anticline before descending through the red mudstone of the Halgaito Shale and the buff-colored Cedar Mesa Sandstone. From the bottom of Comb Wash, the highway climbs east over the Chinle Formation, Wingate Sandstone, and Kayenta Formation before reaching

Cedar Mesa vista

the Navajo Sandstone at the top of Comb Ridge. The reddish Carmel Formation and light-colored Bluff Sandstone are visible near the town of Bluff.

Four miles north of Mexican Hat, Utah State Highway 316 leads to the Goosenecks of the San Juan River, a classic example of incised meanders, contained within the Honaker Trail Formation. Utah State Highway 261 continues north over Halgaito Shale before climbing onto the Cedar Mesa Sandstone.

Monument Valley, visible to the south of Cedar Mesa, contains tall monoliths of De Chelly Sandstone rising out of Organ Rock Shale and capped with a resistant layer of Moenkopi Formation.

The white-colored Navajo Sandstone is a dune deposit with strong

Cedar Mesa Stratification (top to bottom, youngest to oldest)

Formation	Color Highlight	Features	Period Formed
Navajo Sandstone	white	cliffs and domed walls	Jurassic
Kayenta Formation	red	hard, ledgy bands	Jurassic
Wingate Sandstone	tan	cliffs and domed walls	Jurassic
Chinle Formation	pale purple	low-angle slopes	Triassic
Moenkopi Formation	dark brown	low-angle slopes	Triassic
De Chelly Sandstone	peach	cliffs and domed walls	Permian
Organ Rock Shale	red	weak, ledgy bands	Permian
Cedar Mesa Sandstone	buff	alcoves, bridges, and arches	Permian
Halgaito Shale	gray	ledgy cliffs	Pennsylvanian
Honaker Trail Formation	dark gray	cliffs and abundant fossils	Pennsylvanian

wind mechanics similar to the present-day Saharan Desert but weathered to rounded summits and slopes. Navajo Sandstone is widespread and is called Nugget Sandstone in Wyoming and Aztec Sandstone in Arizona and Nevada. The red Kayenta Formation is an accumulation of siltstone and shale river deposits from a wet interlude that formed ledgy bands. The Wingate Sandstone is a tan dune deposit that breaks along vertical joints and forms cliffs. The Wingate, Kayenta, and Navajo Formations are part of the Glen Canyon Group and were deposited 144–208 million years ago during the Jurassic period.

The Chinle Formation alternates between different stream deposits of shale, siltstone, and sandstone. It also contains petrified wood and bentonitic clay formed from volcanic ash deposits. The dark brown Moenkopi Formation is composed of thick mud and sand tidal-flat deposits, and is a notable slope former. Both were deposited during the Triassic, 208–245 million years ago.

De Chelly Sandstone is a peach-colored sand dune formation with many vertical joints and alcoves. Organ Rock Shale is red and consists of mud and silt of lowland and tidal flat deposition; it is identical to the Hermit Shale in the Grand Canyon. Cedar Mesa Sandstone exhibits both dune and beach deposition, and may have been a marine offshore sand bar similar to the Great Bahamas Banks. Cedar Mesa Sandstone is buff colored; contains many alcoves, arches, and bridges; and fractures along vertical joints. These layers were deposited during the Permian period, 245–286 million years ago.

The gray Halgaito Shale was a former marine seaway, while the gray Honaker Trail Formation is limestone from a shallow marine sea. Both layers form ledgy cliffs and contain many fossils. These layers were deposited during the Pennsylvanian period, 286–320 million years ago.

Most of the hiking in Cedar Mesa is on and through Cedar Mesa Sandstone. Exceptions include the Valley of the Gods (Halgaito Shale), Honaker Trail and Lower Johns Canyon (Honaker Trail Formation), and Butler Wash (Navajo Sandstone).

Wilderness Stewardship and Desert Travel

The desert environment is a harsh and hauntingly beautiful landscape that demands respect and responsibility from those who choose to travel there. In addition, Cedar Mesa contains a wealth of well-preserved signs of an ancient civilization. Please follow the proper site visitation protocols below to ensure that Cedar Mesa will remain a desert gem for all of us to visit.

Artifact collections like this have no scientific relevance and are considered vandalism, even if they are left at a site. If you want to examine an object, put it back where you found it!

Visiting Archaeological Sites

— Never climb on, push on, deface, dig into, touch, collect, or otherwise vandalize any components of any of the Ancestral Puebloan structures, rock art panels, or artifacts. The Antiquities Act of 1906 and the Archaeological Resources Protection Act of 1979 specify stiff penalties for anyone vandalizing or damaging these sites. (A number of such offenses have been successfully prosecuted, resulting in substantial fines and even incarceration.)

— Never touch a pictograph or petroglyph since the oils in your skin, perspiration, sunscreens, moisturizers, and insect repellents all remove pigmentation from pictographs and texture from petroglyphs. Do not mark, clean, brush, or deface any rock art. Refrain from using flash photography. Admire from afar.

— Never climb up or down to any site protected by steep walls. Most injuries and fatalities in Cedar Mesa occur when people fall near archaeological sites while trying to get a better view or the best photograph angle. Don't become a fatality yourself.

— Carry binoculars and observe from afar. Use a zoom lens for photography. Observing from outside the immediate site is the safest and least intrusive method for enjoying archaeological resources. The fewer people who enter a site, the less unintentional destruction.

If you feel compelled to explore an archaeological site:

— Remove any backpacks or fanny packs to prevent scratching, bumping, knocking over, or destroying components of the site as you move.
— Enter one at a time to minimize the cracking and settling effects from footfall vibrations. Don't walk on loose soil or near precariously balanced structures.
— Stay on established paths and walk carefully.
— Do not walk on the midden areas. These prehistoric trash mounds provide scientists with many clues to the Ancestral Puebloan culture. They are usually located downslope from the kiva and habitation structures.
— Never remove any pottery sherds, maize cobs, chert, quartz, jacal, masonry, cordage, wood, bones, manos, metates, igneous rocks, or any other artifact. ("If I don't take it, someone else will" is a weak excuse.)
— If you pick up an artifact to inspect it, then you must return it to its exact location and position when you are done, with no exceptions.
— Never build a fire, camp, dig, eat, litter, defecate, or urinate in or near a site.
— Pets and pack stock are not allowed on or in archaeological sites and must be secured at a safe distance.

Report any suspicious activities or vandalism immediately to the nearest BLM personnel or law enforcement officer and call the BLM's Monticello office at (435) 587-1500. Record the vehicle's identifying features (including the license plate), a description of the person(s), and a description of the activities you witnessed. Don't initiate a confrontation, but you might politely educate receptive people on better wilderness stewardship and archaeological site preservation.

The cumulative impact of tourist visitations to archaeological sites is destroying these nonrenewable resources. Practice these visitation protocols scrupulously. "Look but don't touch" and "Inspect from afar" are good rules of thumb when visiting any obvious or suspected archaeological site because they minimize even unintentional damage such as footprints. Take photographs and memories, but leave everything else behind.

Sanitation

Always carry a toilet kit containing a half roll of toilet paper, two resealable plastic bags (one for clean toilet paper, and one for dirty), and a plastic trowel at least six inches long. Disposable towlettes are also good to have but must be packed out as trash.

Urinate on slickrock or sandy surfaces without trampling any flora or cryptogamic soils. Never pee in alcoves, under overhangs, in springs, or in potholes.

Three options exist in Cedar Mesa for human and pet feces: catholes, smearing, and the bag method. The BLM requires the cathole method.

1. Make your cathole 200 feet or 70 paces away from any trail, site, or water source. Use a trowel to dig a six- to eight-inch-deep hole near a sunlit spot next to vegetation. The microorganisms and heat in the soil will speed the breakdown of the waste. Pack out used toilet paper in a resealable plastic bag. Never burn it. Wildfires are a frequent result of burning toilet paper.

2. In an emergency only, if you can't dig a cathole (for instance, when in a slickrock canyon), find a safe talus slope or high ledge and smear your waste thinly on a flat rock facing south. The sunlight and humidity will dry out the feces allowing the wind to blow it away as dust. However, your waste may contaminate the watershed, and catholes should be used whenever possible.

3. Popular rock-climbing and mountaineering areas such as Yosemite and Mount Rainier National Parks require the bag method. Put feces in a resealable plastic bag, add your toilet paper, pack it out, and deposit the waste in an urban flush toilet. This method eventually may be required for all backcountry users in high-traffic areas.

Water

Drink water at regular intervals. Thirst is a sign of dehydration. Not staying hydrated is the most common mistake made by novice and experienced desert adventurers alike. The use of sweetened electrolyte-replacement drinks is recommended.

Acclimatizing to the desert heat and altitude may take up to ten days. Individuals from cooler climates should take it easy for the first few days. Alcohol and caffeine are diuretic and thus contribute to dehydration. One technique for staying hydrated is water loading: drinking several quarts of water before you start to hike in the morning. If temperatures are consistently above 90°F, you may need to drink as much as two gallons in a twenty-four-hour period. During hot weather, get an early start, rest during the midday heat, and resume travel during the cooler evening hours.

Always carry enough potable water to get back to a known source. Water sources, either springs or potholes, can be small, medium, or large, referring not to their physical size but to the likelihood of finding water in them. Water in a small source may dry up within days of a rain, while a medium pothole should hold water for a week or more after a rain. Large potholes will be usable several weeks after a rain. A medium spring will dry up after long periods without moisture, and large springs will dry up after prolonged drought. Springs are shown on most usgs maps. Day-hike descriptions assume you have drinking water in your vehicle and will carry enough to stay hydrated until you return to it.

Contact Kane Gulch Ranger Station for current information on water sources. The Cedar Mesa area generally has a feast or famine water history. For example, in the spring of 1998 and 1999, the streambed springs and potholes in all the major canyons in the Cedar Mesa complex had plenty of water after normal snowfall years. The autumn of 1998 was very wet, and the canyons were frequently in flood. The autumn of 1999, however, had ten rainless weeks after a very wet summer, and the large potholes I saw contained stagnant but organically active water. Many of the medium springs were dry. The Kane Gulch Ranger Station keeps a current water-source report on its information board. Know your water availability before any extended adventuring into the Cedar Mesa area.

All water must be boiled, treated, or filtered. Assume all wilderness water sources contain bacteria, germs, and viral pathogens. *Giardia lamblia,* a hard-shelled protozoan that causes bowel distress in humans, can quickly lead to dehydration. There are three methods for eradicating water-borne microorganisms:

1. Boil your water. Bringing water to a rolling boil will kill most germs, but you must boil it for twenty minutes to kill parasites such as *Giardia.*

2. Effective chemical treatment of water depends on the concentration and length of exposure of the chemical introduced, combined with the effects of water temperature, pH levels, and clarity. Follow the label directions strictly. The 2-percent tincture of iodine works, but follow the instructions on the product's use label carefully. There are medical contraindications to using iodine. Always use fresh iodine tablets because they lose their effectiveness after prolonged exposure to air. Iodine is less effective in the alkaline waters common to the desert Southwest and has not been proven to neutralize

Cryptosporidium. Chlorine and Halazone are effective against viruses and bacteria, but they will not kill *Giardia.* Never add flavored drink mixes to water until after the treatment is complete.

3. Invest in a water filter or purification system. Filters remove germ and bacteria content but are ineffective against viruses; an Environmental Protection Agency–registered water "purifier" combines a protozoa and bacteria filtration process with an iodine resin that kills viruses to guarantee totally safe water. Strain muddy water through a disposable coffee filter or let the sediment settle for a couple of hours in an extra vessel. This prevents the filter from clogging up and slowing the filtration process.

Trash

Pack it in and pack it out. This includes apple cores, orange peels, cigarette butts, peanut shells, and any other organic and nonorganic litter you encounter. If you brought it with you, you can take it out. Collect any litter you may find en route to improve the wilderness appearance of the area. Deposit your trash in an appropriate rubbish bin.

Fires

Fires are prohibited in the canyons of Cedar Mesa. Fire rings and escaped fires leave behind scars that last a lifetime. Instead, use a backpacking stove for cooking. If you must have a campfire when car camping on the mesa top, the BLM requires that you use a firepan, bring your own wood, and transport the ashes to a proper urban refuse facility. Never use live or dead standing wood. These are important habitats for many desert creatures.

Dishwashing

Whether backpacking or car camping, carry out all food scraps and wash all your dinnerware 200 feet or 70 paces away from any water source. Using rubbing alcohol instead of water effectively sanitizes your dinnerware without leaving environmentally damaging soapy wastewater. You can also use baby wipes and pack out the used ones as trash. Always use a strainer to collect food scraps and pack them out. Do not bury food scraps or create gray water areas: both methods attract insects, rodents, and other animals.

Bathing

Swimming, lounging, or bathing in potholes is prohibited. Sunscreens, sweat, insect repellent, deodorant, and other contaminants that humans commonly bear destroy the microbiology of the pothole. Preferably, wait until you get back to an urban area to bathe thoroughly. If you must bathe, use pots and canteens to carry bathing water more than 200 feet or 70 paces from any water source and use only pure soaps (such as Ivory) to minimize environmental damage. Even biodegradable products change the chemistry and biology of the landscape. Baby wipes are an excellent and convenient waterless bathing method. They easily remove sweat and dirt without damaging the environment. Pack out the used baby wipes with your trash.

Campsite Selection

Always camp at least 200 feet or 70 paces from any water source and use an established site where the damage to the immediate environment has already been done. Don't compound the damage by choosing adjacent areas and trampling the flora to oblivion. If an established site is not available, camp in a dry wash, weather permitting, where the next rain will eradicate your presence, or on a dry slickrock area away from cliffs, ledges, potholes, and streams. Never camp on cryptogamic soils. Always return any branches, rocks, pine cones, and leaves to their original locations if you moved them before setting up camp. Avoid visiting isolated water sources after dusk. It prevents the nocturnal desert wildlife from using the pothole or water spring. Leave no trace of your site use.

Many Cedar Mesa access roads are in wilderness study areas, and each new intrusive camping road minimizes the area's "roadless" condition. Over time, the area may be removed from consideration for wilderness designation because of this abuse. When car camping, refrain from creating a new site and accelerating the desert's degradation. Car camp in existing areas or on slickrock surfaces whenever possible. There may be additional restrictions in some areas, and you must obey all signs.

Pets

Dogs must be kept on a leash to minimize environmental damage and wildlife harassment. Pets must be under physical control at all times, and their waste must be buried or bagged for disposal. Don't let your dog muddy isolated potholes: it stresses the microenvironment and corrupts possible drinking water for other hikers. Leave all aggressive animals at home. At this writing, dogs are still allowed, but the BLM is considering banning dogs from all Cedar Mesa canyons "due to numerous visitor complaints and concerns regarding dogs." Other BLM stipulations are that

— Pets are not allowed in Grand Gulch below Collins Spring Canyon or in Slickhorn Canyon.
— Pets are not allowed in alcoves or cultural sites.

Cryptogamic Soil

This soil is a conglomeration of algae, fungi, lichen, and moss that forms a blackish soil throughout Cedar Mesa. This insignificant-looking soil type is extremely important to the desert environment. The slow-growing, living soil checks erosion and locks nutrients into the soil, allowing other plants to take root. The blue-green cyanobacterial algae is dormant when dry but proliferates across and below the soil surface when wet, secreting material and gluing soil particles together into a mucilaginous mat of sticky fibers. The fibers draw up when dry, giving the soil its puffy, wrinkled appearance. The algae recycle dead organic material back into the soil, adding phosphorous, nitrogen, potassium, and calcium. Footsteps and tire tracks compress the soil and break its microscopic physical bonds, undercutting the whole community, which consequently disintegrates with the wind. Stay off of it! Walk on slickrock surfaces, cobbles, or dry, sandy watercourses whenever possible and never drive or camp on cryptogamic soils.

Weather

The best hiking is in the spring—late March, April, and early May—when temperatures rarely reach triple digits or sink below freezing and rainfall is light. The fall months have comfortable hiking temperatures but more precipitation. The summer is hot, with severe thunderstorms, while the winter is cold with moderate snowfall. Even moderate precipitation will muck up most of the Cedar Mesa access roads, making vehicle travel difficult. Severe thunderstorms can occur at any time in the desert, turning dry washes into turbulent channels. Thunder and lightning storms can occur at night even after a clear day. Although the routes described in this guidebook can be hiked during any season, weather extremes in the Cedar Mesa area are not uncommon and may necessitate varying your itinerary.

The desert environment usually reflects solar radiation, causing rising

	Jan.	Feb.	Mar.	Apr.	May	June	July	Aug.	Sept.	Oct.	Nov.	Dec.
Avg. high temp.	39	45	51	60	71	81	90	86	77	63	50	40
Avg. low temp.	17	22	26	32	40	49	58	56	49	37	27	19
Avg. precip. (inches)	.97	.95	1.22	.83	.67	.57	1.45	1.59	1.07	1.48	1.11	1.28

air masses as it heats. Thus, the normal daily cycle for unstable warm air aloft (no jet contrails) is one of clear mornings, late-morning cumulus cloud formation, possible isolated afternoon rain or thundershowers, cloud cover dissipating in the evening, and clear nights. With stable cold air aloft (long jet contrails), mornings and nights are clear with only occasional cumulus cloud formation in the afternoons before dissipating in the evenings. Suspended dust particles creating hazy conditions are common.

Frontal changes bring winds with sharp temperature gradients, defined cloud formations, and frequently precipitation. After the frontal edge moves past, rain or snow squalls usually persist for several hours to days, depending on the strength and size of the storm. Cirrus clouds may indicate the approach of a storm, while patchy cumulus clouds may indicate clearing weather.

The table of weather statistics is from Natural Bridges National Monument's Visitor Center at 6500 feet. The temperatures, on average, are five degrees warmer along the San Juan River at 4000 feet.

In January and February, winter snowstorms are common, and temperatures range from 0°F to 70°F. Access to trailheads is problematic, and there are few people exploring the canyons of Cedar Mesa.

In March, April, and May, enjoyment of spring is tempered with the possibility of precipitation. Temperatures range from freezing to 100°F. These are the most popular months for exploring Cedar Mesa. Gnats, mosquitoes, and biting flies can be a nuisance.

June, July, August, and September, summer heat is in full force with temperatures ranging from 50°F to 115°F, and insects can be irritating. Expect short, intense rainstorms with resulting flash floods. Few people hike beyond the car walks and the northernmost canyons.

In October, November, and December, autumn colors dominate the landscape. Temperatures range from 0°F to 80°F. Snowfall and cold rains are common, creating trailhead access problems. These are popular months for hunters, photographers, and tourists.

Maps

Always carry the appropriate USGS topographic map(s) and keep track of your location at all times. Look behind frequently and note prominent landforms if you have to reverse your route. Thoroughly understand how to use a professional-quality compass and handheld GPS unit before adventuring into the Cedar Mesa area. USGS topographical maps use the true north alignment axis, while compass field bearings will align to magnetic north. Know how to orient your compass and GPS unit relative to declination on a map, how to navigate cross-country to a field or landmark bearing, and how to navigate cross-country to a previously recorded waypoint. Always record a waypoint for your vehicle location before starting any hike. These orienteering skills are best learned from land-navigation instructional materials available at most retail bookstores and urban library systems, or from instructional programs. Maps are sold at Kane Gulch Ranger Station, but they are subject to availability.

Terrain

Take responsibility for your choices. The fastest response from the BLM or San Juan County emergency medical services is usually the folks arriving with the body bag. I am deadly serious. This is not an urban center, and encounters with other folks on even the popular hikes can be infrequent or nonexistent. You must be responsible for your own safety while traversing this rugged environment.

Pay attention and always opt for the conservative choice. Use a belay or a hand-line in any situation where a fall resulting in an injury is possible. If an accident should happen, it may take several days for members of your group to make their way back to a trailhead and notify the authorities. Even more time will elapse before a rescue party can reach you. Take the time to be cautious and safe.

Here are a few skill suggestions to help maximize your safety.

— Avoid walking on loose, spherical concretions that cover some sections of rock and those friable little sandstone ledges that can easily break underfoot. Either can send one slipping and sliding, followed by the "ouch" of a hard landing. On steep slopes, stay squarely on your feet with your weight over them. Transfer your weight slowly and gracefully. Haul heavy packs on steep inclines with hand-lines if necessary. Use ledges, ramps, and bedding planes to traverse slopes.
— It is often easier to climb up a slope than to descend it. When

descending steep inclines, pick a route that contains depressions, small ledges, trees, and bushes that may stop any slip or fall.

— Make sure you can see the entire route down any cliff face or steep talus slope before committing yourself. It's always worth the effort to traverse along the escarpment for some distance to get a good view of the entire route. Be careful around canyon rims with exfoliation and vertical jointing erosion processes. Don't stand on overhanging rock sections that have deep cracks running around their perimeter or slopes with fragments sloughing off. These are blocks of terra firma heading for a descent soon.

— You are a potential target for lightning strikes while on any of the mesa tops or slickrock surface areas. Frequently, you may be taller than the trees and thus the best electrical attraction strike point. Minimize your exposure to lightning by avoiding these areas during stormy weather. Stay in your vehicle if static electricity is high or lightning strikes are hitting nearby. If caught out in the open, crouch on something nonconductive, such as your backpack, away from the highest and lowest spots. Remember to set large metal objects a safe distance away.

— Cedar Mesa Sandstone slickrock can be slippery. Avoid climbing or traversing steep inclines when wet. Flash floods occur in all of the canyons described in this guide. Stay out of narrow canyons when it is raining, or if it starts raining, get out immediately. The slickrock does not absorb moisture, and it takes only a couple of minutes of rain to send a wall of water through any canyon. Be aware that canyons can flash flood even though it is not raining on you. Any ominous rumble from up the canyon may signify a flood and necessitate immediate scrambling to high ground. If you can't safely exit the canyon before the canyon floods, wait until the flood subsides. Be safe and don't make your situation worse by doing something foolish. Hypothermia or injury can be the result of impatience and poor decisions.

— A half hour of steady rainfall or a few minutes of intense shower activity will make most major drainages on Cedar Mesa run with brown water. Never cross a water channel during a flood. Never wade into fast-moving or deep currents. Never wade barefoot. Carry a walking stick or find a suitable stick to probe for deep pools, underwater debris, and uneven terrain if you must wade. Move your feet cautiously and keep them on firm surfaces. Interlock arms with other party members when fording any moving water deeper than one's knees (but below one's waist).

— Many accidents occur when hikers are tired. This can happen in the morning, toward the end of the day's walk, in camp, and especially during the nighttime constitutional. Recognize the hazards of your campsite before going to bed. Fatigue is a precursor to disaster. Pay attention!

— Snow-covered roads are dangerous, and the consequences of a mishap disastrous. When snow melts or after a moderate rain, all the access routes traversing Cedar Mesa become slick, and even 4WD vehicles will have problems. Wet access roads may take several days of sunny weather to dry out. Some roads have short sections of deep sand, clay, or slickrock surfaces. If in doubt, walk the suspect sections before committing your vehicle. Drive slower at night because dark-colored cows, darting deer, washouts, rough sections, and road signs are more difficult to see. Play it safe, drive cautiously, and arrive at the trailhead intact.

Safety

You should leave a complete and detailed itinerary with someone reliable or attach your itinerary to your permit before you drop it into the box at the trail register. If you have a problem, it is often safer to backtrack to the start point since you have a feel for the obstacles of the landscape you've already traveled. Never take a shortcut that may lead you and your party into a more perilous situation. Don't take unnecessary risks. Always make conservative, common-sense decisions. Always!

Be realistic about your skills and motivations before venturing into the Cedar Mesa area. Experiencing difficulties with the terrain or route finding when off-trail can be frustrating and potentially injurious. Stay within your limits and the limitations of the weakest person in your party. Cedar Mesa is not a place to experiment. Avoid difficult routes until you have competent rope-usage, scrambling, and navigation skills acquired from an accredited climbing school and an orienteering course.

I consider myself a safe and cautious hiker. Nevertheless, I've seen and heard rockfall in the canyons of Cedar Mesa. I've waited out flash floods crouched on sandstone knobs. I've had the hair on my body stand up from electrical attraction moments before a thunderbolt hit a slickrock knoll nearby. I've had boulders roll out from underneath my feet. I've taken numerous falls rock climbing and mountaineering. I've been lost in temperate mountains, Southwest deserts, and tropical jungles. Maybe I've just been lucky.

It is not uncommon for a route to take longer than expected or to have access roads become impossible to negotiate after heavy precipitation, delaying hikers for a day or two. Call the Monticello BLM field office at (435) 587-1500 for the latest weather and road conditions, and certainly before initiating a lost person(s) search for overdue hikers.

Fatalities and injures have occurred throughout Cedar Mesa. Be sensible. In 1998 a man fell to his death in McCloyd Canyon trying to reach an inaccessible archaeological site. Grand Gulch had an eighteen-foot-high wall of water rip through the canyon in 1976, and both the South Fork and North Fork of Mule Canyon were stripped to their bedrock by a flashflood in 1999. A man was killed on the San Juan River when the rock overhang he was camping underneath collapsed during a rain shower in August 1999. Fatalities also occur on the narrow highways crisscrossing Cedar Mesa. Additionally, two scout leaders drowned in Kolob Canyon in 1993; a teenage girl drowned in the Black Hole of White Canyon in 1996; eleven tourists were swept away in Antelope Canyon in 1997; two California men drowned in the Virgin Narrows in 1998; and three people died in the Upper Black Box in 1999. Heavy rains falling upstream and flowing through these constrictions all led to these avoidable deaths. The victims of falls, lightning strikes, and flash floods might have avoided their injuries by exercising good judgment.

Rockfall can be deadly. Experienced backcountry hikers Marta Heilbrum and Ron Penner were doing an "easy" backpack trip in Grand Gulch in March 1995 when they were hit by rockfall while they slept. Marta suffered open fractures of her lower legs, and Ron had a split patella. At night and through a snowstorm, Ron was able to contact a nearby NOLS group, who quickly organized a rescue. Through a lucky series of coincidences, both Ron and Marta were able to reach a hospital within eighteen hours of the accident. Marta's legs are scarred but functional. Ron appears no worse for wear. This ordeal strengthened their relationship, but it took several years of rehabilitation before they could return to their trekking and ski-touring activities. They are thankful they had health insurance.

I have stood in the sand where their injuries took place and remembered their calm voices describing the incident. In my judgment, Marta and Ron were enjoying their backpack trip in a safe and prudent manner. I would sleep in the same spot today. But like them, I keep my health insurance premiums paid. You just never know.

You should carry a well-equipped first-aid kit and know how to use its contents. Take a Wilderness First Responder Aid and CPR course. Cellular phones do not work down in the canyons but sometimes work from the mesa top. However, just because you can phone someone and give your GPS coordinates doesn't mean medical care will arrive immediately. It may take hours or days for rescue personnel to reach you, but getting help on the way is crucial.

Know your exact location with distinguishing landmarks and the extent of your party's injuries before calling emergency medical services at 911. Remain calm and answer all of the dispatcher's questions thoroughly. The dispatcher will alert the necessary BLM staff, emergency medical services, or search-and-rescue personnel. You may be asked to stay near the phone in case additional information is needed. Ask the dispatcher for instructions.

Life is full of seemingly random occurrences. We are only a part of the web. You are solely responsible for your behavior and decisions. Prepare for the worst but accept the inevitable. And remember that nature doesn't always accommodate human expectations.

Equipment and Trip Preparation

Desert canyon camping and hiking present different problems than mountain activities. Clues about the weather, field bearings, and satellite communication are more difficult to obtain because of a general lack of vistas when one is down in a canyon (versus on top of a mountain ridge). But many commonalties exist. The following suggestions should help you outfit yourself properly.

I can't emphasize enough that you need to spend extra time testing the fit of boots and backpacks before arriving at the trailhead. You need to lug weighted backpacks around the retail store and have a qualified person make adjustments to the equipment to ensure a proper fit. You need to stand and walk on uneven terrain to test the fit of any pair of boots. Take the time to outfit yourself smartly. The extra four hours spent at the store is worth the investment. An uncomfortable backpack or pair of boots will ruin your chances for a rewarding hiking experience.

Footwear

Expedition-quality leather boots are durable and supportive during long trips with heavy loads. However, these boots need to be broken in with several day hikes before attempting a backpacking trip. Any extended travel in the water will stretch and soften leather boots significantly. Boots constructed with nylon midsoles keep their shape better when wet than those made with leather. Composite boots include synthetics such as nylon and Gore-Tex in their construction, which makes them lighter with better breathability. Take extra time to get boots that fit properly. Everything rides on those feet. Any boot's external stitching will get abraded by the desert environment, but this can be alleviated by coating all of the seams with Barge Cement or Shoe Goop, which acts as a sacrificial layer. It needs to be reapplied from time to time. Invest in orthotics or custom footbeds if you have problems with your feet. Treat your boots with any necessary or recommended weather-proofing applications before getting them wet or dirty.

Camp shoes offer a comfortable respite from your sweaty hiking boots. I prefer light-duty hiking shoes to sandals because of their superior protection against cactus spines and jagged rocks. Also, their smooth soles help to minimize damage to the immediate campsite environment compared to lug-soled boots. Take good care of your feet with moleskin, Second Skin, talcum powder, and moisturizers. Never walk barefoot in the sand or on desert terrain. The use of ankle gaiters will keep your socks cleaner by keeping out the dirt, sand, and water.

Day hikes require high-cut (over the ankle) lightweight hiking boots. The additional ankle support is necessary for walking over uneven terrain. A soft compound sole will give you better traction on slickrock surfaces, but they tend to wear faster. Find synthetic blended socks that wick away moisture, with flat seams that appropriately pad your feet. Take at least three pairs of socks for extended trips, and rotate them as necessary. Stop immediately and remedy hot spots before any blisters can form.

Backpacks

The standard external-frame backpack works well, but a good internal-frame pack is beneficial for most routes in Cedar Mesa. An internal frame pack does not throw you off balance as often on uneven sections and allows greater freedom of movement while scrambling or butt scooting down sandstone slabs and boulder dams. Buy a backpack with an abrasion-resistant bottom and water-resistant fabric. Moisture-wicking properties in the shoulder straps and hip belt are preferred. Many specialty retailers will make fit adjustments or suggest modifications for a custom fit. A properly adjusted backpack is essential to enjoying any hike. A good midsize day pack or large fanny pack is necessary for enjoying many Cedar Mesa hikes. Find one that fits properly.

Tents

Both freestanding and tie-down-style tents work well in the desert. I like tents that are lightly colored with enough height to sit in. They're not as gloomy if you're stuck in the tent all day because of bad weather, and it's easier to change clothes if you can sit up. Generous windows increase ventilation and decrease condensation. They also help to minimize claustrophobic tendencies. Make sure your tent can withstand winds in excess of fifty miles per hour. A taut rainfly will also minimize condensation and the irritating flapping of the fly against the tent body during windy periods. Avoid lubricating the tent's zippers since these products frequently catch the sand, which can lead to prematurely worn out metal and plastic sliders.

Many campsites will be on slickrock where tent pegs will not work. Tie six-foot lengths of parachute cord to all of the tent hold-down loops whether it's a freestanding tent or not. The cords can be tied to rocks to secure the tent better. Return any rocks that were moved to their original positions before breaking camp. Remember to check for little critters by rolling the rock over and inspecting its underside first.

Invest in a good ground cloth. It will minimize abrasion to the floor and prolong the life of the tent. The metallic plastic-composite emergency shelter blankets available at many retailers make durable ground cloths. You can also get a sewing shop to custom fit a ground cloth to the exact dimensions of your tent and vestibule. Bivy sacks are a lightweight alternative, but many don't keep out sand on windy nights or pesky insects attracted to headlamp readers as tents do They can also be dangerous: in 1999 a young man in Arizona suffocated in a bivy sack that was improperly closed over his face.

Sleeping Bags

A two-season bag might get you by in the summer, and a four-season bag is preferable for winter trips. I use three- and four-season bags because I'm thin and I sleep cold. Down is compactable and light but doesn't insulate when wet. Many synthetics provide good compromises in compactability, weight, and insulation value, both wet and dry. Always bring a sleeping pad to insulate you from the ambient temperature of the terrain you're sleeping on. It will also provide some cushion for those imperfections in the surface you're lying on.

Stoves

A stove is essential for preparing most backpacking-style dehydrated food. Because wind robs heating efficiency, and fine airborne particles can clog stoves, invest in a thick foil windscreen. They work better than makeshift sandstone slab windbreaks. Know how to fix your stove, and bring a repair kit with spare parts and the proper tools. Strands of copper wire can be used to clean out the jets on most stoves. Any fuel, whether it is white gas, kerosene, or gasoline, has a short shelf life, and old fuel will clog your stove with carbon deposits. Use fresh fuel for every trip, and dispose of your old fuel in an environmentally friendly manner. Remember to pack and eat nutritionally balanced meals with plenty of calories, vitamins, and minerals.

Clothing

There are many waterproof and breathable garments available. Invest in a parka and pair of pants. Check to make sure the waistband is smooth to avoid creating pressure points from your backpack's hip belt. Mesh linings and armpit zippers increase ventilation. Jacket pocket locations shouldn't interfere with the alignment of backpack shoulder straps. Knee-high side zips in your rain pants allow you to add or remove the pants without having to remove your boots. Avoid nylon ponchos that flap around your legs and make it difficult to negotiate terrain obstacles safely. Ankle gaiters can keep the water streaming down your rain pants from leaking into the top of your boots and soaking your socks.

Windproof fleece wear insulates well and is water repellent, making it my choice over wool for foul weather and camp wear. A down vest or jacket does wonders in the early morning pre-sun hours. Synthetic underwear is a great first layer. It insulates and wicks away perspiration. A fleece hat, gloves, and socks are all worthwhile investments. Good rainwear is essential for keeping your insulating layers dry.

A long-sleeved, light-colored cotton shirt protects against insects and sunlight. A wide-brimmed, light-colored hat provides excellent protection against the sun. Loose-fitting, abrasion-resistant cotton pants with ankle cinches work well in the desert environment abounding with scraggly plants, brush-choked canyon bottoms, and strong sunshine. Buy shorts and pants that have smooth waistbands that won't create pressure points when your backpack's hip belt is buckled over them. Having a T-shirt to sleep in will help keep your sleeping bag from getting dirty.

Water Systems

On multiple-day routes you should have the capacity to carry at least six quarts of water per person. Use stout plastic containers. The smoke-colored Nalgene water bottles do not pick up and hold the taste of drink mixes or iodine the way standard plastic bottles do.

Invest in a water purifier. Water purifiers combine filtration that removes protozoa and bacteria with an iodine resin that kills viruses for EPA-registered "totally safe" water. Potable water is a must for any backpacking adventure. Day hikes require one to eight quarts of water per person, depending on the weather and the length of the route. Always err toward too much water.

Insect Protection

Gnats, mosquitoes, and no-see-ums can be controlled with DEET- or citronella-based repellents. Mosquito netting for the head, a long-sleeved shirt that can be cinched at the wrists, and baggy pants cinched at the ankles work best and avoid any potential repellent-toxicity reactions. Remember to do thorough tick checks at least once a day during the spring and early summer months.

Toiletries

A half roll of toilet paper kept in a resealable plastic bag and a plastic trowel are sufficient for six to ten average user days. Women should remember to bring feminine hygiene products, also kept in a resealable plastic bag, and a spare garbage bag for used products. Better safe than sorry.

Carry a toothbrush, a small tube of toothpaste, and dental floss in a small resealable bag. If necessary, take contact-lens supplies, hand lotion, sunscreen, lip balm, and a nail clipper or emery board. I like to carry three baby wipes per day in a separate baggie for personal hygiene.

Food

You can go simple or elaborate. My partner Wendy did an eighteen-day walk in Glacier National Park eating oatmeal and ramen with a Power-bar for lunch each day. I carried a watermelon up to a glaciated summit for lunch on Mount Adams, and numerous bottles of red wine while tramping in New Zealand. But we generally opt for simplicity. We boil water, fill our mugs for tea, dump some dehydrated food substance into the pot, let it hydrate, and then we eat.

I prefer going to a health-food store and buying gourmet chocolate, bulk oatmeal, gorp, couscous, and instant rice because they tend to taste better and are hearty food sources. I study labels for diet balance (30 percent protein/40 percent carbohydrate/30 percent fat), caloric intake (a minimum of 2500 cal/day/person) and nutritional needs (vitamins and minerals). I avoid glutamates and sulfur dioxide preservatives (respectively, they give me headaches and smelly farts). I strip the unnecessary packaging away. Spend some time reading backpacking manuals and cookbooks or browsing through grocery stores for inspiration for your own meal combinations.

Miscellaneous

A good headlamp is ideal for finding things at night, cooking in the dark, or reading. Headlamps free up the hands for other uses and are superior to flashlights. You only need enough candlelight power to illuminate close objects, not the other side of the canyon. Square, clear plastic containers make great personal mess kits. All your utensils, beverage bags, and favorite spices can be kept in them. A one-liter backpacking pot, lid, and a six-inch vise grip pot holder are necessary for each pair of hikers. Ditty bags and/or resealable plastic bags help keep things organized inside your backpack. A walking stick or two will assist during water crossings or on uneven terrain, especially when carrying a heavy backpack. A good compass, the correct topographical map(s), a pocketknife, Gerber or Leatherman tools, and a functional wristwatch are required. And don't forget your sunglasses!

A camera, binoculars, compact disc or cassette personal stereo, and a handheld GPS unit are optional. A paperback book, a writing or drawing pad, playing cards, and a backpacking checker/chess set are nice luxuries for in-camp activities.

Exercise

The trail is not the place to get in shape. A month before any extended backpacking trip, you should start an exercise program to build up your leg muscles and, more importantly, the joints in your hips, knees, and, especially, ankles. Health clubs are great places to build flexibility, strength, and endurance, but you need to build up the tendons in your leg joints by walking on broken, uneven terrain. Break in those new hiking boots by walking to the grocery store wearing your new backpack and buying the next week's worth of groceries. Take your mail to the post office and return those overdue books to the library by hiking there. Get your body accustomed to hiking with additional weight on your back, but limit it to a third of your body weight to avoid injury.

You can skimp and borrow a sleeping bag, insulating pad, stove, mess kit, water purifier, rain gear, and fleece clothing, but your boots and backpack have to fit comfortably to make for an enjoyable trip. Test your rain gear in the next squall. Set up camp in your backyard and learn how everything works. Then do it again with only moonlight. Load up your backpack, hike over to a friend's house, cook dinner with your backpacking gear, and spend the night in the backyard. Practice increases familiarity and efficiency that might be crucial during your desert sojourn. Learn climbing techniques such as smearing, mantling, shimmying, and rope skills at an indoor climbing gym. Learn map navigation skills from an orienteering course.

Vehicle

Your vehicle should be in good operating condition and reliable. Always carry extra water, food, clothing, fuel, motor oil, spare tire, shovel, and tow strap, just in case. Weather changes and road hazards can strand you, and accidents happen. Keep your valuables out of sight to minimize vandalism. Be wary of hitchhikers, especially those without hiking equipment.

Books

Following are a few suggestions from the plethora of material out there. Ann Zwinger's *Wind in the Rock,* Kent Frost's *My Canyonlands,* and David Roberts's *In Search of the Old Ones* are collections of natural history essays about Cedar Mesa. David Grant Noble's *Ancient Ruins of the Southwest: An Archaeological Guide,* Alex Patterson's *A Field Guide to Rock Art Symbols of the Greater Southwest,* and Donald Baars's *Canyonlands Country: Geology of Canyonlands and Arches National Parks* are good references. Stewart Udall's *The Quiet Crisis and the Next Generation,* Rachel Carson's *Silent Spring,* Aldo Leopold's *Sand County Almanac,* and Henry David Thoreau's *Walden* are conservation classics. Other good reads are W. L. Rusho's biography *Everett Ruess: A Vagabond for Beauty* and Edward Abbey's novel *The Monkey Wrench Gang.* Ray Jardine's *PCT Hiker's Handbook* is part philosophy and part technical backpacking manual.

Permits and Regulations

In January 1999 the BLM began operating an advance-reservation permit system for all overnight trips to Cedar Mesa, whether commercial, educational, or private. This includes Grand Gulch, and Fish, Johns, Lime Creek, McCloyd, Mule, Owl, Road, and Slickhorn Canyons. You must contact the BLM office in Monticello, Utah, at (435) 587-1532 for permits between March 1 and June 15, and September 2 and October 31. At all other times, permits are issued on a first-come, first-served basis from 8 A.M. to noon at the Kane Gulch Ranger Station. There is an $8.00 per person backpacker use fee. Stock groups and large private overnight groups (eight to twelve people) must make advance reservations regardless of the season. For small overnight groups (up to seven), a walk-in permit might be available from the Kane Gulch Ranger Station. It is best to call ahead to reserve your trip dates.

Day users must pay a $2.00 per person single-day use fee for Grand Gulch, and Fish, Johns, Lime Creek, McCloyd, Mule, Owl, Road, and Slickhorn Canyons, or $5.00 per person for seven consecutive days. This fee is collected at roadside kiosks, the Monticello office, or the Kane Gulch Ranger Station. The BLM accepts cash, credit cards, money orders, and personal checks for user fees. The revenue is returned to the BLM San Juan Resource Area for the management of the Grand Gulch Primitive Area and the surrounding Cedar Mesa area. The Butler Wash, Arch Canyon, and Comb Wash areas are currently exempt from user fees, but this is subject to change.

On all trailhead signs, the BLM has "Cedar Mesa Use Stipulations" posted. Read these carefully. Copies of the stipulations are also included with any advance reservation or walk-in permit. There is also a Web site with current regulatory information maintained by the BLM for the Grand Gulch Primitive Area. At this writing, the address is www.blm.gov/utah/monticello/cedarmesa.htm.

Group size is limited to twelve individuals and ten animals year-round in Grand Gulch, and Arch, Dry Wash, Fish, Johns, Lime Creek, McCloyd, Mule, Owl, Road, and Slickhorn Canyons. Only twenty-five animals total are allowed in Grand Gulch or Fish and Owl Canyons at any time. Camping is restricted to two consecutive nights at the Junction, Turkey Pen, mouth of Bullet, and Jailhouse areas. Split Ruin and the surrounding bench area is closed to camping. No camping is allowed within one mile of the San Juan River in Slickhorn Canyon and Grand Gulch. Use only well established campsites, and never pioneer a new site. There is a fourteen-day camping limit on Cedar Mesa. Use of climbing gear to access archaeological sites is strictly prohibited.

Bicycles and all motorized vehicles must stay on established roads. Bicycles are not allowed on hiking trails. Illegal use of off-road vehicles is currently the biggest problem associated with recreation in the Cedar Mesa area. Obey all road closure signs and never make a new trail into the desert. Damage from all types of tires to the desert soils can last a century or more.

Trash (including food debris and toilet paper) must be packed out. No campfires are allowed in the canyons. Mesa-top users must use a metal fire pan for campfires and pack out all fire debris. The use of even biodegradable soaps near or in any water source is prohibited. Dishwater must be strained and deposited two hundred feet away from any water source. Again, never bathe in any water source. Catholes must be dug two hundred feet away from any water source, at least six inches deep and covered with soil.

This is the minimum standard for desert behavior. The BLM "Cedar Mesa Use Stipulations" may seem onerous, but they are a response to human usage. I expect they will become more restrictive as visits increase and inevitable abuses escalate. Remember that it is your responsibility to know the current regulations.

How to Use This Guide

I define Cedar Mesa as the area bordered on the east by the Comb Ridge monocline and on the west by the Red House Cliffs. The southern boundary is the San Juan River, and the northern boundary is the Elk Ridge Highlands. Utah State Highway 95 provides access to the northern portion of Cedar Mesa, while Utah State Highway 163 gives access to the southern sections. Utah State Highway 261 cuts through the middle, forming a north-south axis. The San Juan County Routes Butler Wash 230 and Lower Butler Wash 262 provide access to the eastern part of Cedar Mesa. Utah State Highway 276 gives access to the western part. Services and water sources are limited in the Cedar Mesa area.

I have divided the routes for this guidebook into three categories. Car walks, indicated with a ●, are less than one mile round-trip, usually to a BLM or State of Utah developed site. Day hikes, indicated with a ■, are one to sixteen miles round-trip over periodically maintained trails. Backpack routes, indicated with a ◆, are multiple-day walks averaging eight miles per day and ranging from twelve to fifty-two miles. Route descriptions are prefaced by a summary of pertinent aspects of the hike.

"But they did it in the commercial...." Walk suspect road sections before committing your vehicle.

There is no reason why you can't enjoy routes from all three categories. I certainly do.

The "Access" section provides detailed instructions to the carpark for each hike, the type of vehicle that can make it there (when driven carefully and competently), and available camping sites. I classify vehicles as follows:

— All vehicles: including recreational vehicles, touring vehicles, and cars towing trailers.
— Standard vehicles: sedans, minivans, pickups, and vehicles towing trailers.
— High-clearance vehicles: full-size vans, full-size pickups, and mini pickups.
— Four-wheel drive (4WD): I'm talking about the real thing, which does not include the smaller all-wheel-drive cars and vans that do not have the necessary ground clearance or engine torque to negotiate uneven terrain, steep slopes, or loose ground surfaces.

The Utah state highways can accommodate all vehicles. The clay-based surface roads, when periodically maintained by a grader, can accommodate standard vehicles, including most sedans and pickups towing trailers. The numerous tracks, which are not maintained by graders, require high-clearance vehicles to negotiate their inherent obstacles. Many tracks are for 4WD vehicles only. High-clearance and 4WD tracks will rattle your vehicle incessantly, test your suspension, wheels, and tires, and unceremoniously scratch the exterior paint. Rain or snow can make all of the access roads impassable, even for 4WD vehicles. If in doubt, walk the suspect sections of the road or track before committing your vehicle.

All mileage is cumulative and includes a description of where the mileage starts. All the important side roads have GPS coordinates and mileage listed for their intersections. Every trailhead is listed with GPS coordinates and mileage information. Note that signs have a habit of disappearing. Access roads change after each storm or grading event. Keep track of your mileage and follow the road descriptions assiduously. Check with the Kane Gulch Ranger Station personnel before venturing too far from the beaten path and after severe storms.

The "Trail Statistics" section provides the length of the described route, overall elevation changes, and the time for a fit, competent person to complete the hike while enjoying the route's highlights. However, the times listed in the route narratives and charts is actual walking time between points. It does not include time for rest stops, sight-seeing, photography, and the like. Trail statistics also includes a quality rating, terrain classification, effort rating, and route-finding skill rating. A "fair" quality rating is a typical desert canyon without remarkable archaeo-logical or geological features. A "good" quality rating indicates at least one remarkable archaeological or geological feature. An "excellent" quality rating indicates remarkable archaeological or geological features plus ambience.

Terrain classifications use the Yosemite Decimal Scale. This system describes the characteristics of the route's terrain and rates the hardest, most technical part of the route into five classes.

Class 1: Trail or flat walking with no objective dangers.
Class 2: Off-trail walking with some scrambling and boulder hopping in steeper terrain.
Class 3: Definite scrambling where hands may be needed for balance. Exposure to heights is possible.
Class 4: Large hand and foot holds are used where a fall could have serious consequences. Ropes could be used here.
Class 5: Roped, technical climbing on near-vertical walls, requiring physical skills and familiarity with climbing ropes and protection devices.

Ratings for the effort to accomplish the described route are "easy" (relatively flat), "moderate" (elevation changes and/or scrambling), or "strenuous" (steep terrain with extended scrambling sections). Ratings for route-finding skill level are "easy" (following an obvious trail), "moderate" (following cairns across extended slickrock sections or stepping over streambed cobbles), or "difficult" (scrambling routes or extended streambed cobbles sections).

I've summarized each route's featured attractions, whether archaeological, geological, or other; described any specific cautions about the route; and listed the appropriate maps under separate subheadings.

The following cautions apply to all routes:

— You must take your own drinking water or water purifier and wear good footwear.
— Stay on the major paths to avoid increasing erosion.
— All typical water hazards can be avoided.
— Slickrock gets slippery when wet.
— Always use proper site visitation stewardship.

The maps provided in this guide are for illustrative purposes only; they are not drawn to scale or intended for navigation. It is important to read the complete route description before committing yourself and others to the hazards of the route.

The navigation terms in this guide use three layers of coordinates. The simplest is time measurements between described locations; the second is standard compass directions; the third is GPS coordinates. My theory is the more exact the coordinates, the less interpretative confusion while on route.

The route narratives use the abbreviation LDC (looking down-canyon) and LUC (looking up-canyon). The term "down-canyon" refers to the direction water would flow: water goes downslope. "Up-canyon" refers to the direction the water flows from. Thus, "turn north (left LUC)" means while looking up-canyon, take your left route option north. The route narratives also use standard compass directions (e.g., north, southwest, east-northeast) to describe travel instructions.

Common abbreviations used in this guide include UTM (Universal Transverse Mercator), BLM (Bureau of Land Management), NPS (National Park Service), NBNM (Natural Bridges National Monument), USGS (United States Geological Society), GPS (Global Positioning System), SJC (San Juan County), WSA (Wilderness Study Area), NRA (National Recreation Area), SUWA (Southern Utah Wilderness Alliance), and AN (author's name for a site or attraction). Note that "Moqui" is spelled "Mokee," "Moke," and "Moki" on different maps and in published articles.

Cairns, trail-marker signs, and alluvial bank trails change with flash floods, rainfall, snowfall, winds, rockfall, fires, earthquakes, wildlife behavior, and human behavior. Any hike missing these trail indicators will make the route-finding more difficult. Check with the Kane Gulch Ranger Station after any unusual natural phenomena to find out if any changes to the routes have been reported. The canyons of Cedar Mesa are dynamic, evolving systems. The routes will change.

I used the UTM idiom for GPS coordinates. Note that GPS readings vary depending on the datum format choice, longitudinal and latitudinal idioms, the military-designed random-dithering, selective-availability "error" feature, programmable magnetic declination software features, the proximity of the canyon walls impeding communication with satellites, the seasons, and the usual paranormal stuff. Even good 1999 hand-held GPS units err by ten to three hundred feet horizontally and between ten and one thousand feet vertically. The GPS coordinates in this guide are for approximation only.

Field benchmark errors, improved high-altitude photography, an oscillating earth orbit axis, fluctuating magnetic fields, coordinate idioms, and cartographic manipulations all affect individual USGS 7.5-minute map accuracy. Be aware that field GPS coordinates taken from the surface of a sphere don't always precisely fit the manipulated contours and linear grids of commercial two-dimensional topographical maps.

All GPS coordinates listed for each hike are within sight of the feature described and usually within an easy stone's toss. (Please, no throwing stones in any of the canyons.) GPS units will display coordinate readings within a 250-foot radius of the true topographical coordinates 90 percent of the time. The GPS coordinates in this guide are within that circle of accuracy to the real topographical coordinate.

I day-hike at 3 mph over cobbled terrain, and backpack at 2 mph on flat terrain. Your speed will differ from mine. If you don't see the described feature within the described time period, turn on your GPS unit and get a set of coordinates. Compare your coordinate set with those listed in the guide. Determine which direction you need to go. Navigate to the listed coordinates while searching the landscape for the described feature. Remember to turn off your GPS unit when not in use to avoid draining the batteries.

Thoroughly understand how to use a professional-quality compass and hand-held GPS unit. USGS topographical maps use the true north alignment axis while compass field bearings will align to magnetic north. Know how to orient your compass and GPS unit relative to declination. I used a declination of 12.5 degrees east while doing field research in 1998–99. Know how to navigate cross-country to a field or landmark bearing. Know how to navigate cross-country to a previously recorded waypoint. Always record a waypoint for your vehicle location before starting any hike.

I did not cover Whirlwind Draw, Steer Gulch, or Dry Wash Canyon because they have rather long, featureless, waterless approach routes. The upper tributary forks of Fish Canyon are difficult canyoneering sections I chose not to include in this guide. I did not drive the sometimes 4WD Mormon Trail that traces the original Hole-in-the-Rock migration route from Escalante to Bluff, Utah, through the Muley Twist.

Mountain-bike options include the technical ascent along San Juan County Route 094 Hotel Rock, and descent on San Juan County Route Trail Canyon 205, or the grueling, sandy ride up San Juan County Trail 002 in Arch Canyon. San Juan County Route Comb Wash 235 from Utah State Highway 163 to the San Juan River, San Juan County Route Snow Flat Springs 237, San Juan County Route Mormon Trail 230A, and San Juan County Route Valley of the Gods 242 are easier possibilities. Use safe riding techniques, take lots of water, and follow stewardship rules for the area assiduously.

I used a Garmin 45XL model GPS unit and a Silva Ranger model compass. I drove a 1984 full-size, half-ton, two-wheel drive, high-clearance pickup with seven inches of ground clearance at the front suspension components and rear differential. This truck had a limited slip rear end, a granny gear, all-terrain-load tires, and dual fuel tanks with a four-hundred-mile driving range. I maimed a deer going 25 mph below the speed limit midday along Utah State Highway 95. Drive carefully! Wildlife and cattle graze along and in the roads at all times of day and night.

In creating this guide, I used the following methodology: I walked each route noting GPS coordinates, archaeological sites, rock art panels, natural features, and personal impressions. Later, I traced the routes with the digital USGS topographical maps provided in the "All Topo Utah" CD software to confirm each route's accuracy and to estimate elevations. The accuracy and precision of these coordinates are well within hiking and backpacking navigational needs but are not intended for scientific or legal site descriptions. Originally I included GPS coordinates for only previously published and popular Ancestral Puebloan structures and rock art sites. After a good deal of pressure from folks who regard publication of any coordinates whatsoever as sacrilege, I have reluctantly removed even those for such well-known places as Moon House. I think this makes the book somewhat less useful, but I have retained trailhead coordinates and waypoints that do not have cultural significance. Some will say this is still insufficient; others that it is pedantic. I'm sure I will hear from both sides!

The "author's name" abbreviation (AN) in the route narratives is used to describe sites for which I couldn't find an existing name.

Cedar Mesa has a local tradition of self-discovery in its canyons and on its mesa tops. In this spirit I have designed a guidebook that includes the most popular hikes of the area but is not a comprehensive map to the region. I have deleted references to minor archaeological sites or sites still well preserved. Nor have I pioneered any new routes. Whether a guidebook can claim to promote self-discovery is for you to decide, but if you have purchased this book chances are you would say yes. The difference between now and the days when there were fewer visitors is that today you're required to leave what's there there!

There are 1700 BLM-documented archaeological sites in the Cedar Mesa area. I probably saw 200 of them. I am sure I missed a few things in the routes I describe, and I know I haven't included everything. Many areas were intentionally left out for exploration by the adventuresome. The publisher and I have also agreed to not include any photographs of archaeological sites except for a few in this section that are unidentified.

I hope the self-discovery tradition will continue unhindered throughout Cedar Mesa. Keep on exploring!

Best of the Best

Car Walk: Mule Canyon Indian Ruin
Short Day Hike: Monarch Cave
Long Day Hike: NBNM Bridges Loop
Backpack Route: Kane Gulch–Bullet Canyon
Campsite: Muley Point Overlook

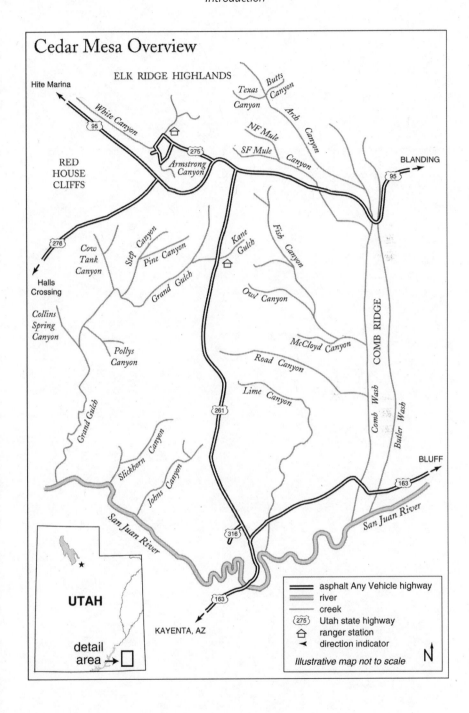

Cedar Mesa Overview

ELK RIDGE HIGHLANDS

Hite Marina

White Canyon

95

RED HOUSE CLIFFS

276

Halls Crossing

Collins Spring Canyon

Cow Tank Canyon

Step Canyon

Pine Canyon

Grand Gulch

Armstrong Canyon

275

Texas Canyon

Butts Canyon

Arch Canyon

NF Mule

SF Mule Canyon

BLANDING

95

Kane Gulch

Fish Canyon

Owl Canyon

McCloyd Canyon

Road Canyon

COMB RIDGE

Comb Wash

Butler Wash

Pollys Canyon

Lime Canyon

261

Grand Gulch

Slickhorn Canyon

Johns Canyon

BLUFF

163

San Juan River

San Juan River

316

163

KAYENTA, AZ

UTAH

detail area →

asphalt Any Vehicle highway
river
creek
275 Utah state highway
⌂ ranger station
◄ direction indicator

Illustrative map not to scale

N

Hike Summaries

Car Walks

	Location	Quality	Skill	Effort	Time	Vehicle
● 1 NBNM Loop Road	Hwy. 95	excellent	easy	easy	2 hr.	All
● 8 Salvation Knoll	Hwy. 95	good	moderate	moderate	20 min.	All
● 9 Mule Canyon Indian Ruin	Hwy. 95	good	easy	easy	10 min.	All
● 10 Dry Wash Canyon Overlook	Hwy. 95	fair	easy	easy	10 min.	Standard
● 14 Arch Canyon Overlook	Hwy. 95	good	easy	easy	30 min.	High Clearance
● 15 Mule Canyon Cave Towers Ruin	Hwy. 95	good	easy	easy	30 min.	Standard
● 28 Arch Canyon Ruin	Hwy. 95	good	easy	easy	30 min.	High Clearance
● 29 Walnut Knob Petroglyph Panel	Hwy. 95	fair	moderate	moderate	30 min.	All
● 16 Butler Wash Ruin Overlook	Hwy. 95	good	easy	easy	30 min.	All
● 23 Sand Island Petroglyph Panel	Hwy. 163/191	good	easy	easy	20 min.	All
● 24 Wolfman Petroglyph Panel	Hwy. 163	fair	easy	easy	30 min.	Standard
● 52 Valley of the Gods Loop	Hwy. 163/261	fair	easy	easy	2 hr.	All
● 46 Muley Point Overlook	Hwy. 261	good	easy	easy	30 min.	All
● 51 Goosenecks Overlook	Hwy. 316	good	easy	easy	15 min.	All

Day Hikes

	Location	Quality	Skill	Class	Effort	Time	Miles (r-t)
■ 2 Upper White Canyon	NBNM	good	moderate	2	moderate	5–7 hr.	11
■ 3 White Canyon	NBNM	fair	easy	2	easy	5–7 hr.	9.8
■ 4 Upper Armstrong Canyon	NBNM	fair	easy	2	easy	2–3 hr.	4.2
■ 5 NBNM Bridges Loop	NBNM	excellent	moderate	2	moderate	5–6 hr.	8.6
■ 6 Step-Pine Canyon Loop	Hwy. 95	fair	difficult	4	strenuous	6–8 hr.	9
■ 7 Grand Gulch Rim	Hwy. 95	fair	easy	1	easy	1–2 hr.	2.4
■ 11 South Fork Mule Canyon	Hwy. 95	good	moderate	2	moderate	3–4 hr.	8
■ 12 Mule Canyon Loop	Hwy. 95	fair	easy	2	easy	2–3 hr.	3.1
■ 13 North Fork Mule Canyon	Hwy. 95	good	moderate	2	moderate	7–9 hr.	10.8

	Access	Road	Trail		Rating	Time	Miles
17 Ballroom Cave	Hwy. 95	fair	easy	1	easy	1–2 hr.	2
26 Comb Wash Cave	Comb Wash	fair	moderate	2	easy	1–2 hr.	1
27 Arch Canyon	Comb Wash	good	easy	2	moderate	8–11 hr.	15.4
30 Lower Mule Canyon	Comb Wash	good	moderate	3	moderate	8–11 hr.	15.4
31 Lower Fish Canyon	Comb Wash	good	easy	2	easy	3–5 hr.	6.3
18 Fish Mouth Cave	Butler Wash	excellent	easy	2	easy	1–2 hr.	2
19 Cold Springs Cave	Butler Wash	good	easy	2	easy	2–3 hr.	3
20 Monarch Cave	Butler Wash	excellent	easy	1	easy	1–2 hr.	1
21 Procession Petroglyph Panel	Butler Wash	excellent	easy	2	easy	1–2 hr.	2
22 Double Stack Ruin Loop	Butler Wash	good	easy	3	easy	1–2 hr.	2.5
25 River Petroglyph Panel	Butler Wash	excellent	easy	2	easy	2–4 hr.	3
32 Kane Gulch	Hwy. 261	excellent	easy	2	easy	6–8 hr.	9.8
33 Owl Canyon	Hwy. 261	good	moderate	3	moderate	5–7 hr.	10
34 Todie Canyon	Hwy. 261	good	moderate	4	strenuous	2–4 hr.	4.6
35 Shieks Canyon	Hwy. 261	excellent	moderate	4	moderate	2–4 hr.	4
36 McCloyd Canyon	Hwy. 261	excellent	moderate	3	moderate	3–4 hr.	5.5
37 Bullet Canyon	Hwy. 261	excellent	moderate	3	strenuous	8–10 hr.	15
38 Government Trail–Big Man Panel	Hwy. 261	good	moderate	3	moderate	5–7 hr.	12.2
39 Government Trail–Pollys Canyon Loop	Hwy. 261	fair	difficult	4	moderate	4–6 hr.	9.6
40 Slickhorn Canyon #1–#2 Loop	Hwy. 261	good	moderate	3	moderate	6–8 hr.	9.8
41 Slickhorn Canyon #4–#6 Loop	Hwy. 261	good	moderate	3	moderate	6–8 hr.	10.8
42 Road Canyon	Hwy. 261	good	moderate	3	moderate	8–11 hr.	14.2
43 Lime Creek Canyon	Hwy. 261	good	moderate	3	moderate	8–10 hr.	15.4
44 Upper Johns Canyon Loop	Hwy. 261	fair	moderate	4	moderate	4–6 hr.	6.7

	Location	Quality	Skill	Class	Effort	Days	Miles (r-t)
■ 45 West Fork Johns Canyon	Hwy. 261	fair	difficult	4	moderate	3–4 hr.	5.2
■ 47 Honaker Trail	Hwy. 261	good	moderate	2	strenuous	3–4 hr.	3.8
■ 48 Johns Canyon Rim	Hwy. 261	fair	easy	1	easy	5–7 hr.	10.4
■ 49 Middle Johns Canyon	Hwy. 261	fair	easy	1	easy	5–7 hr.	9.5
■ 50 Lower Johns Canyon	Hwy. 261	fair	moderate	3	moderate	8–10 hr.	14.6
■ 53 Cow Tank Canyon	Hwy. 276	fair	easy	2	easy	5–7 hr.	10
■ 54 Collins Spring–Banister Ruin	Hwy. 276	good	easy	2	easy	6–8 hr.	10.1
Backpack Routes	*Location*	*Quality*	*Skill*	*Class*	*Effort*	*Days*	*Miles (r-t)*
◆ 55 Step Canyon	Hwy. 95	good	difficult	4	moderate	2–4	12.6
◆ 56 Arch-Texas-Butts Canyons	Hwy. 95	excellent	easy	1	easy	3–5	15.4
◆ 57 Kane Gulch–Bullet Canyon	Hwy. 261	excellent	moderate	3	moderate	3–5	22.8
◆ 58 Kane Gulch–Government Trail							
◆ 59 Kane Gulch–Collins Spring	Hwy. 261	excellent	easy	2	easy	4–6	28
◆ 60 Owl-McCloyd-Fish Canyons Loop	Hwy. 261	excellent	easy	2	easy	5–8	38
◆ 61 Slickhorn #1 – #6 Loop	Hwy. 261	excellent	moderate	3	strenuous	3–5	17
◆ 62 Slickhorn #1–Johns Canyon Loop	Hwy. 261	good	moderate	3	moderate	2–4	15.5
◆ 63 Collins Spring–San Juan River	Hwy. 261	fair	moderate	4	moderate	6–8	51
◆ 64 San Juan River–Kane Gulch	Hwy. 276	good	moderate	3	moderate	5–8	35.4
	San Juan	excellent	moderate	3	moderate	8–10	51.7

1

Natural Bridges
National Monument

Utah State Hwy. 275 and the Natural Bridges National
Monument (NBNM) loop road are paved all-vehicle surfaces. The
National Park Service (NPS) has a length limit for the loop road, but
recreational vehicles or trailers can be parked temporarily in the visitor
center carpark. Overnight parking is not permitted on the loop road. All
viewpoints are handicapped accessible with sidewalk surfaces. Drinking
water and flush toilets are available at the visitor center, which also has
two pay phones and a mailbox.

Any visit to NBNM is worth the effort. A leisurely drive around the
scenic loop with walks out to the viewpoints takes 2 hours. In 4–6 hours,
one could hike down and back to each of the three bridges. In a full day,
one could hike the NBNM Natural Bridges Loop and visit all the viewpoints in 7–9 hours.

The NPS has the following regulations for the national monument in
addition to those for the surrounding BLM-administered lands: (1) Pets
must be on a short leash and are not allowed in the canyon bottoms; (2)
Camping is only permitted in the designated campground of 13 spaces
for $10.00/night. The fee covers access to the vault toilet and a campsite
with a picnic table, tent pad, and one 26-foot combined vehicle length
parking space. Campsites are limited to 10 people and one vehicle only;
(3) Entrance fees are $6.00/vehicle or $3.00/person or bicyclist and are
paid at the visitor center. These are valid for 7 days; (4) Bicycles are only
allowed on paved surfaces.

The canyon bottoms are littered with chert, petrified wood, and
igneous precipitates from the Elk Ridge Highlands to the north. No
cattle are allowed and, consequently, there are fewer insects in the
national monument than in the surrounding BLM rangeland. The
abundant tree species include Fremont cottonwood, Gambel oak, piñon
pine, and Utah juniper, and the monument has a plethora of flowering
plants. Wildlife roams freely throughout the landscape. There are great
desert vistas, and sculpted sandstone canyons contorting the landscape.
Natural bridges are very rare geological features, and having three large
ones in such proximity is incredible. Because of the scenic, geological,

and archaeological values of the area, President Theodore Roosevelt created Natural Bridges National Monument on April 16, 1908. However, in the 1960s the monument's southern boundary was moved north from Snow Flat to the current location. The area's protection and preservation allow its unique aesthetic values to be enjoyed by everyone today and tomorrow.

Cass Hite, a prospector who settled the town of Hite (now under the waters of Lake Powell), is credited with being the first Anglo to discover the three natural bridges, which he named President, Congressman, and Senator in 1883. In 1904 they were renamed Augusta, Caroline, and Edwin. In 1908 President Roosevelt proclaimed Natural Bridges the first Utah site to be administered by the NPS. In 1909 President William Howard Taft gave the natural bridges more appropriate Hopi names. Kachina, Spirit or Sacred Dance, was chosen because of the dance symbols on the abutments. Sipapu, Place of Emergence, was chosen because of the bridge's unusual shape, while Owachomo, Flatrock Mound, was named after a geological feature atop the bridge. White Canyon was probably named after the white sandstone layers it cuts through.

For more information, call the NPS at (435) 629-1234; write Natural Bridges National Monument, P.O. Box 1, Lake Powell, UT 84533; or surf to www.nps.gov/nabr/.

Car Walk	Quality	Skill	Effort	Time	Vehicle
● 1 NBNM Loop Road	excellent	easy	easy	2 hr.	All

Day Hikes	Quality	Skill	Class	Effort	Time	Miles (r-t)
■ 2 Upper White Canyon	good	moderate	2	moderate	5–7 hr.	11
■ 3 White Canyon	fair	easy	2	easy	5–7 hr.	9.8
■ 4 Upper Armstrong Canyon	fair	easy	2	easy	2–3 hr.	4.2
■ 5 NBNM Bridges Loop	excellent	moderate	2	moderate	5–6 hr.	8.6

● 1 NBNM Loop Road

Access: The NBNM Loop Road is located in Natural Bridges National Monument. Take Utah State Hwy. 95 to mile 91, GPS coordinates 0,595,932 E; 4,159,734 N; Elevation 6840'. Turn north and follow Utah State Hwy. 275 for 4.4 miles to the NBNM visitor center.

Natural Bridges National Monument

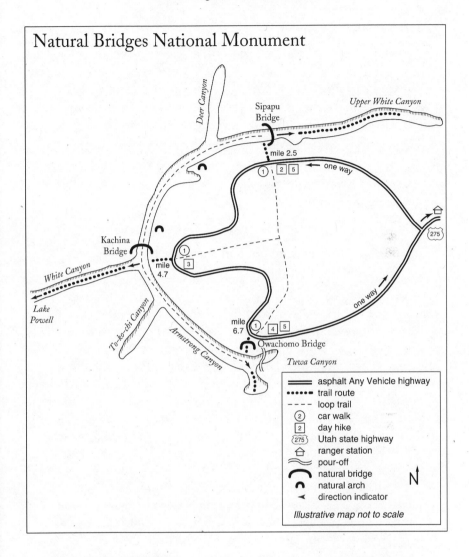

Trail Statistics: The route is ½-mile round-trip with a nominal elevation change requiring 1–2 hours to complete. This is an excellent walk over Class 1 terrain requiring easy effort and easy route-finding skills.

Attractions: Sipapu, Kachina, and Owachomo Natural Bridges.

Cautions: There is no midday shade.

■ 2 Upper White Canyon

Access: Upper White Canyon is located in Natural Bridges National Monument. Take Utah State Hwy. 95 to mile 91, GPS coordinates 0,595,932 E; 4,159,734 N; Elevation 6840'. Turn north and follow Utah State Hwy. 275 for 4.4 miles to the NBNM visitor center. Drive another 2.5 miles on the one-way loop road to the Sipapu Natural Bridge carpark.

Trail Statistics: The route is 11 miles round-trip with an elevation change of 500 feet requiring 5–7 hours to complete. This is a good hike over Class 1–2 terrain requiring moderate effort and moderate route-finding skills.

Attractions: Sipapu Natural Bridge.

Cautions: There is moderate midday shade.

Description: Descend the maintained NBNM trail to the Sipapu Natural Bridge in 20 minutes. Behind the NPS trail registry, head up-canyon northeast (right LUC) under the Sipapu Natural Bridge and onto the floor of White Canyon. It is 65 minutes to a north-trending tributary junction (left LUC). Follow the northeast stem (right LUC) and in 20 minutes, White Canyon bends sharply to the east (right LUC) with a beautiful dryfall and lower amphitheater directly north. I followed only deer tracks through the mud and vegetation from here. It is 15 minutes to north-northeast tributary junction (left LUC). Go east-southeast (right LUC) to reach a plunge pool and boulder dam obstacle. Bushwhack up the south wall (right LUC) to pass the boulder dam. It is 15 minutes to a north-trending tributary junction (left LUC). Bushwhack through the junction island vegetation in an easterly direction (right LUC). The last tributary junction is just ahead approximately 15 more minutes through greasy mud and thick vegetation. I chose to turn around at the island. The side tributaries were all choked with thick brush. The fall deciduous vegetation was beginning to turn yellow and contrasted strongly with the blue skies. I enjoyed the sense of walking in a canyon where no one else had walked for a while. I felt like an explorer surrounded by only nature and the sounds of my own footsteps. Return the way you came.

Upper White Canyon UTM GPS Coordinates

Sipapu carpark	0,587,415 E; 4,163,135 N	Elevation 6370'	00 min.
Sipapu Bridge	0,587,317 E; 4,163,467 N	Elevation 5870'	20 min.
North tributary junction	0,589,197 E; 4,164,700 N	Elevation 6000'	85 min.
North dryfall amphitheater	0,589,812 E; 4,164,793 N	Elevation 6050'	105 min.

Sipapu Natural Bridge

N-NE tributary junction	0,590,416 E; 4,164,964 N	Elevation 6100'	120 min.
North island junction	0,590,431 E; 4,164,969 N	Elevation 6150'	135 min.
Sipapu carpark	0,587,415 E; 4,163,135 N	Elevation 6370'	270 min.

■ 3 White Canyon

Access: White Canyon is located in Natural Bridges National Monument. Take Utah State Hwy. 95 to mile 91, GPS coordinates 0,595,932 E; 4,159,734 N; Elevation 6840'. Turn north and follow Utah State Hwy. 275 for 4.4 miles to the NBNM visitor center. Drive another 4.7 miles on the one-way loop road to the Kachina Natural Bridge carpark.

Trail Statistics: The route is 9.8 miles round-trip with an elevation change of 500 feet requiring 5–7 hours to complete. This is a fair hike over Class 1–2 terrain requiring easy effort and easy route-finding skills.

Attractions: Kachina Natural Bridge.

Cautions: Take your own drinking water and wear good footwear. Slickrock surfaces are slippery when wet. Stay on the major paths to avoid increasing erosion. All typical water hazards can be avoided. There is moderate midday shade.

Maps: USGS Blanding and Hite Crossing (1:100,000) or USGS Moss Back Butte (1:62,500)

Kachina Natural Bridge

Description: Descend the maintained NBNM trail to the Kachina Natural Bridge in 15 minutes noticing the small arch alongside the descent trail en route. Enjoy the rock art, Conical Ruin and natural beauty of Kachina Bridge. Follow White Canyon downstream past the Conical Ruin area and underneath the red "wrong way" sign suspended above the streambed by the NPS. This takes about 5 minutes. A small arch catches the morning light nicely just down-canyon from the "wrong way" sign on the north wall (right LDC). I call it the Morning Arch. Continue down-canyon for 60 minutes to a north-northeast-trending tributary junction (right LDC). Continue down the main canyon (left LDC) for 35 minutes to a south-trending tributary junction (left LDC) with a sloped pour-off at its mouth and a thick dead cottonwood on the outwash sand bar. Walk another 35 minutes down-canyon to a junction with a northeast-trending tributary (right LDC), where I chose to turn around. Enjoy a snack and return the way you came.

White Canyon UTM GPS Coordinates

Sipapu carpark	0,587,415 E; 4,163,135 N	Elevation 6370'	00 min.
Kachina carpark	0,585,986 E; 4,161,594 N	Elevation 6500'	00 min.
NPS trail marker	0,585,615 E; 4,160,745 N	Elevation 6060'	10 min.
Kachina Bridge	0,585,630 E; 4,161,618 N	Elevation 6040'	15 min.
Morning Arch junction	0,585,439 E; 4,161,570 N	Elevation 6020'	20 min.
NPS boundary	0,584,498 E; 4,161,331 N	Elevation 6000'	60 min.
N-NE tributary	0,583,723 E; 4,162,496 N	Elevation 5800'	80 min.
South tributary junction	0,581,899 E; 4,162,964 N	Elevation 5700'	115 min.
NE junction	0,581,558 E; 4,163,988 N	Elevation 5580'	150 min.
Kachina carpark	0,585,986 E; 4,161,594 N	Elevation 6500'	300 min.

■ 4 Upper Armstrong Canyon

Access: Upper Armstrong Canyon is located in Natural Bridges National Monument. Take Utah State Hwy. 95 to mile 91, GPS coordinates 0,595,932 E; 4,159,734 N; Elevation 6840'. Turn north and follow Utah State Hwy. 275 for 4.4 miles to the NBNM visitor center. Drive another 6.7 miles on the one-way loop road to Owachomo Natural Bridge carpark.

Trail Statistics: The route is 4.2 miles round-trip with an elevation change of 200 feet requiring 2–3 hours to complete. This is a fair hike over Class 1–2 terrain requiring easy effort and easy route-finding skills.

Attractions: Owachomo Natural Bridge.

Cautions: There is moderate midday shade.

Maps: USGS Blanding and Hite Crossing (1:100,000) or USGS Moss Back Butte (1:62,500)

Owachomo Natural Bridge

Description: Descend the maintained NBNM trail to the Owachomo Natural Bridge in 5 minutes. Pass underneath the natural bridge and turn east (left) on the floor of Armstrong Canyon. Walk up-canyon for 10 minutes to the junction of Tuwa Canyon (left LUC). Tuwa Canyon ends in a sloped 40′ pour-off and plunge pool almost immediately. Go up Armstrong Canyon (right LUC) for 20 minutes to an east-trending tributary (left LUC). It is another 40 minutes of walking to a wide junction with southeast- and east-trending tributaries. The east-trending tributary (left LUC) ends with a 25′ pour-off and garden seep in 5 minutes, while the southeast tributary (right LUC) ends with a 30′ pour-off and garden seep, also in 5 minutes. On one occasion, I walked this canyon section on a hot day in early October with strong sunshine. I remember lying in the shade of a Fremont cottonwood tree mesmerized by the harvest full moon in a blue sky. The scene was framed by the fluttering yellow leaves of the overhead canopy. Return the way you came.

Upper Armstrong Canyon UTM GPS Coordinates

Owachomo carpark	0,587,220 E; 4,160,014 N	Elevation 6500'	00 min.
Owachomo Bridge	0,587,171 E; 4,159,765 N	Elevation 6320'	05 min.
Tuwa & Armstrong junction	0,587,239 E; 4,159,672 N	Elevation 6300'	15 min.
Tuwa pour-off	0,587,502 E; 4,159,629 N	Elevation 6400'	20 min.
East tributary	0,587,663 E; 4,159,234 N	Elevation 6350'	35 min.
SE & East tributary junction	0,587,844 E; 4,158,492 N	Elevation 6400'	75 min.
Owachomo carpark	0,587,220 E; 4,160,014 N	Elevation 6500'	150 min.

■ 5 NBNM Bridges Loop

Access: The NBNM Bridges Loop is located in Natural Bridges National Monument. Take Utah State Hwy. 95 to mile 91, GPS coordinates 0,595,932 E; 4,159,734 N; Elevation 6840'. Turn north and follow Utah State Hwy. 275 for 4.4 miles to the NBNM visitor center. Drive another 2.5 miles to the Sipapu Natural Bridge carpark along the one-way loop road.

Trail Statistics: The route is 8.6 miles with an elevation change of 650 feet requiring 5–6 hours to complete. This is an excellent hike over Class 1–2 terrain requiring moderate effort and moderate route-finding skills.

Attractions: Sipapu, Kachina, and Owachomo Natural Bridges.

Cautions: There is moderate midday shade in White Canyon, limited midday shade in Armstrong Canyon, and almost no shade on the mesa top.

Maps: USGS Blanding and Hite Crossing (1:100,000) or USGS Moss Back Butte and Kane Gulch (1:62,500)

Description: This hike connects all three bridges in White and Armstrong Canyons with an overland leg. I started at Sipapu Natural Bridge and walked the exposed Armstrong Canyon and overland sections, under cloudy afternoon skies. On hot days, one should consider hiking from Owachomo to Sipapu for more shade, with a car or bike shuttle back to Owachomo.

Descend the steep trail to Sipapu Natural Bridge in 15 minutes. Take your time on the tricky sections of the descent. Continue down-canyon (left LDC at the trail registry) for 20 minutes to the junction of Deer Canyon (right LDC). Continue down White Canyon (left LDC) for 5 minutes to Horse Collar Ruin on a high alcove along the west wall (right LDC). However, this ruin is best seen from the rim-top viewpoint along the loop road above with binoculars. Continue for 25 minutes to an arch along the southeast canyon wall (left LDC). Kachina Natural Bridge is reached in 10 minutes. Rock art panels can be seen along each abutment surface, with both pictograph and petroglyph figures. The Conical Ruin and rock art panel are immediately downstream in White Canyon on the north wall (right LDC) along the high sandy deposition bank. There are plenty of cottonwoods here, so you can enjoy a lunch in the shade and make your best guess about the meanings of the rock art panels.

Continue southeast up-canyon (left LUC at the Armstrong/White Canyon junction from underneath Kachina Bridge), which puts you in Armstrong Canyon, and follow the NPS trail marker to avoid the sculpted 30' pour-off immediately upstream from Kachina Bridge. This is the same route up to the Kachina view area carpark, but traverse along the sandstone ledge following the rock cairns (starting at the NPS trail marker sign) instead of continuing the climb to the loop road.

It is 20 minutes of walking to a southwest-trending tributary junction (right LUC). Follow the main drainage bottom or the sandy bank trail east up-canyon (left LUC) for 10 minutes to an east-trending tributary canyon junction (left LUC). Go south up-canyon (right LUC) for 10 more minutes to the south-trending To-ko-chi Canyon junction (right LUC). Walk south-southeast up-canyon (left LUC) for 15 minutes to a north-northeast-trending tributary junction (left LUC). Go southeast up-canyon (right LUC) and avoid a boulder dam by following the cairns (left LUC). Watch for the NPS trail marker sign on the east wall (left LUC) in 10 minutes. It marks the ascent trail, which uses a high slickrock ledge to avoid several pour-offs and plunge pools in Armstrong Canyon. It is 10 minutes to Owachomo Natural Bridge, and 5 minutes to the Owachomo Natural Bridge carpark from the NPS trail marker sign. The mesa-top trail is across the pavement to the north and marked with a NPS sign. Follow the trail and cairns for 35 minutes to the NPS trail junction for all three bridges. Sipapu Natural Bridge carpark is only 20 more minutes of walking north.

NBNM Bridges Loop UTM GPS Coordinates

Sipapu carpark	0,587,415 E; 4,163,135 N	Elevation 6370'	00 min.
Sipapu Bridge	0,587,317 E; 4,163,467 N	Elevation 5870'	15 min.
Deer Canyon junction	0,586,615 E; 4,163,198 N	Elevation 6300'	35 min.
Horse Collar Ruin		Elevation 6300'	40 min.
Rim top arch	0,585,786 E; 4,162,135 N	Elevation 6200'	65 min.
Kachina Bridge	0,585,630 E; 4,161,618 N	Elevation 6040'	75 min.
NPS trail sign	0,585,615 E; 4,160,745 N	Elevation 6060'	80 min.
Southwest tributary junction	0,585,545 E; 4,161,072 N	Elevation 6090'	95 min.
East tributary junction	0,585,995 E; 4,161,092 N	Elevation 6120'	105 min.
To-ko-chi Canyon junction	0,586,044 E; 4,160,779 N	Elevation 6150'	115 min.
N-NE tributary junction	0,586,556 E; 4,160,258 N	Elevation 6200'	130 min.
Owachomo Bridge	0,587,171 E; 4,159,765 N	Elevation 6320'	150 min.
Owachomo carpark	0,587,220 E; 4,160,014 N	Elevation 6500'	155 min.
Overland trail junction	0,587,263 E; 4,161,901 N	Elevation 6600'	190 min.
Sipapu carpark	0,587,415 E; 4,163,135 N	Elevation 6370'	210 min.

2

Utah State Highway 95 Section

THE ALL-VEHICLE EAST-WEST UTAH STATE HWY. 95 IS PAVED, WITH narrow lanes and no shoulders from Hanksville to Blanding and few passing lanes. The road climbs over the rather blank sage flats between the Clay Hill cliffs and Salvation Knoll before descending to Comb Wash. A steep climb takes you over the Comb Ridge monocline and past Butler Wash to a second steep section at Cottonwood Wash before arriving in Blanding. Most of the access roads into Cedar Mesa are topped with clay soils that get exceedingly slick and mucky when soaked. Utah State Hwy. 95 is the major thoroughfare for folks heading to Lake Powell from the east. The hikes along Utah State Hwy. 95 are organized from west to east (Hanksville to Blanding) with numbered circles indicating car walks and numbered squares indicating day hikes. Numerous camping pullout tracks for standard and high-clearance vehicles intersect the highway.

After getting lost in midwinter during the 1879 Hole-in-the-Rock expedition, George Hobbs, Lemuel Redd, George Sevy, and George Morrill scouted a route around the forbidding barrier of Grand Gulch from a high point they named Salvation Knoll. The same scouts named Grand Gulch. Mule Canyon was named after the wild mules that once inhabited the canyon, and Arch Canyon for the natural arches it contains. Comb Ridge was named by the Hole-in-the-Rock expedition, probably after its resemblance to the comb on a rooster. Butler Wash was named after John Butler, one of the first scouts from the Hole-in-the-Rock expedition to enter San Juan County.

Access Points along Utah State Highway 95

Hwy. 95 & Hwy. 276	mile 83.8	0,586,727 E; 4,157,522 N	Elevation 6200'
Step & Pine Canyons	mile 87.2	0,591,455 E; 4,155,116 N	Elevation 6640'
Grand Gulch Rim	mile 88.6	0,593,469 E; 4,155,974 N	Elevation 6620'
Hwy. 275	mile 91.0	0,595,932 E; 4,159,734 N	Elevation 6840'
Hwy. 95 & Hwy. 261	mile 93.2	0,598,414 E; 4,159,525 N	Elevation 6800'
Salvation Knoll	mile 97.3	0,604,338 E; 4,157,984 N	Elevation 7200'
Mule Canyon Indian Ruin	mile 100.9	0,610,911 E; 4,155,335 N	Elevation 6000'
Dry Wash Canyon Overlook	mile 101.1	0,609,854 E; 4,155,697 N	Elevation 6000'

South Fork Mule Canyon	mile 102.3	0,611,598 E; 4,154,999 N	Elevation 6000'
Mule Canyon Loop	mile 102.3	0,611,598 E; 4,154,999 N	Elevation 6000'
North Fork Mule Canyon	mile 102.3	0,611,598 E; 4,154,999 N	Elevation 6000'
Arch Canyon Overlook	mile 102.3	0,611,598 E; 4,154,999 N	Elevation 6000'
Mule Canyon Cave Towers	mile 102.6	0,612,003 E; 4,154,755 N	Elevation 5980'
Northbound SJC #235	mile 107.4	0,618,801 E; 4,152,277 N	Elevation 4900'
Southbound SJC #235	mile 107.5	0,619,045 E; 4,152,248 N	Elevation 4900'
Butler Wash Overlook Ruin	mile 111.2	0,620,918 E; 4,153,443 N	Elevation 5200'
Ballroom Cave	mile 111.4	0,621,196 E; 4,153,911 N	Elevation 5200'
Hwy. 95 & SJC #230	mile 112.3	0,621,941 E; 4,154,875 N	Elevation 5400'

Car Walks	Quality	Skill	Effort	Time	Vehicle
● 8 Salvation Knoll	good	moderate	moderate	20 min.	All
● 9 Mule Canyon Indian Ruin					
	good	easy	easy	10 min.	All
● 10 Dry Wash Canyon Overlook					
	fair	easy	easy	10 min.	Standard
● 14 Arch Canyon Overlook					
	good	easy	easy	30 min.	High Clearance
● 15 Mule Canyon Cave Towers					
	good	easy	easy	30 min.	Standard
● 16 Butler Wash Ruin Overlook					
	good	easy	easy	30 min.	All

Day Hikes	Quality	Skill	Class	Effort	Time	Miles (r-t)
■ 6 Step-Pine Canyon Loop						
	fair	difficult	4	strenuous	6–8 hr.	9
■ 7 Grand Gulch Rim	fair	easy	1	easy	1–2 hr.	2.4
■ 11 SF Mule Canyon	good	moderate	2	moderate	3–4 hr.	8
■ 12 Mule Canyon Loop	fair	easy	2	easy	2–3 hr.	3.1
■ 13 NF Mule Canyon	good	moderate	2	moderate	7–9 hr.	10.8
■ 17 Ballroom Cave	fair	easy	1	easy	1–2 hr.	2

■ 6 Step-Pine Canyon Loop

Access: The Step-Pine Canyon complex is located south of Utah State Hwy. 95. At mile 87.2 turn onto San Juan County Route Mormon Trail #230A, GPS coordinates 0,591,455 E; 4,155,116 N; Elevation 6620'. Follow the standard-vehicle road surface for 3 miles to the dead-end slickrock rim carpark at GPS coordinates 0,588,092 E; 4,152,489 N; Elevation 6200'. Parking/camping is limited to several vehicles.

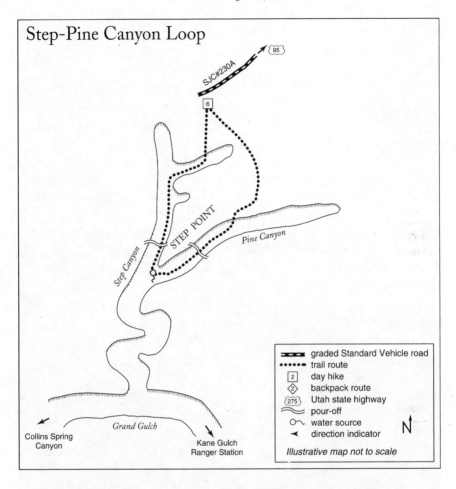

Trail Statistics: The route is 9 miles round-trip with an elevation change of 900 feet requiring 6–8 hours to complete. This is a good canyon hike over Class 1–4 terrain requiring moderate effort and difficult route-finding skills.

Attractions: An abandoned cowboy cache.

Cautions: There are two pour-offs in Step Canyon and a double-drop pour-off in Pine Canyon that require stacked rock booster steps or tree-limb ladders to circumnavigate. These helpers are occasionally removed by human and weather phenomena. Their absence will make this hike impassable. Check in with the Kane Gulch Ranger Station for the current status of these canyons and their helper stations. Take 30 feet of nylon line or tubular webbing for hauling packs or pets. There is minimal midday shade.

Step Canyon pour-off

Maps: USGS Blanding, Navajo Mountain and Hite Crossing (1:100,000), or USGS Black Moss Butte, Pollys Pasture (1:62,500), or Trails Illustrated Grand Gulch Plateau (1:62,500)

Description: From the carpark, traverse east-southeast to a small cleft and follow the slickrock runoff rivulets south (straight LDC) for 10 minutes to a shallow drainage. Go west (right LDC) and follow the streambed down-canyon for 10 minutes to a 10′ pour-off. Avoid this pour-off by traversing 5 minutes south (left LDC) into the next adjacent drainage and descending its 2' pour-off instead. Continue down-canyon for 10 minutes to a north-trending tributary junction (right LDC). Keep going south (left LDC) for another 25 minutes to a northeast-trending tributary junction (left LDC) followed by another 10 minutes to an east-trending tributary junction (left LDC) with two deep plunge pools. Go south for 10 minutes to another east-trending tributary junction (left LDC) followed by 35 minutes to a junction with a northeast-trending tributary (left LDC). Persist in a southerly direction (right LDC) for 5 more minutes to an old cowboy encampment along a low southeast-facing alcove in the western wall (right LDC) surrounded by barb-wire fence remnants.

It is 30 minutes to an 8' pour-off, but traverse along the eastern wall (left LDC) to a down-climb route. You will need either a rock pile step or a tree-limb ladder already at the bottom to overcome this obstacle. Otherwise, return the way you came!

It is 20 minutes to the confluence with Pine Canyon near a solitary hoodoo on the south rim. Go east (left LDC) up Pine Canyon for 60 minutes to a north-trending but short tributary dryfall (left LUC) just past an easily negotiated 4' pour-off. It is 45 minutes to the scalloped 40' Double Drop dryfall (AN) requiring some friction scrambling and a stack of rocks to create a booster step to overcome each drop. Return through Step Canyon if this obstacle is beyond your abilities.

Once on top, continue 15 minutes to a ledgy slope on the north wall (left LUC) immediately past a short, north-trending dryfall tributary (left LUC). This tributary immediately cliffs out but zigzag your way up the cross-bedding ledges to the rim of the inner gorge just up-canyon from this tributary. Walk north (left LUC) across the bench and find an ascent route through the broken 15' high cliff bands. Once on the mesa top, continue north across Step Point and follow the slickrock rim around the two eastern-trending tributaries of Step Canyon to the carpark. The rim walk to your vehicle takes 60 minutes.

Step-Pine Canyon Loop UTM GPS Coordinates

Step Point carpark	0,588,092 E; 4,152,489 N	Elevation 6200'	00 min.
Streambed path	0,587,956 E; 4,151,899 N	Elevation 6100'	10 min.
Pour-off traverse bottom	0,587,419 E; 4,151,894 N	Elevation 6000'	25 min.
North tributary junction	0,586,815 E; 4,151,757 N	Elevation 5900'	35 min.
NE tributary junction	0,586,195 E; 4,150,675 N	Elevation 5800'	60 min.
East tributary junction	0,585,981 E; 4,150,454 N	Elevation 5700'	70 min.
East tributary junction	0,584,913 E; 4,150,000 N	Elevation 5600'	105 min.
Cowboy encampment	0,584,347 E; 4,149,976 N	Elevation 5600'	110 min.

Pour-off traverse	0,583,924 E; 4,148,955 N	Elevation 5550′	140 min.
Pine Canyon junction	0,583,732 E; 4,148,443 N	Elevation 5300′	160 min.
North-trending dryfall	0,586,155 E; 4,149,182 N	Elevation 5350′	220 min.
Double Drop dryfall	0,588,078 E; 4,150,617 N	Elevation 5400′	265 min.
Pine Canyon exit	0,588,848 E; 4,151,448 N	Elevation 5500′	280 min.
Step Point carpark	0,588,092 E; 4,152,489 N	Elevation 6200′	340 min.

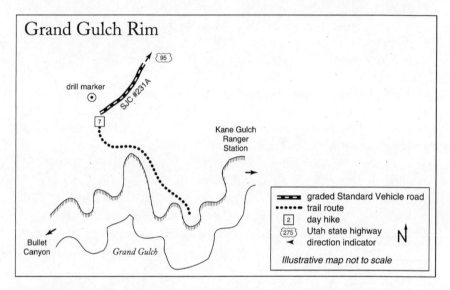

■ 7 Grand Gulch Rim

Access: Grand Gulch Rim is located south of Utah State Hwy. 95. At mile 88.6, turn onto San Juan County Route Harmony Flat #231A, GPS coordinates 0,593,469 E; 4,155,974 N; Elevation 6620′. Follow the standard-vehicle road surface south for 4.3 miles to the carpark adjacent to the drill marker at GPS coordinates 0,590,148 E; 1,149,808 N; Elevation 5980′. Parking/camping is limited to several vehicles.

Trail Statistics: The route is 2.4 miles round-trip with an elevation change of 50 feet requiring 1–2 hours to complete. This is a fair surface hike over Class 1 terrain requiring easy effort and easy route-finding skills.

Attractions: Grand Gulch vistas.

Cautions: There is no midday shade.

Maps: USGS Blanding (1:100,000), or USGS Cedar Mesa North (1:62,500), or Trails Illustrated Grand Gulch Plateau (1:62,500)

Description: Record a waypoint before leaving your vehicle and another atop the sandstone knob immediately to the east of the carpark. Avoid trampling the cryptogamic soils on the mesa surface. Descend the eastern face of the knob and contour down into the runoff rivulet trails. Follow these to the main wash and descend the sandy and slickrock streambed surfaces south (right LDC) to the rim of Grand Gulch. There are abandoned meanders, fins, hoodoos, and intricate Cedar Mesa sandstone wall formations to see from the rim. Traverse across the southeastern peninsula (left LDC) for other views. Take binoculars with you. Return the way you came.

Grand Gulch Rim UTM GPS Coordinates

Grand Gulch Rim carpark	0,590,148 E 1,149,808 N	Elevation 5980′	00 min.
First overlook	0,590,801 E 1,149,359 N	Elevation 5980′	20 min.
Second overlook	0,591,289 E 1,149,052 N	Elevation 6000′	30 min.
Grand Gulch Rim carpark	0,590,148 E 1,149,808 N	Elevation 5980′	60 min.

● 8 Salvation Knoll

Access: Salvation Knoll is located south of Utah State Hwy. 95 on the crest at mile 97.3, GPS coordinates 0,604,338 E; 4,157,984 N; Elevation 7200′. There is an information sign here. Parking is limited to six vehicles.

Trail Statistics: From the gravel carpark, the ⅛-mile trail climbs steeply up the 40′ tall knoll. This is a good walk over Class 1–2 terrain requiring moderate effort and moderate route-finding skills.

Attractions: Stunning desert vistas.

Cautions: If the trail is wet, the mud is slippery! Stay on the major paths to avoid increasing erosion. There is minimal midday shade along this route.

● 9 Mule Canyon Indian Ruin

Access: The Mule Canyon Indian Ruin is located north of Utah State Hwy. 95 at mile 100.9, GPS coordinates 0,610,911 E; 4,155,335 N; Elevation 6000′. There is a pit toilet but no potable water or refuse collection.

Trail Statistics: A ⅛-mile concrete path leads from the carpark to the ruin and information board. This is a good walk over Class 1 terrain requiring easy effort and easy route-finding skills. It is handicapped accessible.

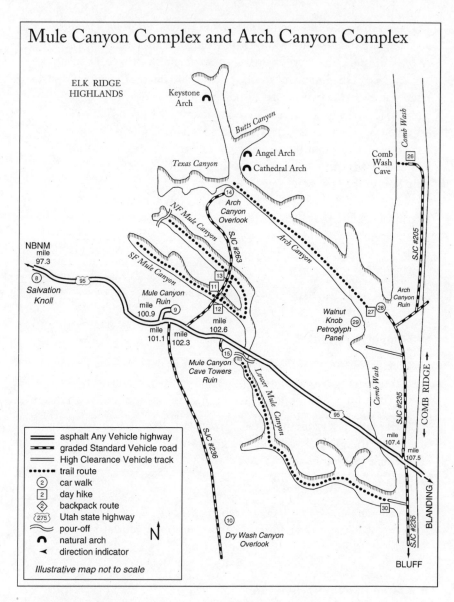

Mule Canyon Complex and Arch Canyon Complex

ELK RIDGE
HIGHLANDS

Keystone Arch

Butts Canyon

Texas Canyon

Angel Arch

Cathedral Arch

Comb Wash Cave

Comb Wash

Arch Canyon Overlook

NF Mule Canyon

SJC #263

Arch Canyon

SJC #205

NBNM mile 97.3

Salvation Knoll

SF Mule Canyon

Mule Canyon Ruin
mile 100.9

mile 101.1

mile 102.3

mile 102.6

Walnut Knob Petroglyph Panel

Arch Canyon Ruin

Mule Canyon Cave Towers Ruin

Lower Mule Canyon

Comb Wash

SJC #235

COMB RIDGE

mile 107.4

mile 107.5

SJC #236

BLANDING

SJC #235

Dry Wash Canyon Overlook

BLUFF

asphalt Any Vehicle highway
graded Standard Vehicle road
High Clearance Vehicle track
trail route
2 car walk
2 day hike
backpack route
275 Utah state highway
pour-off
natural arch
direction indicator

N

Illustrative map not to scale

Attractions: Stabilized tower, kiva, and habitat structures with informative sign.

● 10 Dry Wash Canyon Overlook

Access: The Dry Wash Canyon Overlook is located south of Utah State Hwy. 95. At mile 101.1, turn onto San Juan County Route Lower

Bailey Road #236, GPS coordinates 0,609,854 E; 4,155,697 N; Elevation 6000'. Follow the standard-vehicle road surface south for 6.6 miles to the Dry Wash Canyon rim. Refer to map.

Trail Statistics: The route is ¼-mile round-trip with nominal elevation changes that takes 10 minutes to complete. This is a fair walk over Class 1 terrain requiring easy effort and easy route-finding skills.

Attractions: Comb Ridge vista.

■ 11 South Fork Mule Canyon

Access: The South Fork of Mule Canyon is located north of Utah State Hwy. 95. At mile 102.3, turn onto San Juan County Route Arch Canyon #263, GPS coordinates 0,611,598 E; 4,154,999 N; elevation 6045'. Follow the standard-vehicle road surface for 0.3 mile to the carpark. Parking is limited to several vehicles. There are good camping sites farther north up the road.

Trail Statistics: The route is 8 miles round-trip with an elevation change of 400 feet requiring 3–4 hours to complete. This is an good canyon hike over Class 1–2 terrain requiring moderate effort and moderate route-finding skills.

Attractions: Sandstone canyon in an alpine setting.

Cautions: There is minimal midday shade along this route. A flash flood ripped through this canyon in the summer of 1999 stripping the streambed down to bedrock in many places.

Maps: USGS Blanding (1:100,000), or USGS South Long Point and Hotel Rock (1:62,500), or Trails Illustrated Grand Gulch Plateau (1:62,500)

Description: From the trailhead registry, hike up-canyon for 20 minutes. There are structures under an overhang along the north wall (right LUC). In 40 minutes you'll see structures high on the northern wall (right LUC) that you can admire from the slickrock slope below with binoculars. Continue 40 minutes up-canyon to another inaccessible alcove containing structures high on the north wall (right LUC). You can use binoculars to see details of the site.

The prominent bench below is an excellent place to enjoy a snack and bask in the sunshine. From this bench, one can find the roaring lion figure maiden (AN) pinnacle on the north canyon wall (right LUC) before the South Fork of Mule Canyon blends into the piñon pines crowding each other on top of Cedar Mesa. Play the imagination game and name objects seen in the clouds and rock formations around you. Return the way you came.

South Fork Mule Canyon UTM GPS Coordinates

SF Mule Canyon carpark	0,612,091 E; 4,155,082 N	Elevation 5900′	00 min.
Twenty-minute ruin		Elevation 5950′	20 min.
High alcove ruin	0,608,722 E; 4,156,672 N	Elevation 6200′	60 min.
Roaring lion figure maiden	0,607,981 E; 4,157,487 N	Elevation 6425′	100 min.
SF Mule Canyon carpark	0,612,091 E; 4,155,082 N	Elevation 5900′	200 min.

■ 12 Mule Canyon Loop

Access: The Mule Canyon loop is located north of Utah State Hwy. 95. At mile 102.3, turn onto San Juan County Route Arch Canyon #263, GPS coordinates 0,611,598 E; 4,154,999 N; Elevation 6045′. Follow the standard-vehicle road surface for 0.3 mile to the carpark. Parking is limited to several vehicles. There are good camping spots within the next mile on Arch Canyon #263. Refer to map.

Trail Statistics: The route is 3.1 miles with an elevation change of 200 feet requiring 2–3 hours to complete. This is a fair canyon hike over Class 1–2 terrain requiring easy effort and easy route-finding skills.

Attractions: Gentle canyon loop walk.

Cautions: There is minimal midday shade along this route. A flash flood ripped through this canyon in the summer of 1999 stripping the streambed down to bedrock in many places. Do not venture too close to the lip of the Mule Canyon waterfall since gusty winds are common through here.

Maps: USGS Blanding (1:100,000), or USGS South Long Point (1:62,500), or Trails Illustrated Grand Gulch Plateau (1:62,500)

Description: This hike begins at the carpark for the South Fork of Mule Canyon and heads down-canyon by walking down the San Juan County Route Arch Canyon #263 fill slope. Notice the pre-atomic-era rusted automobile shell resting at the bottom on the north side of the stream (left LDC). Walk down-canyon for 30 minutes to the junction of the North and South Forks of Mule Canyon. The highway can be seen to the south (right LDC). If you're interested, go south down-canyon and walk through the eerie culvert pipe and listen to the vibrations of your

Mule Canyon waterfall in flood

footsteps in the metal ribs. It is 5 minutes to the top of the 30' Mule Canyon dryfall and 100' tall amphitheater chamber below. Gusty winds are common in here. Don't go peering over the lip.

Return back up-canyon and explore the North Fork of Mule Canyon (right LUC). Weave your way through flash-flood debris for 20 minutes until reaching an undercut sandstone pour-off ledge that requires backtracking a few steps and scrambling up onto the channel ledge (left LUC) to navigate around this obstacle. It is another 20 minutes to the North Fork of Mule Canyon carpark through water-polished sandstone surfaces. From the bridge over the North Fork of Mule Canyon, it is 15 minutes walking along San Juan County Route Arch Canyon #263 south (left LUC) to the South Fork of Mule Canyon carpark.

Mule Canyon Loop UTM GPS Coordinates

SF Mule Canyon carpark	0,612,091 E; 4,155,082 N	Elevation 5900'	00 min.
North and South Forks junction	0,612,559 E; 4,154,740 N	Elevation 5800'	35 min.
NF Mule Canyon carpark	0,612,320 E; 4,155,759 N	Elevation 6000'	75 min.
SF Mule Canyon carpark	0,612,091 E; 4,155,082 N	Elevation 5900'	90 min.

■ 13 North Fork Mule Canyon

Access: The North Fork of Mule Canyon is located north of Utah State Hwy. 95. At mile 102.3, turn onto San Juan County Route Arch Canyon #263, GPS coordinates 0,611,598 E; 4,154,999 N; Elevation 6045'. Follow the standard-vehicle road surface for 1 mile to the carpark near the bridge. Parking is limited to several vehicles. There are good camping sites along Arch Canyon #263. Refer to map.

Trail Statistics: The route is 10.8 miles round-trip with an elevation change of 400 feet requiring 7–9 hours to complete. This is a good canyon hike over Class 1–2 terrain requiring moderate effort and moderate route-finding skills.

Attractions: Sandstone canyon in an alpine setting.

Cautions: There is minimal midday shade along this route. A flash flood ripped through this canyon in the summer of 1999 stripping the streambed down to bedrock in many places.

Maps: USGS Blanding (1:100,000), or USGS South Long Point and Hotel Rock (1:62,500), or Trails Illustrated Grand Gulch Plateau (1:62,500)

Description: From the trailhead registry, hike up-canyon for 75 minutes to structures high on the northern wall near the skyline (right

LUC). Continue up-canyon for another 15 minutes to more structures near the skyline (right LUC). There are no trails to these inaccessible ruins, which must be admired from below with binoculars.

For the adventuresome, continue up-canyon for 45 minutes to the start of the North Fork's narrow section. In another 45 minutes, a junction with the brief north-trending tributary is encountered. Stay in the main streambed channel (left LUC) and continue 10 minutes to a 30' serpentine dryfall. This is an excellent place to enjoy a snack and bask in the sunshine. Return the way you came.

North Fork Mule Canyon UTM GPS Coordinates

NF Mule Canyon carpark	0,612,320 E; 4,155,759 N	Elevation 6000'	00 min.
High alcove ruin		Elevation 6150'	75 min.
Skyline ruin		Elevation 6200'	90 min.
30' dryfall	0,607,396 E; 4,159,598 N	Elevation 6375'	190 min.
NF Mule Canyon carpark	0,612,320 E; 4,155,759 N	Elevation 6000'	380 min.

North Fork of Mule Canyon, Cedar Mesa Sandstone cross-bedding planes

● 14 Arch Canyon Overlook

Access: Arch Canyon Overlook is located north of Utah State Hwy. 95. At mile 102.3, turn onto San Juan County Route Arch Canyon #263, GPS coordinates 0,611,598 E; 4,154,999 N; Elevation 6045'. Go north on the high-clearance road for 6.4 miles to a 4WD track (right). It is a steep 0.2 mile to the overlook. Parking is limited to six vehicles. Refer to map.

Trail Statistics: The route is a 1/8-mile round-trip with nominal elevation changes that takes 30 minutes to complete. This is a good walk over Class 1–2 terrain requiring easy effort and easy route-finding skills.

Attractions: Stunning vistas of Angel Arch and Cathedral Arch.

● 15 Mule Canyon Cave Towers Ruin

Access: The Mule Canyon Cave Towers Ruin is located south of Utah State Hwy. 95 at a gated turnout at mile 102.6, GPS coordinates 0,612,003 E; 4,154,755 N; Elevation 5980'. Follow the high-clearance-vehicle road 0.6 mile south to the carpark. Parking/camping is limited to a dozen vehicles. Refer to map.

Trail Statistics: It is a ¾-mile round-trip requiring 30 minutes of walking with nominal elevation changes. This is a good walk over Class 1–2 terrain requiring easy effort and easy route-finding skills.

Attractions: Mule Canyon Cave Towers Ruin.

Description: From the carpark, follow the worn path to the head of the canyon. Explore the surface ruin on each side. There are three circular structures on the west rim and five circular and linear structures on the east rim. The walls are partially intact on two of the structures, and there is one intact door on the west rim tower structure. Please don't climb on the structures; they have not been stabilized. Walk along each canyon rim to get better views of the six alcove structures below, three under each rim. A good set of binoculars would be useful here. There is no route down to the structures. Don't stand on the cliff edges that are undercut. Gusty winds are typical. Return the way you came.

● 16 Butler Wash Ruin Overlook

Access: The Butler Wash Ruin Overlook is located northwest of Utah State Hwy. 95 at mile 111.2, GPS coordinates 0,620,918 E; 4,153,443 N; Elevation 5200'. There is a pit toilet but no potable water or refuse collection.

Trail Statistics: It is 1 mile round-trip, climbs 80 feet, and takes 30–60 minutes to complete. This is a good walk over Class 1–2 terrain requiring easy effort and easy route-finding skills.

Attractions: Butler Wash Ruin.

Ballroom Cave and Butler Wash Ruin Overlook

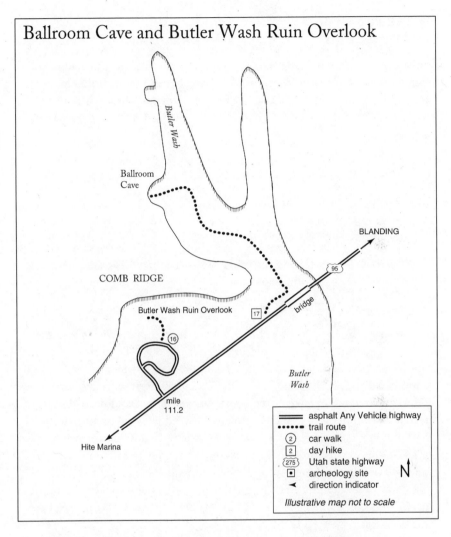

Butler Wash

Ballroom
Cave

BLANDING

COMB RIDGE

95

Butler Wash Ruin Overlook 17 bridge

16

*Butler
Wash*

mile
111.2

Hite Marina

	asphalt Any Vehicle highway
••••••	trail route
②	car walk
2	day hike
{275}	Utah state highway
▣	archeology site
◄	direction indicator

N

Illustrative map not to scale

Description: From the carpark, follow the ½-mile path to the overlook area as it ascends on slickrock surfaces. For the best photography, visit the ruin in the morning so the early light will illuminate the alcove ruin sufficiently. A good set of binoculars is necessary to see the details of the structures since the overlook is on the east rim looking across the draw 100' to the ruin under the west rim. Return the way you came.

■ 17 Ballroom Cave

Access: The Ballroom Cave is located north of Utah State Hwy. 95, mile 111.4, GPS coordinates 0,621,196 E; 4,153,911 N; Elevation 5200′. You can hike down the short access trail starting behind the pit toilet to the small off-highway carpark near the bridge. Parking is limited to several vehicles. Campsites are available along Butler Wash #230 nearby. Refer to map.

Trail Statistics: The route is 2 miles round-trip with an elevation change of 100 feet requiring 1–2 hours to complete. This is a fair canyon hike over Class 1 terrain requiring easy effort and easy route-finding skills.

Attractions: Ballroom Cave Ruin.

Cautions: There is moderate midday shade along this route.

Maps: USGS Blanding (1:100,000), or USGS Hotel Rock (1:62,500), or Trails Illustrated Grand Gulch Plateau (1:62,500)

Description: Follow the path up the northern drainage for 5 minutes to a northeast-trending tributary junction (right LUC). Go north-northwest (left LUC) for 15 minutes through tall willows and small cottonwood trees. The trail crosses the Butler Wash rivulet several times. From the junction of a west-trending tributary (left LUC), follow the steep trail to Ballroom Cave in the head alcove. Avoid walking on the soft soils near the precariously balanced walls. The alcove has no artifacts or rock art. For the curious, Butler Wash continues up-canyon for another 10 minutes before reaching a terminal junction between a west-trending tributary (left LUC) that leads to a small amphitheater pour-off and the north-trending main stem (right LUC) that also ends in a pour-off. Return the way you came.

Ballroom Cave UTM GPS Coordinates

Hwy. 95 carpark	0,621,089 E; 4,153,994 N	Elevation 5200′	00 min.
N-NW & N-NE junction	0,621,025 E; 4,154,170 N	Elevation 5220′	05 min.
Ballroom Cave		Elevation 5300′	20 min.
Terminal junction	0,620,006 E; 4,155,530 N	Elevation 5300′	30 min.
Highway 95 carpark	0,621,089 E; 4,153,994 N	Elevation 5200′	60 min.

3

Butler Wash Section:
San Juan County Routes 230 and
Lower Butler Wash 262

THE EAST SIDE OF THE COMB RIDGE MONOCLINE CONTAINS MANY SIDE drainages climbing through the 750' tall hogbacks of Navajo Sandstone. The eastern rim of Butler Wash is composed of successive layers of Entrada Sandstone, Summerville Formation, Curtis Formation, Morrison Formation, and Dakota Sandstone. The Comb Wash side of Comb Ridge is composed of Moenkopi Formation, Chinle Formation, Wingate Sandstone, Kayenta Formation, and Navajo Sandstone on top. The Ancestral Puebloan peoples farmed the alluvial fill of Butler Wash extensively, and many artifacts of their culture exist in these side canyons. Interestingly, many sites display Kayenta ceramic and masonry influences here. Every fissure has a little something. One could spend a week hiking these side canyons and enjoy their rewards and frustrations.

Numerous camping pullouts can be found along this section. The standard-vehicle road surface, composed of clays and sands, is slick when wet. San Juan County Route Butler Wash #230 and San Juan County Route Lower Butler Wash #262 have many steep wash crossings that may make towing trailers difficult. I have included a sampling of the more popular sites in Butler Wash. The hikes are organized from north to south (Blanding to Bluff) with numbered circles indicating car walks and numbered squares indicating day hikes.

Access Points along San Juan County Routes #230 and #262

Hwy. 95 & SJC #230	mile 0.0	0,621,941 E; 4,154,875 N	Elevation 5400'
Fish Mouth Cave	mile 8.4	0,620,633 E; 4,142,890 N	Elevation 4800'
Cold Springs Cave	mile 13.5	0,621,230 E; 4,136,166 N	Elevation 4700'
Monarch Cave	mile 13.8	0,621,430 E; 4,135,396 N	Elevation 4700'
Procession Petroglyph Panel	mile 14.4	0,621,445 E; 4,134,542 N	Elevation 4680'
Double Stack Ruin	mile 17.2	0,621,416 E; 4,130,426 N	Elevation 4600'
Wolfman Petroglyph Panel	mile 20.0	0,621,337 E; 4,124,974 N	Elevation 4400'
Hwy. 163 & SJC #262	mile 21.0	0,621,337 E; 4,124,974 N	Elevation 4400'

Access Points along Utah State Hwy. 191/163 (East-West)

Sand Island Petroglyph Panel	mile 22.6	0,623,246 E; 4,125,199 N	Elevation 4300'
Hwy. 163 & Hwy. 191	mile 21.4	0,621,915 E; 4,125,008 N	Elevation 4450'
River Petroglyph Panel	mile 40.5	0,620,450 E; 4,124,774 N	Elevation 4280'
Valley of the Gods Loop	mile 29.0	0,605,245 E; 4,121,388 N	Elevation 4500'
Hwy. 163 & Hwy. 261	mile 24.9	0,600,764 E; 4,116,920 N	Elevation 4500'

Car Walks	Quality	Skill	Effort	Time	Vehicle
● 23 Sand Island Petroglyph Panel					
	good	easy	easy	20 min.	All
● 24 Wolfman Petroglyph Panel					
	fair	easy	easy	30 min.	All

Day Hikes	Quality	Skill	Class	Effort	Time	Miles (r-t)
■ 18 Fish Mouth Cave	excellent	easy	2	easy	1–2 hr.	2
■ 19 Cold Springs Cave	good	easy	2	easy	2–3 hr.	3
■ 20 Monarch Cave	excellent	easy	1	easy	1–2 hr.	1
■ 21 Procession Petroglyph Panel						
	excellent	easy	2	easy	1–2 hr.	2
■ 22 Double Stack Ruin Loop						
	good	easy	3	easy	1–2 hr.	2.5
■ 25 River Petroglyph Panel						
	excellent	easy	2	easy	2–4 hr.	3

■ 18 Fish Mouth Cave

Access: Fish Mouth Cave is located east of San Juan County Route Butler Wash #230 between Utah State Hwy. 95 and Utah State Hwy. 163.

From the north, take Utah State Hwy. 95 to mile 112.3 and San Juan County Route Butler Wash #230, GPS coordinates 0,621,941 E; 4,154,875 N; Elevation 5400'. Turn onto San Juan County Route #230, drive past the BLM sign at 0.2 mile, and turn right onto the south branch of the intersection at 0.3 mile. Continue south to a fence at 8.4 miles and turn west (right) onto a standard-vehicle track (GPS coordinates 0,620,633 E; 4,142,890 N; Elevation 4800').

From the south, take Utah State Hwy. 163 to mile 40.5 and turn north onto San Juan County Route Lower Butler Wash #262, GPS coordinates 0,621,337 E; 4,124,974 N; Elevation 4400'. Drive 9.9 miles and turn left onto San Juan County Route Butler Wash #230 (GPS coordinates 0,622,313 E; 4,139,071 N; Elevation 4800'). Continue north to mile 12.6 and turn left

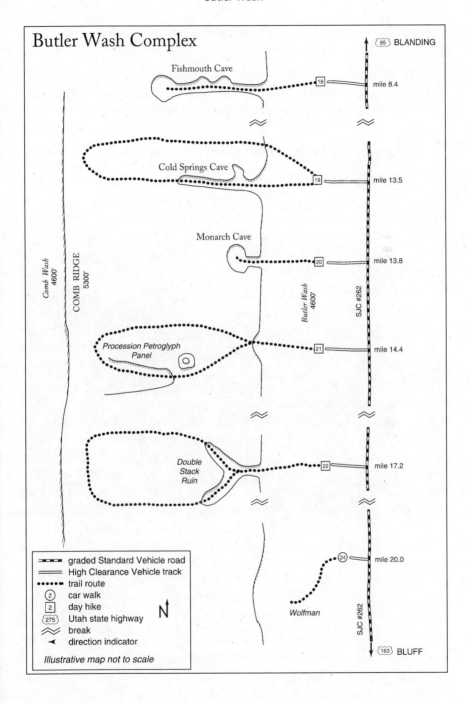

Butler Wash Complex

95 BLANDING

Fishmouth Cave

18   mile 8.4

Cold Springs Cave

19   mile 13.5

Monarch Cave

20   mile 13.8

Comb Wash 4600'

COMB RIDGE 5300'

Butler Wash 4600'

SJC #262

Procession Petroglyph Panel

21   mile 14.4

Double Stack Ruin

22   mile 17.2

24   mile 20.0

Wolfman

SJC #262

163 BLUFF

Legend:

- ▰▰▰ graded Standard Vehicle road
- ═══ High Clearance Vehicle track
- •••••• trail route
- ② car walk
- ② day hike
- ⟮275⟯ Utah state highway
- ≋ break
- ◄ direction indicator

N

Illustrative map not to scale

(west) onto the standard-vehicle track before crossing the fence and cattle guard. Parking/camping is limited to several vehicles.

Trail Statistics: The route is 2 miles round-trip with an elevation change of 50 feet requiring 1–2 hours to complete. This is an excellent hike over Class 1–2 terrain requiring easy effort and easy route-finding skills.

Attractions: Fish Mouth Cave Ruin.

Cautions: There is limited midday shade along this route.

Maps: USGS Blanding and Bluff (1:100,000), or USGS Bluff Northwest (1:62,500), or Trails Illustrated Grand Gulch Plateau (1:62,500)

View of La Sal Mountains from Butler Wash

Description: Follow the path up the western draw for 15 minutes to a rim alcove in the north wall (right LUC). In another 5 minutes of up-canyon walking, there is a second south-facing alcove (right LUC). Fish Mouth Cave is 15 minutes further up-canyon (straight LUC). Return the way you came.

Fish Mouth Cave UTM GPS Coordinates

Fish Mouth Cave carpark	0,620,633 E; 4,142,890 N	Elevation 4800′	00 min.
First alcove		Elevation 4860′	15 min.

Second alcove		Elevation 4880'	20 min.
Fish Mouth Cave		Elevation 4920'	35 min.
Fish Mouth Cave carpark	0,620,633 E; 4,142,890 N	Elevation 4800'	70 min.

■ 19 Cold Springs Cave

Access: Cold Springs Cave is located east of San Juan County Route Lower Butler Wash #262 between Utah State Hwy. 95 and Utah State Hwy. 163.

From the north, take Utah State Hwy. 95 to mile 112.3 and San Juan County Route Butler Wash #230, GPS coordinates 0,621,941 E; 4,154,875 N; Elevation 5400'. Turn onto Butler Wash #230, drive past the BLM sign at 0.2 mile, and turn right onto the south branch of the intersection at 0.3 mile. Continue south to a junction with San Juan County Route Lower Butler Wash #262 at mile 11.1 (GPS coordinates 0,622,313 E; 4,139,071 N; Elevation 4800'). Continue south (right) and turn west (right) at mile 13.5 onto a standard-vehicle track (GPS coordinates 0,621,230 E; 4,136,166 N; Elevation 4700').

From the south, take Utah State Hwy. 163 to mile 40.5 and turn north onto San Juan County Route Lower Butler Wash #262, GPS coordinates 0,621,337 E; 4,124,974 N; Elevation 4400'. Drive north for 7.5 miles and turn left (west) onto the standard-vehicle track. Parking/camping is limited to several vehicles. Refer to Butler Wash Complex map.

Trail Statistics: This route is 3 miles round-trip with an elevation change of 500 feet requiring 2–3 hours to complete. This is a good hike over Class 1–2 terrain requiring easy effort and easy route-finding skills.

Attractions: Cold Springs Cave Ruin.

Cautions: There is limited midday shade along this route.

Maps: USGS Bluff (1:100,000), or USGS Bluff Southwest (1:62,500), or Trails Illustrated Grand Gulch Plateau (1:62,500)

Description: Follow the obvious cattle/human trail across Butler Wash. The exit canyon is immediately south (left) of the prominent east-facing cave midway up the slickrock slope. The canyon to Cold Springs Cave is the second one south of this cave (left) with a prow of red rock near the ridgeline. Gain access to the bottom of the Cold Springs Cave tributary and follow the trail through the sandy bottom to a junction with a northwest-trending drainage (right LUC) in 10 minutes. It has a 4' pour-off at its mouth with a traverse trail on its west wall (left LUC). Cold Springs Cave is immediately up-canyon in the southeast-facing alcove (right LUC). Notice the concentric circle petroglyph on a wall block. Speculate on its significance. Return the way you came, or continue up to Comb Ridge by following the main drainage west-southwest (left LUC) from the junction with the 4' pour-over. It is 35 minutes over mostly slickrock surfaces to the north escarpment above the saddle with the exit canyon. Head northeast down to the saddle and around the prominent cliff to the north. The exit canyon has a few simple rock fall obstacles to negotiate. It is 35 minutes to the bottom of the drainage and another 10 minutes back to the carpark.

Cold Springs Cave UTM GPS Coordinates

Cold Springs Cave carpark	0,621,230 E; 4,136,166 N	Elevation 4700'	00 min.
Cold Springs Cave		Elevation 4720'	10 min.
Comb Ridge Vista	0,619,304 E; 4,136,118 N	Elevation 5200'	45 min.
Cold Springs Cave carpark	0,621,230 E; 4,136,166 N	Elevation 4700'	90 min.

■ 20 Monarch Cave

Access: Monarch Cave is located east of San Juan County Route Lower Butler Wash #262 between Utah State Hwy. 95 and Utah State Hwy. 163.

From the north, take Utah State Hwy. 95 to mile 112.3 and San Juan County Route Butler Wash #230 on the southeast side of the highway, GPS coordinates 0,621,941 E; 4,154,875 N; Elevation 5400'. Turn onto San Juan County Route #230, drive past the BLM sign at 0.2 mile, and turn right onto the south branch of the intersection at 0.3 mile. Continue south to a junction with San Juan County Route Lower Butler Wash #262 at mile 11.1 with GPS coordinates 0,622,313 E; 4,139,071 N; Elevation 4800'. Continue south (right) and turn right (west) at mile 13.8 onto a standard-vehicle track (GPS coordinates 0,621,430 E; 4,135,396 N; Elevation 4700').

From the south, take Utah State Hwy. 163 to mile 40.5 and turn north onto San Juan County Route Lower Butler Wash #262, GPS coordinates 0,621,337 E; 4,124,974 N; Elevation 4400'. Drive north for 7.2 miles and turn left (west) onto the standard-vehicle track. Parking/camping is limited to several vehicles. Refer to the Butler Wash Complex map.

Trail Statistics: The route is 1 mile round-trip with an elevation change of 150 feet requiring 1–2 hours to complete. This is an excellent hike over Class 1 terrain requiring easy effort and easy route-finding skills.

Attractions: Monarch Cave Ruin.

Cautions: There is limited midday shade along this route.

Maps: USGS Bluff (1:100,000), or USGS Bluff Southwest (1:62,500), or Trails Illustrated Grand Gulch Plateau (1:62,500)

Artifacts displayed out of context have no value. Please refrain from creating artifact displays; it is illegal.

Description: Follow the trail to the draw directly west and continue up-canyon into the draw itself. In 20 minutes you will reach the Monarch Cave amphitheater. The ruin is eroding away, and there is evidence of vandalism, but pictographs and petroglyphs still remain. The water in the plunge pool is oily, cold, and stagnant but the amphitheater harbors many flowering plants. Traverse the amphitheater along the north perimeter carefully. The incised name from the Illustrated America Exploring Expedition of 1892 is on the western cave wall. Return the way you came.

Monarch Cave UTM GPS Coordinates

Monarch Cave carpark	0,621,430 E; 4,135,396 N	Elevation 4700′	00 min.
Monarch Cave		Elevation 4850′	20 min.
Monarch Cave carpark	0,621,430 E; 4,135,396 N	Elevation 4700′	40 min.

■ 21 Procession Petroglyph Panel

Access: The Procession Petroglyph Panel is located east of San Juan County Route Lower Butler Wash #262 between Utah State Hwy. 95 and Utah State Hwy. 163.

From the north, take Utah State Hwy. 95 to mile 112.3 and San Juan County Route Butler Wash #230, GPS coordinates 0,621,941 E; 4,154,875 N; Elevation 5400'. Turn onto Butler Wash #230, drive past the BLM sign at 0.2 mile, and turn right onto the south branch of the intersection at 0.3 mile. Continue south to a junction with San Juan County Route Lower Butler Wash #262 at mile 11.1 (GPS coordinates 0,622,313 E; 4,139,071 N; Elevation 4800'). Continue south (right) and turn west (right) at mile 14.4 onto a standard-vehicle track (GPS coordinates 0,621,445 E; 4,134,542 N; Elevation 4655').

From the south, take Utah State Hwy. 163 to mile 40.5 and turn north onto San Juan County Route Lower Butler Wash #262, GPS coordinates 0,621,337 E; 4,124,974 N; Elevation 4400'. Drive north for 6.6 miles and turn west (left) onto the standard-vehicle track. Parking/camping is limited to several vehicles. Refer to the Butler Wash Complex map.

Trail Statistics: The route is 2 miles round-trip with an elevation change of 720 feet requiring 1–2 hours to complete. This is an excellent hike over Class 1–2 terrain requiring easy effort and easy route-finding skills.

Attractions: Procession Petroglyph Panel.

Cautions: There is no midday shade along this route.

Maps: USGS Bluff (1:100,000), or USGS Bluff Southwest (1:62,500), or Trails Illustrated Grand Gulch Plateau (1:62,500)

Description: Follow the trail immediately south from the carpark and go west across Butler Wash. Head toward the low-angled slickrock slope immediately to your southwest with two rounded domes on its upper slopes. There is a red prow near the ridge top of the canyon immediately south of the rounded domes. Reaching the slickrock slope from the carpark takes 5 minutes. The first ascent section is on these slickrock slopes until the upper south drainage is reached. Walk up the slickrock slope for 10 minutes toward the lower dome, but contour around it to the south, above a pour-off (left LUC), and drop into the south drainage bottom. Continue up this shallow canyon for 15 minutes until the red and black desert varnish of the northern wall comes into view. Work

Comb Ridge monocline near the Butler Wash Procession Panel

your way up toward Comb Ridge on the ascending north-side canyon ledges (right LUC) for 10 minutes. There are 179 petroglyph figures in a procession on this panel, hence its name. Comb Ridge is a 5- minute climb to the west. Return the way you came.

Procession Petroglyph Panel UTM GPS Coordinates

Procession Petroglyph Panel carpark	0,621,445 E; 4,134,542 N	Elevation 4655′	00 min.
Procession Petroglyph Panel		Elevation 5240′	40 min.
Comb Ridge Vista	0,619,665 E; 4,134,582 N	Elevation 5375′	45 min.
Procession Petroglyph Panel carpark	0,621,445 E; 4,134,542 N	Elevation 4655′	90 min.

■ 22 Double Stack Ruin Loop

Access: The Double Stack Ruin Loop is located east of San Juan County Route Lower Butler Wash #262 between Utah State Hwy. 95 and Utah State Hwy. 163.

From the north, take Utah State Hwy. 95 to mile 112.3 and San Juan County Route Butler Wash #230, GPS coordinates 0,621,941 E; 4,154,875 N; Elevation 5400′. Turn onto Butler Wash #230, drive past the BLM sign at 0.2 mile, and turn right onto the south branch of the intersection at 0.3 mile. Continue south to a junction with San Juan County Route Lower Butler Wash #262 at mile 11.1 (GPS coordinates 0,622,313 E; 4,139,071 N; Elevation 4800′). Continue south (right) and turn west (right) at mile 17.2 onto a standard-vehicle track (GPS coordinates 0,621,416 E; 4,130,426 N; Elevation 4600′).

From the south, take Utah State Hwy. 163 to mile 40.5 and turn north onto San Juan County Route Lower Butler Wash #262, GPS coordinates

0,621,337 E; 4,124,974 N; Elevation 4400'. Drive north for 3.8 miles and turn west (left) onto the standard-vehicle track. Parking/camping is limited to several vehicles. Refer to the Butler Wash Complex map.

Trail Statistics: The route is 2.5 miles round-trip with an elevation change of 600 feet requiring 1–2 hours to complete. This is a good hike over Class 1–3 terrain requiring easy effort and easy route-finding skills.

Attractions: Different erosion features in each drainage.

Cautions: There is no midday shade along this route.

Maps: USGS Bluff (1:100,000), or USGS Bluff Southwest (1:62,500), or Trails Illustrated Grand Gulch Plateau (1:62,500)

Description: The most difficult part is finding a path across Butler Wash. Traverse the base of the low-angle slickrock slopes northwestward to the Y-shaped draw. Follow the trail up the draw itself. In 20 minutes you should reach the Y junction between the northern and southern tributaries. The Double Stack Ruin (AN) is up the north tributary (right LUC).

Continue up-canyon for another 5 minutes to a large, empty alcove and pour-off that can be traversed on the south (left LUC) talus slope. It is another 10 minutes through cobbles, boulders, and vegetation before gaining the slickrock drainage fan for the final 10-minute push to the vista from the top of Comb Ridge. Traverse south along the ridge (left LUC), route-finding over the short ledges to the saddle nearest the red-colored south canyon wall. Walk around this outcrop and descend into the adjacent drainage, which is the south fork of the Y from below. Two pour-off ledges can be traversed on the north wall (left LDC). The descent back to the Y junction takes 45 minutes. The north branch of the Y is narrow and cobbled, while the south branch is open slickrock walking with scalloped walls revealing cross-bedding planes and shaded potholes. These two tributaries contain quite different erosion characteristics for being within the same drainage.

Double Stack Ruin Loop UTM GPS Coordinates

Double Stack Ruin Loop carpark	0,621,416 E; 4,130,426 N	Elevation 4600'	00 min.
Double Stack Ruin (AN)		Elevation 4670'	20 min.
Comb Ridge Vista	0,619,626 E; 4,131,260 N	Elevation 5200'	45 min.
Double Stack Loop carpark	0,621,416 E; 4,130,426 N	Elevation 4600'	90 min.

● 23 Sand Island Petroglyph Panel

Access: The Sand Island Petroglyph Panel is located south of Utah State Hwy. 191 on San Juan County Route Sand Island #275, at mile 22.6. Drive down the paved access road to the cattle-guard crossing at 0.3 mile. To the west (right) are the petroglyph panels behind protective cyclone fencing. To the east (left) are the BLM boat launch ramps, information signs, pit toilets, and developed picnic areas. Parking/camping is available for several dozen vehicles.

Trail Statistics: The route is ¼-mile round-trip with no elevation changes, requiring 10–60 minutes to thoroughly photograph and ponder the different rock art panels. This is a good walk over Class 1 terrain requiring easy effort and easy route-finding skills.

Attractions: Several hundred rock art figures, with styles ranging from the Archaic through the Pueblo III periods and mixed with more recent Native American, cowboy, and modern inscriptions.

● 24 Wolfman Petroglyph Panel

Access: The Wolfman Petroglyph Panel is located north of Utah State Hwy. 163 on San Juan County Route Lower Butler Wash #262, mile 40.5, GPS coordinates 0,621,337 E; 4,124,974 N; Elevation 4400'. Drive north for 1 mile and turn left (west) onto the standard-vehicle track. Parking/camping is limited to several vehicles. Refer to the Butler Wash Complex map.

Trail Statistics: The route is ½-mile round-trip with an elevation change of 50 feet requiring 10–30 minutes to complete. This is a fair walk over Class 1–2 terrain requiring easy effort and easy route-finding skills.

Attractions: Wolfman Petroglyph Panel.

Description: Head across the surface slickrock in a southwesterly direction to the rim. Follow the cairns down the rock ledge/ramp into Butler Wash and head south for 2 minutes to Wolfman Petroglyph Panel, complete with the requisite bullet marks. Return the way you came.

■ 25 River Petroglyph Panel

Access: The River Petroglyph Panel is located west of San Juan County Route Bluff Airport #269A. Take Hwy. 163 to mile 40.5, GPS

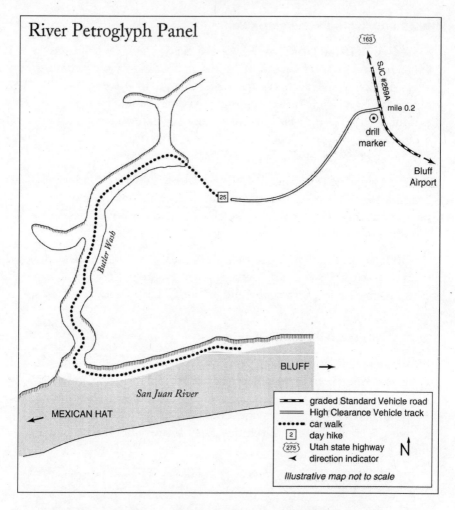

River Petroglyph Panel

graded Standard Vehicle road
High Clearance Vehicle track
car walk
② day hike
㉗ Utah state highway
◄ direction indicator

Illustrative map not to scale

coordinates 0,620,450 E; 4,124,774 N; Elevation 4400'. Go south on San
Juan County #269A and turn west (right) onto a high-clearance-vehicle
track at the drill marker at mile 0.2 (GPS coordinates 0,620,465 E;
4,124,457 N; Elevation 4375'). Follow this track to a slickrock rim marked
with small cairns at mile 1.6 (GPS coordinates 0,618,794 E; 4,123,205 N;
Elevation 4350'). Parking/camping is limited to a dozen vehicles.

Trail Statistics: The route is 3 miles round-trip with an elevation
change of 100 feet requiring 2–4 hours to complete. This is an excellent
canyon hike over Class 1–2 terrain requiring easy effort and easy route-
finding skills.

Attractions: River Petroglyph Panel.

Cautions: There is limited midday shade along this route. This is a popular sight-seeing stop and campsite for river runners.

Maps: USGS Bluff (1:100,000), or USGS Bluff Southwest (1:62,500), or Trails Illustrated Grand Gulch Plateau (1:62,500)

Description: Head west from the carpark and follow the cairns down the ramp into Butler Wash along a wagon trail built in 1908–1910. Go south down-canyon (left LDC) to a northwest-trending tributary junction (right LDC) in 15 minutes. Stay in the main channel and continue south (left LDC) for 10 minutes to a large solitary cottonwood. There are three inaccessible structures (right LDC) in the west wall. It is 10 minutes to the rock art panel on the northeastern river wall (left LDC) at the confluence, passing through a popular river-runner campsite. These panels contain several hundred figures. Continue east upstream for 20 minutes (left LUC) to four sets of moqui steps chiseled into the sandstone river wall (left LUC) below the small pour-off cleft. Return the way you came.

River Petroglyph Panel UTM GPS Coordinates

Carpark	0,618,794 E; 4,123,205 N	Elevation 4350'	00 min.
NW tributary junction	0,618,623 E; 4,122,518 N	Elevation 4300'	15 min.
River Petroglyph Panel		Elevation 4280'	35 min.
Moqui steps		Elevation 4295'	55 min.
Carpark	0,618,794 E; 4,123,205 N	Elevation 4350'	110 min.

4

Comb Wash Section: San Juan County Routes 235 and 205

THE EAST SIDE OF COMB WASH IS COMPOSED OF MOENKOPI FORMATION, Chinle Formation, Wingate Sandstone, Kayenta Formation, and Navajo Sandstone in stark relief atop Comb Ridge. There are numerous camping pullouts along this section. The road surface, composed of clays and sands, is slick when wet. The northern portion of the road, immediately south of Utah State Hwy. 95, has some long sandy sections, and the southern section has some steep wash crossings.

Obey all private-property signs protecting the rights of the Mountain Utes' tribal lands in Comb Wash. Arch Canyon is also the site of the annual Jeep Jamboree festival, usually held in the spring.

The hikes are organized from north to south (Blanding to Bluff) with numbered circles indicating car walks and numbered squares indicating day hikes.

Access Points along Comb Wash #235 and Trail Canyon #205

Comb Wash Cave	mile 5.6	0,616,183 E; 4,159,841 N	Elevation 5400'
Arch Canyon	mile 2.5	0,617,563 E; 4,156,120 N	Elevation 5000'
Walnut Knob Panel	mile 2.1	0,617,436 E; 4,155,784 N	Elevation 5200'
Hwy. 95 & SJC #235	mile 0.0	0,618,801 E; 4,152,277 N	Elevation 4900'
Lower Mule Canyon	mile 0.8	0,618,746 E; 4,150,659 N	Elevation 4900'
Lower Fish Canyon	mile 9.0	0,617,731 E; 4,138,950 N	Elevation 4600'
Hwy. 163 & SJC #235	mile 23.0	0,621,337 E; 4,124,974 N	Elevation 4400'

Car Walks	Quality	Skill	Effort	Time	Vehicle
● 28 Arch Canyon Ruin	good	easy	easy	30 min.	High Clearance
● 29 Walnut Knob Panel	fair	moderate	moderate	30 min.	All

Day Hikes	Quality	Skill	Class	Effort	Time	Miles (r-t)
■ 26 Comb Wash Cave	fair	moderate	2	easy	1 hr.	1
■ 27 Arch Canyon	good	easy	2	moderate	8–10 hr.	15.4
■ 30 Lower Mule Canyon	good	moderate	3	moderate	8–10 hr.	15.4
■ 31 Lower Fish Canyon	good	easy	2	easy	3–5 hr.	6.3

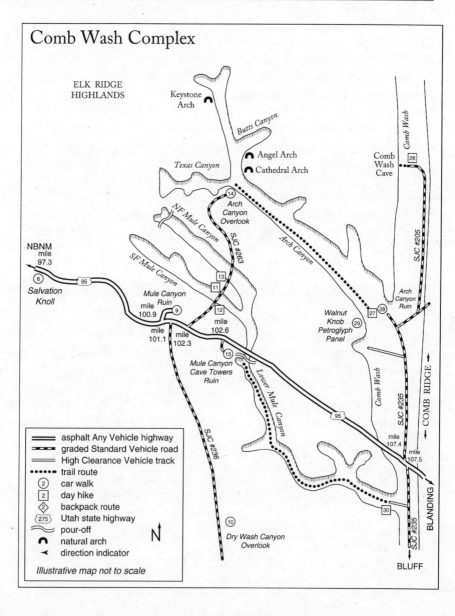

Comb Wash Complex

ELK RIDGE
HIGHLANDS

Keystone
Arch

Butts Canyon

Texas Canyon

Angel Arch
Cathedral Arch

Comb Wash

Comb
Wash
Cave

26

NF Mule Canyon

Arch
Canyon
Overlook

14

SJC #263

Arch Canyon

SJC #205

NBNM
mile
97.3

Salvation
Knoll

SF Mule Canyon

8

95

13

11

Mule Canyon
Ruin

mile
100.9

9

12

mile
102.6

mile
101.1

mile
102.3

15

Mule Canyon
Cave Towers
Ruin

Walnut
Knob
Petroglyph
Panel

29

Arch
Canyon
Ruin

27

28

Lower Mule Canyon

Comb Wash

SJC #235

COMB RIDGE

95

mile
107.4

mile
107.5

SJC #236

10

Dry Wash Canyon
Overlook

30

SJC #235

BLANDING

BLUFF

Legend

═══	asphalt Any Vehicle highway
▄▄▄	graded Standard Vehicle road
≣≣≣	High Clearance Vehicle track
••••	trail route
②	car walk
2	day hike
◇	backpack route
275	Utah state highway
∼∼∼	pour-off
∩	natural arch
◄	direction indicator

N

Illustrative map not to scale

■ 26 Comb Wash Cave

Access: Comb Wash Cave is located northwest of San Juan County Route Trail Canyon #205. Take Hwy. 95 to mile 107.4, GPS coordinates 0,618,870 E; 4,152,180 N; Elevation 4900'. There are pit toilets but no potable water in the south-side camping area. Drive north on the standard-vehicle surface of San Juan County Route Comb Wash #235 to a gated fence on a hill at mile 2. Go through the gate to an immediate junction at mile 2.1. Take the east branch (right) and cross Comb Wash at mile 2.3. Turn northwest (left) at the junction onto San Juan County Route Trail Canyon #205 at mile 3.1. Go north to mile 5.4 and turn west (left) onto a standard-vehicle track. The carpark is at mile 5.6. Several camping sites are available between Utah State Hwy. 95 and Comb Wash Cave.

Trail Statistics: The route is 1 mile round-trip with an elevation change of 200 feet requiring about 1 hour to complete. This is a fair hike over Class 1–2 terrain requiring easy effort and moderate route-finding skills.

Attractions: Stalagmites.

Cautions: There is limited midday shade along this route.

Maps: USGS Blanding (1:100,000), or USGS Hotel Rock (1:62,500), or Trails Illustrated Grand Gulch Plateau (1:62,500)

Description: Go west across Comb Wash and follow the ATV tracks to the drainage below the prominent cave seen from the carpark. Pick your way carefully into the drainage bottom and follow it west (left LUC) up-canyon for 10 minutes. Use the developing trail on the south canyon wall (left LUC) to access the cave. There are several stalagmites on the floor of the cave. Return the way you came.

Comb Wash Cave UTM GPS Coordinates

Comb Wash Cave carpark	0,616,934 E; 4,160,027 N	Elevation 5200'	00 min.
Comb Wash Cave	0,616,183 E; 4,159,841 N	Elevation 5400'	10 min.
Comb Wash Cave carpark	0,616,934 E; 4,160,027 N	Elevation 5200'	20 min.

■ 27 Arch Canyon

Access: Arch Canyon is located northwest of San Juan County Route Comb Wash #235. Take Hwy. 95 to mile 107.4 (GPS coordinates 0,618,870

Angel Arch

E; 4,152,180 N; Elevation 4900′). There is a camping area south of the highway that has pit toilets but no potable water. Turn north onto San Juan County Route Comb Wash #235 and go 2 miles to a gated fence on a hill. Go through the gate to an immediate junction at mile 2.1. Take the east branch (right) and turn north (left) at mile 2.3, before crossing Comb Wash, and drive past the BLM sign for Arch Canyon Trail #002. The trail registry is at the cattle guard at mile 2.4. There is a steep wash crossing and a sandy section immediately before the Arch Canyon Ruin carpark that may require a high-clearance vehicle, but otherwise the access route is on a standard-vehicle road surface. Several camping sites are available between Utah State Hwy. 95 and Arch Canyon. Refer to the Comb Wash Section map.

Trail Statistics: The route is 15.4 miles round-trip with an elevation change of 600 feet requiring 8–10 hours to complete. This is a good hike over Class 1–2 terrain requiring moderate effort and easy route-finding skills.

Attractions: Natural arches in an alpine setting with red-rock sandstone walls.

Cautions: There is limited midday shade along this route. This is a multiple-use corridor.

Maps: USGS Blanding (1:100,000), or USGS Hotel Rock, Kigalia Point and South Long Point (1:62,500), or Trails Illustrated Grand Gulch Plateau (1:62,500)

Description: The road to Arch Canyon is a popular 4WD track that crosses a perennial stream and its steep banks repeatedly for 7.7 miles. Go northwest up Arch Canyon Trail #002 to the fenced turnstile and the old BLM information sign. There are structures, pictographs, petroglyphs, and cowboy glyphs along the wall. Notice the many circular wall indentations from the supports of the upper-level structures now missing. Walk up-canyon 5 minutes to a cobbled section of the road. Look north (to your right LUC) and across the streambed to Arch Cobble Ruin (AN) under the alcove facing southeast. Continue up-canyon for 20 minutes to a junction with a north-trending tributary (right LUC) that leads to Hotel Rock.

It is 30 minutes to Dream Speaker Spire (left LUC) at the junction of a west-trending tributary. Continue up-canyon for another 20 minutes toward a prominent ruin in an alcove high along the north wall (right LUC). Use binoculars to see details because the site is inaccessible. Head up-canyon to a north-trending tributary junction (right LUC) in 20 minutes, noticing that ponderosa pines are now thriving along the streambed.

A small arch on the north wall (right LUC) is reached in 15 minutes. It is another 30 minutes to the junction with Texas Canyon (left LUC) and the end of the road. Cathedral Arch is seen from this point along the northeast wall (right LUC). It is a short scramble to climb up to its abutments. Angel Arch is another 10 minutes up-canyon along the northeast wall (right LUC). Return the way you came.

Arch Canyon UTM GPS Coordinates

Arch Canyon carpark	0,617,563 E; 4,156,120 N	Elevation 5000'	00 min.
North tributary junction	0,614,378 E; 4,157,320 N	Elevation 5180'	50 min.
Dream Speaker Spire	0,612,047 E; 4,158,720 N	Elevation 5250'	80 min.
North tributary junction	0,610,964 E; 4,160,943 N	Elevation 5450'	120 min.
Small arch	0,610,297 E; 4,161,564 N	Elevation 5500'	135 min.
Texas Canyon junction	0,609,273 E; 4,162,279 N	Elevation 5600'	165 min.
Cathedral Arch	0,609,551 E; 4,163,109 N	Elevation 5700'	170 min.
Angel Arch	0,609,420 E; 4,163,914 N	Elevation 5720'	180 min.
Arch Canyon carpark	0,617,563 E; 4,156,120 N	Elevation 5000'	360 min.

Cathedral Arch

Keystone Arch

● 28 Arch Canyon Ruin

Access: Arch Canyon Ruin is located northwest of San Juan County Route Comb Wash #235. Take Hwy. 95 to mile 107.4 (GPS coordinates 0,618,870 E; 4,152,180 N; Elevation 4900′). There are pit toilets but no potable water in the south-side camping area. Drive north on San Juan County Route Comb Wash #235 to a gated fence on a hill at mile 2. Go through the gate to an immediate junction at mile 2.1. Take the east branch (right) and turn north (left) at mile 2.3, before crossing Comb Wash, and drive past the BLM sign for Arch Canyon Trail #002. The trail registry is at the cattle guard at mile 2.4. A steep wash crossing and a sandy section immediately before the Arch Canyon Ruin carpark at mile 2.5 may require a high-clearance vehicle, but otherwise the access route is on standard-vehicle road surface. Several campsites are available between Utah State Hwy. 95 and Arch Canyon. Refer to the Comb Wash Section map.

Trail Statistics: The route is ¼-mile round-trip with nominal elevation changes requiring 30 minutes to complete. This is a good hike over Class 1–2 terrain requiring easy effort and easy route-finding skills.

Attractions: Arch Canyon Ruin.

Description: Go northwest up Arch Canyon Trail #002 to the fenced turnstile and the old BLM information sign. There are structures, pictographs, petroglyphs, and cowboy glyphs along the wall. Notice the many circular wall indentations from the supports of the upper-level structures now missing. Return the way you came.

● 29 Walnut Knob Petroglyph Panel

Access: The Walnut Knob Petroglyph Panel is located west of San Juan County Route Comb Wash #235. Take Hwy. 95 to mile 107.4, GPS coordinates 0,618,870 E; 4,152,180 N; Elevation 4900'. There are pit toilets but no potable water in the south-side camping area. The carpark for Walnut Knob Petroglyph Panel is at mile 2.1 on the standard-vehicle-surface San Juan County Route Comb Wash #235. Drive north to a gated fence on a hill at mile 2. Go through the gate to an immediate junction at mile 2.1. The west branch (left) goes to Dog Tanks along the old highway roadbed that predates the current route of Utah State Hwy. 95 through the big cut in Comb Ridge. The east branch (right) continues to Arch Canyon Trail #002 and San Juan County Route Trail Canyon #205. Parking is limited to just one vehicle at this interception. Refer to the Comb Wash Section map.

Trail Statistics: Walnut Knob Petroglyph Panel is ½-mile round-trip, climbing 200 feet in 10–30 minutes. This is a fair walk over Class 1–2 terrain requiring moderate effort and moderate route-finding skills.

Attractions: Walnut Knob Petroglyph Panel.

Cautions: There is no midday shade along this route.

Description: Walnut Knob Petroglyph Panel is 15 minutes west up the slickrock slopes to the prominent knob seen from the carpark. Return the way you came.

■ 30 Lower Mule Canyon

Access: Lower Mule Canyon is located west of San Juan County Route Comb Wash #235.

From the north, take Utah State Hwy. 95 until reaching mile 107.4 and San Juan County Route Comb Wash #235, GPS coordinates 0,618,870 E; 4,152,180 N; Elevation 4900'. Turn south onto Comb Wash #235 and drive 0.8 mile, crossing Comb Wash twice en route. Turn west (right)

Contemporary petroglyphs; notice mounted rider figure.

onto a high-clearance-vehicle track. Descend this track for 0.3 mile to the carpark area.

From the south, take Utah State Hwy. 163 to mile 37.6, GPS coordinates 0,617,290 E; 4,125,828 N; Elevation 4400'. Turn north onto San Juan County Route Comb Wash #235 and drive 22.2 miles to the carpark access track. There is space for a dozen vehicles. Refer to the Comb Wash Section map.

Trail Statistics: The route is 15.4 miles round-trip with an elevation change of 700 feet requiring 8–10 hours to complete. This is a good canyon hike over Class 1–3 terrain requiring moderate effort and moderate route-finding skills.

Attractions: A precipitating chert bed.

Cautions: There is minimal midday shade along this route. A flash flood ripped through this canyon in the summer of 1999 stripping the streambed down to bedrock in many places.

Maps: USGS Blanding and Bluff (1:100,000), or USGS Bluff Northwest and Hotel Rock (1:62,500), or Trails Illustrated Grand Gulch Plateau (1:62,500)

Description: From the carpark area, follow the ATV trail across the streambed to a cattle-guard gate in 5 minutes. Continue up-canyon along the road surface to a north-trending tributary (right LUC) in 10 minutes. Turn north (right LUC) into this tributary to explore the precipitating chert bed layer.

Return to the previous intersection, turn west (right LDC) and go up-canyon. It is another 10 minutes to a northwest-trending tributary (right LUC). Continue up-canyon (left LUC) to a junction with a southwest-trending tributary (left LUC) near some tall cottonwoods. Proceed northwest (right LUC) as the canyon begins to narrow and passes through some gray limestone layers. It is 30 minutes of steady walking to a minor pinnacle (right LUC). The streambed becomes more littered with boulders for the next 30 minutes, with a hanging spring and pinnacle hoodoo on the west wall (both left LUC). Another 35 minutes of scrambling brings you to a northwest tributary junction.

It is northwest (left LUC) for 25 minutes to the Mule Canyon cave tower ruin or northeast (right LUC) for 20 minutes to the Mule Canyon waterfall and amphitheater. Return the way you came.

Bear print petroglyphs

Lower Mule Canyon UTM GPS Coordinates

Lower Mule Canyon carpark	0,618,321 E; 4,150,723 N	Elevation 4900′	00 min.
Cattle gate	0,617,941 E; 4,150,957 N	Elevation 4920′	05 min.
North tributary junction	0,617,787 E; 4,151,302 N	Elevation 4950′	15 min.
Northwest tributary junction	0,616,782 E; 4,151,424 N	Elevation 4950′	25 min.
Southwest tributary junction	0,615,073 E; 4,150,308 N	Elevation 5080′	60 min.
Boulder choke-stones	0,612,832 E; 4,152,780 N	Elevation 5300′	130 min.
Upper tributary junction	0,612,588 E; 4,153,350 N	Elevation 5400′	165 min.
Mule Canyon waterfall	0,612,705 E; 4,154,135 N	Elevation 5500′	185 min.
Lower Mule Canyon carpark	0,618,321 E; 4,150,723 N	Elevation 4900′	370 min.

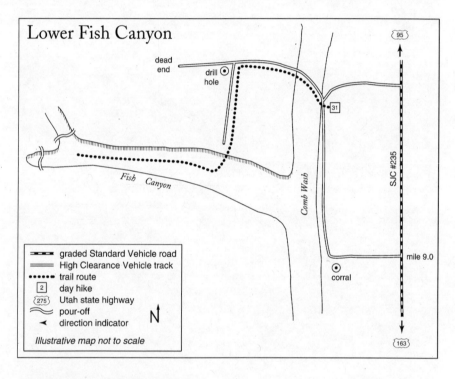

■ 31 Lower Fish Canyon

Access: Lower Fish Canyon is located west of San Juan County Route Comb Wash #235.

From the north, take Utah State Hwy. 95 to mile 107.4, GPS coordinates 0,618,870 E; 4,152,180 N; Elevation 4900′. Turn south onto San Juan County Route Comb Wash #235. Drive 9 miles and turn west (right) onto a standard-vehicle track with a BLM fee-collection site. San Juan County

Route Comb Wash #235 crosses Comb Wash three times and traverses several sandy spots en route to the trailhead. Descend this track to the corral at 9.5 miles and turn north to parallel the wash until reaching the crossing of Comb Wash at mile 10 (GPS coordinates 0,617,731 E; 4,138,950 N; Elevation 4600').

From the south, take Utah State Hwy. 163 to mile 37.6, GPS coordinates 0,617,290 E; 4,125,828 N; Elevation 4400'. Turn north onto San Juan County Route Comb Wash #235 and drive 16 miles to the carpark. There is parking space for a dozen vehicles.

Trail Statistics: The route is 6.3 miles round-trip with an elevation change of 100 feet requiring 3–5 hours to complete. This is a good canyon hike over Class 1–2 terrain requiring easy effort and easy route-finding skills.

Attractions: Ancestral Puebloan structure sites.

Cautions: There is minimal midday shade along this route.

Maps: USGS Blanding and Bluff (1:100,000), or USGS Bluff Northwest (1:62,500), or Trails Illustrated Grand Gulch Plateau (1:62,500)

Description: Go west across Comb Wash and ascend the slopes along the high-clearance-vehicle track for 20 minutes until reaching a south-trending high-clearance-vehicle track near a drill marker. Turn south (left) and follow this track into the bottom of Fish Canyon in 10 minutes. Turn west (right) and travel up-canyon through thick tamarisk cover and shallow beaver ponds. Fortunately, the cattle have created some good trails through this area. A southeast-facing alcove is reached in 30 minutes (right LUC). Unfortunately, the same cattle that made the trails have almost completely destroyed the structures on the lower level.

Walk 5 more minutes up-canyon to a second alcove, where both positive and negative handprint pictographs can be seen above the structure remnants on both levels. The BLM livestock gate is immediately up-canyon. It is 35 minutes to the terminal pour-offs at the junction with a southwest-trending tributary (left LUC) across flats thick with Russian thistle. Both drainages have impassable dryfalls. Return the way you came.

Lower Fish Canyon UTM GPS Coordinates

Lower Fish Canyon carpark	0,617,731 E; 4,138,950 N	Elevation 4600'	00 min.
South-trending track junction	0,616,810 E; 4,139,154 N	Elevation 4640'	20 min.

Fish Canyon streambed	0,617,034 E; 4,138,613 N	Elevation 4600′	30 min.
First alcove		Elevation 4600′	60 min.
Second alcove		Elevation 4600′	65 min.
Terminal pour-off junction	0,614,654 E; 4,138,409 N	Elevation 4640′	100 min.
Lower Fish Canyon carpark	0,617,731 E; 4,138,950 N	Elevation 4600′	200 min.

5

Utah State Highway 261 North Section

THE PAVED NORTH-SOUTH UTAH STATE HWY. 261 HAS NARROW LANES AND no shoulders for most of its 32.5 miles, and no passing lanes. The 3-mile Moqui Dugway section, a graded gravel road surface with a 10% grade descending 1100 feet, connects Cedar Mesa to the lower tablelands. The northern section of highway rolls over the rather blank juniper highlands and sage flats with little indication of the marvelous sandstone canyons surrounding you until reaching the Moqui Dugway. The southern section crosses the red-rock tablelands of Halgaito Shale. The access roads to the carparks are either maintained standard-vehicle or high-clearance-vehicle clay surfaces that get exceedingly slick when wet. The hikes are organized from north to south (Kane Gulch to Muley Point Overlook) with numbered circles indicating car walks and numbered squares indicating day hikes.

There are pit toilets but no potable water or garbage collection at the Kane Gulch Ranger Station. The seasonal and/or volunteer BLM ranger(s) can answer questions about current hiking, weather, water availability and road conditions from 8 A.M. to noon. You can also find books, maps, and memorabilia for sale, and learn about wilderness and archaeological stewardship. Updated weather forecasts and information on water availability are usually written on the chalkboard on the front porch for after-hours visitors. The BLM does not organize vehicle shuttles between carparks.

Kane Gulch was probably named after the great friend of the Mormon people, Colonel Thomas L. Kane. Norm Neville started running the San Juan River in 1934 and quickly became known as "the river rat" with his wooden boats and adventure travel company; the prominent arch in Owl Canyon was renamed in tribute to Neville, who promoted the Four Corners to tourists and conservationists alike. McCloyd Canyon was named after rancher Charles McCloyd. Bullet Canyon, prior to 1894, was called Graham Canyon after prospector Charles Cary Graham. Both McCloyd and Graham were on the first Grand Gulch archaeology expedition in January 1891. The Hole-in-the-Rock expedition scouts George Hobbs, Lemuel Redd, George Sevy, and

George Morrill named Road Canyon after their attempt to put a wagon road down its course. Lime Creek Canyon is named after the large lime deposits through which the creek flows. A herd of longhorn cattle in Slickhorn Canyon gave that canyon its name. Johns Canyon was first known as Douglas Canyon after an early 1900s prospector but was changed when Jimmy Palmer killed cattle rancher John Oliver in the same canyon.

Access Points along Utah State Highway 261

Hwy. 261 & Hwy. 95	mile 32.5	0,598,414 E; 4,159,525 N	Elevation 6800'
Kane Gulch Ranger Station	mile 28.7	0,597,584 E; 4,153,458 N	Elevation 6400'
Fish & Owl Canyons	mile 27.7	0,596,551 E; 4,148,042 N	Elevation 6600'
Todie Flat	mile 25.2	0,596,551 E; 4,148,042 N	Elevation 6460'
Sheiks Flat	mile 24.2	0,596,063 E; 4,146,565 N	Elevation 6530'
Snow Flat	mile 22.6	0,595,351 E; 4,144,146 N	Elevation 6500'
Bullet Canyon	mile 21.7	0,594,317 E; 4,143,029 N	Elevation 6425'
Cigarette Spring/Slickhorn	mile 18.1	0,593,537 E; 4,139,176 N	Elevation 6500'
Johns Canyon	mile 17.3	0,594,112 E; 4,136,339 N	Elevation 6520'
Muley Point Overlook	mile 9.6	0,593,761 E; 4,125,991 N	Elevation 6400'
Moqui Dugway sign	mile 9.3	0,594,049 E; 4,125,615 N	Elevation 6100'
Valley of the Gods Loop	mile 5.4	0,594,717 E; 4,124,508 N	Elevation 5300'
Hwy. 261 & Hwy. 316	mile 0.9	0,599,529 E; 4,117,333 N	Elevation 4680'
Hwy. 261 & Hwy. 163	mile 0.0	0,600,764 E; 4,116,920 N	Elevation 4500'

Car Walk		Quality	Skill	Effort	Time	Vehicle
● 46 Muley Point Overlook		good	easy	30 min.	easy	All

Day Hikes	Quality	Skill	Class	Effort	Time	Miles (r-t)
■ 32 Kane Gulch	excellent	easy	2	easy	6–8 hr.	9.8
■ 33 Owl Canyon	good	moderate	3	moderate	5–7 hr.	10
■ 34 Todie Canyon	good	moderate	4	strenuous	2–4 hr.	4.6
■ 35 Sheiks Canyon	excellent	moderate	4	moderate	2–4 hr.	4
■ 36 McCloyd Canyon	excellent	moderate	3	moderate	3–4 hr.	5.5
■ 37 Bullet Canyon	excellent	moderate	3	strenuous	8–10 hr.	15
■ 38 Government Trail–Big Man Panel						
	good	moderate	3	moderate	5–7 hr.	12.2
■ 39 Government Trail–Pollys Canyon Loop						
	fair	difficult	4	moderate	4–6 hr.	9.6

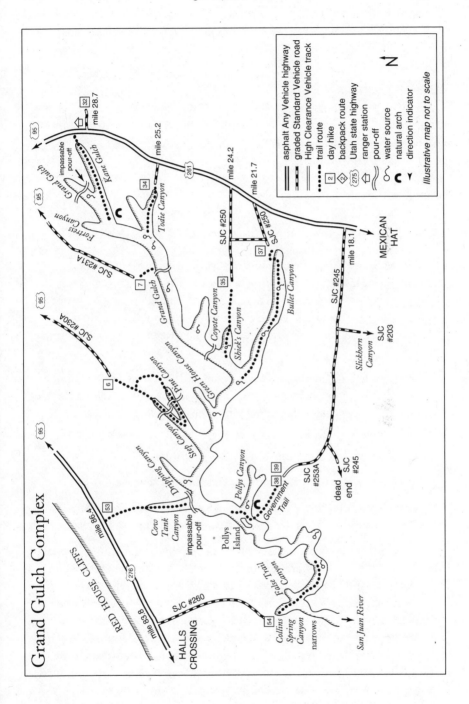

Grand Gulch Complex

Legend:
asphalt Any Vehicle highway
graded Standard Vehicle road
High Clearance Vehicle track
trail route
day hike
backpack route
Utah state highway
ranger station
pour-off
water source
natural arch
direction indicator
Illustrative map not to scale

Day Hikes	Quality	Skill	Class	Effort	Time	Miles (r-t)
■ 40 Slickhorn Canyon #1–#2 Loop						
	good	moderate	3	moderate	6–8 hr.	9.8
■ 41 Slickhorn Canyon #4–#6 Loop						
	good	moderate	3	moderate	6–8 hr.	10.8
■ 42 Road Canyon	good	moderate	3	moderate	8–10 hr.	14.2
■ 43 Lime Creek Canyon	good	moderate	3	moderate	8–10 hr.	15.4
■ 44 Upper Johns Canyon Loop						
	fair	moderate	4	moderate	4–6 hr.	6.7
■ 45 West Fork Johns Canyon						
	fair	difficult	4	moderate	3–4 hr.	5.2

■ 32 Kane Gulch

Access: The Kane Gulch Ranger Station and carpark are located east of Utah State Hwy. 261 at mile 28.7 (GPS coordinates 0,597,584 E; 4,153,458 N; Elevation 6400′). There is a pit toilet but no potable water or refuse collection facilities. There are camping pullouts along Hwy. 261. Parking is available for several dozen vehicles. Refer to the Grand Gulch map.

Trail Statistics: The route is 9.8 miles round-trip with an elevation change of 500 feet requiring 6–7 hours to complete. This is an excellent canyon hike over Class 1–2 terrain requiring easy effort and easy route-finding skills.

Attractions: Junction Ruin and Turkey Pen Ruin.

Cautions: There is limited midday shade along this route.

Maps: USGS Blanding (1:100,000), or Kane Gulch and Cedar Mesa North (1:62,500), or Trails Illustrated Grand Gulch Plateau (1:62,500)

Description: The trail starts on the western side of the highway. Look both ways TWICE for oncoming vehicular traffic before crossing the pavement. Head in a southwesterly direction down the wash. It is 50 minutes to a steep slickrock boulder section. Luckily, a north traverse route (right LDC) passes the Wilderness Study Area BLM sign en route before crossing the streambed and continuing down the south side of the canyon (left LDC). However, stop in the slickrock basin before crossing the streambed to notice the sombrero-looking rim rock on the south wall.

It is 30 more minutes to the confluence with Grand Gulch and its sandy alluvial banks shaded by mature cottonwood trees. To get to Junction Ruin, go through the camping area (right LDC) to the southeast-

Stimper Arch

facing alcove (left LDC), which also has yellow, red, and white hand-prints and some petroglyphs. Walk down-canyon for 20 minutes to Turkey Pen Ruin in the south-facing alcove (right LDC). Stay off the midden areas at both Junction and Turkey Pen Ruin sites. Stimper Arch is around the bend another 5 minutes down-canyon along the south wall (left LDC) near the rim. Return the way you came.

Kane Gulch UTM GPS Coordinates

Kane Gulch Ranger Station	0,597,584 E; 4,153,458 N	Elevation 6400'	00 min.
Junction Ruin		Elevation 6060'	95 min.
Turkey Pen Ruin		Elevation 6040'	115 min.
Stimper Arch	0,593,342 E; 4,151,678 N	Elevation 6040'	120 min.
Kane Gulch Ranger Station	0,597,584 E; 4,153,458 N	Elevation 6400'	240 min.

■ 33 Owl Canyon

Access: The Owl Canyon carpark is located east of Utah State Hwy. 261 on San Juan County Route Long Spike #253. Take Hwy. 261 to mile 27.7 and the junction with Long Spike #253 (GPS coordinates 0,596,551 E; 4,148,042 N; Elevation 6600'). Turn east onto a standard-vehicle road surface with an "Owl Creek 5" BLM sign. It is 5.1 miles to the carpark. Parking/camping is limited to a dozen vehicles. The trailhead, information board, and registry are directly north of the carpark.

Fish-Owl-McCloyd Canyon Complex

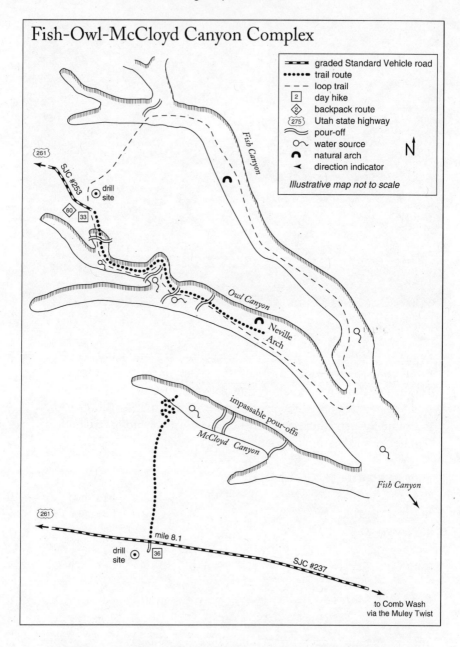

Trail Statistics: The route is 10 miles round-trip with an elevation change of 1000 feet requiring 5–7 hours to complete. It is a good canyon hike over Class 1–3 terrain requiring moderate effort and moderate route-finding.

Attractions: Neville Arch.

Cautions: This route requires a lot of slickrock scrambling. There is moderate midday shade in Owl Canyon. Leave your pets behind for this walk.

Maps: USGS Bluff and Blanding (1:100,000), or USGS Snow Flat Spring Cave and Cedar Mesa North (1:62,500), or Trails Illustrated Grand Gulch Plateau (1:62,500)

Neville Arch

Description: The trail down Owl Canyon starts behind the BLM information board and follows the shallow drainage to the head of Owl Canyon proper in 5 minutes. Follow the cairns carefully as you descend the steep slickrock surfaces. It is a 15-minute descent to a northwest-trending tributary junction (left LDC). Continue another 10 minutes to a west-trending tributary junction (right LDC). Proceed southeast (left LDC) for 25 minutes to a dished-out pour-off and plunge pool. Walk up-canyon north (left LDC) for 10 minutes into the tributary to detour around the pour-off. Notice the small natural bridge on the south side of the dished-out pour-off. It is 10 minutes to the main stem junction of Owl Canyon and its west-trending south fork tributary (right LDC). The pour-off and plunge pool are traversed on the north wall (left LDC). Proceed east down-canyon for 20 minutes to a spring and pour-off with a south wall (right LDC) traverse route. In 10 minutes, the canyon begins to widen. Neville Arch is seen in an additional 10 minutes. The large arch is on the north wall near the rim (left LDC). For the curious, it is another 45 minutes of grassy sand flats walking to the junction with Fish Canyon. Return the way you came.

Owl Canyon UTM GPS Coordinates

Fish & Owl Canyon carpark	0,604,483 E; 4,147,880 N	Elevation 6200'	00 min.
Descent path	0,604,776 E; 4,147,602 N	Elevation 6180'	05 min.
West tributary junction	0,604,883 E; 4,146,715 N	Elevation 5400'	30 min.
Dished pour-off	0,606,210 E; 4,146,398 N	Elevation 5300'	55 min.
West tributary junction	0,606,312 E; 4,146,008 N	Elevation 5000'	75 min.
Neville Arch	0,608,077 E; 4,145,249 N	Elevation 4900'	115 min.
Fish Canyon confluence	0,610,584 E; 4,143,150 N	Elevation 4850'	160 min.
Fish & Owl Canyon carpark	0,604,483 E; 4,147,880 N	Elevation 6200'	320 min.

■ 34 Todie Canyon

Access: The Todie Canyon carpark is located west of Utah State Hwy. 261 on the Todie Flat Road at mile 25.2, GPS coordinates 0,596,551 E; 4,148,042 N; Elevation 6460'. Turn west onto the standard-vehicle track, which is narrow, not signed, and obscured by sage bushes. It is 1.8 miles to the car park. Parking/camping is limited to several vehicles. Refer to the Grand Gulch map.

Trail Statistics: This route is 4.6 miles round-trip with an elevation change of 800 feet requiring 2–4 hours to complete. This is a good canyon combination hike over Class 1–4 terrain requiring strenuous effort and moderate route-finding skills.

Attractions: Canyoneering-style hiking.

Cautions: There is limited midday shade along this route. Leave your pets behind for this walk.

Maps: USGS Bluff and Navajo Mountain (1:100,000), or USGS Cedar Mesa North (1:62,500), or Trails Illustrated Grand Gulch Plateau (1:62,500)

Description: Head west initially over the mesa top to the south rim section and follow the stacked cairns carefully. Step Point is seen to the west, while the Bear's Ears and Elk Ridge Highlands are to the north. In 5 minutes, two structures with intact doors can be seen under the far north rim of Todie Canyon. Binoculars are needed to see details of the structures. Continue west another 5 minutes to the steep descent route

A fire scar at Todie Canyon confluence with Grand Gulch

near a juniper tree and many cairns. Carefully pick your way around the exfoliated boulders and across the slickrock slopes, working your way down through the thorny thicket near the bottom. Follow the cairns west (left LDC) down-canyon for 15 minutes to a pour-off tributary trending northwest on the north wall (right LDC). Continue southwest (left LDC) 25 minutes to another northwest-trending tributary on the north wall (right LDC). It is 25 minutes to the confluence with Grand Gulch. The burnt cottonwoods in this area should be a reminder to be careful with fires and backpacking stoves. The rounded amphitheater-like confluence is a good lunch spot. Notice the difference in the walls and gradients between Grand Gulch (sloped and flat) and Todie Canyon (vertical and steep). Return the way you came.

Todie Canyon UTM GPS Coordinates

Todie carpark	0,594,766 E; 4,148,618 N	Elevation 6400′	00 min.
Descent path	0,593,971 E; 4,149,154 N	Elevation 6340′	10 min.
NW tributary junction	0,593,869 E; 4,149,232 N	Elevation 6100′	25 min.
NW tributary junction	0,593,010 E; 4,149,593 N	Elevation 5800′	50 min.
Grand Gulch confluence	0,592,113 E; 4,149,466 N	Elevation 5605′	75 min.
Todie carpark	0,594,766 E; 4,148,618 N	Elevation 6400′	150 min.

■ 35 Sheiks Canyon

Access: The Sheiks Canyon carpark is located west of Utah State
Hwy. 261. At mile 24.2, turn west onto San Juan County Route North
Road #250, GPS coordinates 0,596,063 E; 4,146,565 N; Elevation 6530′.
It is 4.7 miles to the carpark along a standard-vehicle road surface.
Parking/camping is limited to several vehicles. Refer to the Grand
Gulch map.

Trail Statistics: The route is 4 miles round-trip with an elevation
change of 800 feet requiring 3–5 hours to complete. This is an excellent
canyon hike over Class 1–4 terrain requiring moderate effort and
moderate route-finding skills for difficult terrain.

Attractions: Green Mask Pictograph Panel.

Cautions: There is limited midday shade along this route. Don't
touch or climb on either the structures or the rock art. Leave your pets
behind for this walk.

Maps: USGS Bluff and Navajo Mountain (1:100,000), or USGS Pollys
Pasture and Cedar Mesa North (1:62,500), or Trails Illustrated Grand
Gulch Plateau (1:62,500). The canyon is not marked on these maps.

Description: From the carpark with its cowboy hearth, head west
along the slickrock and sand canyon bottom. Three pour-offs are easily
avoided. Proceed for 40 minutes to the top of a scalloped slickrock
dryfall. It takes 5 minutes to descend this and 15 more minutes of
scrambling over boulders and cobbles choking the streambed to the
north-south T tributary junction.

Proceed south (left LDC) for 10 minutes to the top of the last dryfall
series. This descent requires some shimmying and mantling skills with
exposure. Descend through the boulders and traverse the east wall (left
LDC) to the talus slopes south of the dryfall to avoid the plunge pool.
Descend to the bottom of the canyon and scan the southeast-facing wall
(right LDC) for a large alcove. Inside are structures on two different
ledges. The most amazing element of this site is the pictographs of
white, black, and red on the walls and ceilings. The campsite opposite
Green Mask Ruin is an excellent lunch spot with a great view of the
alcove. Use binoculars to see details of the rock art. The confluence with
Grand Gulch is 5 minutes farther down-canyon. Return the way you
came.

Sheiks Canyon UTM GPS Coordinates

Sheiks Canyon carpark	0,589,894 E; 4,144,984 N	Elevation 6315′	00 min.
T junction		Elevation 5775′	60 min.
Green Mask Ruin		Elevation 5600′	70 min.
Grand Gulch	0,586,298 E; 4,145,319 N	Elevation 5500′	75 min.
Sheiks Canyon carpark	0,589,894 E; 4,144,984 N	Elevation 6315′	170 min.

■ 36 McCloyd Canyon

Access: The McCloyd Canyon carpark is located east of Utah State Hwy. 261. Take Hwy. 261 to mile 22.6 and turn east onto San Juan County Route Snow Flat Springs #237, GPS coordinates 0,595,351 E; 4,144,146 N; Elevation 6500′. It is 8.1 miles on a standard-vehicle road surface to the carpark. Take the northeast fork at 0.4 mile, pass a BLM bulletin board at 1 mile, and cross a cattle fence at 5.2 miles. Snow Flat Springs #237 is part of the Mormon Trail. There is parking/camping space for a dozen vehicles. Refer to the Owl Canyon map.

Trail Statistics: The route is 5.5 miles round-trip with an elevation change of 400 feet requiring 3–4 hours to complete. This is an excellent canyon hike over Class 1–3 terrain requiring moderate effort and moderate route-finding skills.

Attractions: Moon House Ruin.

Cautions: There is limited midday shade along this route. Leave your pets behind for this walk.

Maps: USGS Bluff and Navajo Mountain (1:100,000), or USGS Snow Flat Spring Cave (1:62,500), or Trails Illustrated Grand Gulch Plateau (1:62,500). The canyon is unmarked on these maps.

Description: Head north over the mesa top in the left track for 25 minutes to the canyon rim. Perhaps in time the desert will reclaim the other track, and instead of a road scar, only a hiking trail will remain. Follow the stacked cairns closely on the descent. It takes 20 minutes to reach the bottom from the rim. Five minutes into the descent, look for a north-facing alcove; Moon House Ruin is obvious in the alcove. Take the time to use binoculars to study the ruin and the ascent route. Once in the canyon bottom, turn east (right LDC) and head down-canyon along the north wall to the ascent route in the talus slope near the plunge pools. It is 5 minutes to reach the ledge where Moon House ruin is located. There is usually a BLM official monitoring visitors at this site. Descend the same route.

Up-canyon, it is 30 minutes to the twin terminus 15′ pour-offs in a cottonwood oasis. Down-canyon, it is 25 minutes to a terminus 30′ pour-off. Return the way you came.

McCloyd Canyon UTM GPS Coordinates

McCloyd Canyon carpark	0,606,224 E; 4,141,570 N	Elevation 5700′	00 min.
Canyon rim	0,606,575 E; 4,143,545 N	Elevation 5700′	25 min.
Bottom of canyon		Elevation 5450′	45 min.
Moon House Ruin		Elevation 5600′	50 min.
McCloyd Canyon carpark	0,606,224 E; 4,141,570 N	Elevation 5700′	100 min.

■ 37 Bullet Canyon

Access: The Bullet Canyon carpark is located west of Utah State Hwy. 261. Take Hwy. 261 to mile 21.7 and turn west onto San Juan County Route South Road #251, GPS coordinates 0,594,317 E; 4,143,029 N; Elevation 6425′. It is 1.2 miles on a standard-vehicle road surface to the carpark. There is limited camping space in the carpark area, and parking for a dozen vehicles. Refer to the Grand Gulch map.

Trail Statistics: The route is 15 miles round-trip with an elevation change of 1100 feet requiring 9–11 hours to complete. This is an excellent canyon hike over Class 1–3 terrain requiring strenuous effort and moderate route-finding skills.

Attractions: Perfect Kiva Ruin and Jailhouse Ruin.

Cautions: There is limited midday shade. This route has extended steep slickrock sections; do not attempt to hike it in adverse weather conditions.

Maps: USGS Bluff and Navajo Mountain (1:100,000), or USGS Cedar Mesa North and Pollys Pasture (1:62,500), or Trails Illustrated Grand Gulch Plateau (1:62,500)

Description: Head west initially over the mesa top along the path to the north rim descent section. Follow the stacked cairns closely. It takes 5 minutes to reach the bottom from the carpark. Proceed west (right LDC) down the streambed for 15 minutes. You'll be able to see a structure on the north rim that stands out starkly against the skyline. A zoom lens for photography and binoculars are necessary to see much detail. Continue down-canyon for 10 minutes to a junction with a southeast-trending tributary (left LDC). Proceed west (right LDC) 5 minutes to a staircase slope. Use your friction skills to navigate down the slope following the cairns. In 5 minutes you are at the bottom. Walk for 10 minutes in the streambed full of cobbles and boulders. Immediately below a 6' pour-off that drops into a large plunge pool is a path that follows a ledge high along the north wall (right LDC) and avoids some of the boulder-choked streambed. Otherwise, continue to weave your way downstream through the maze of rocks for 5 minutes to a junction with a southeast-trending tributary (left LDC).

Continue west (right LDC) down-canyon for 35 minutes to Perfect Kiva Ruin. It is in the north amphitheater along a southeast-facing alcove (right LDC). This is an incredible site, so treat it with the utmost respect. Walk down-canyon another 10 minutes to Jailhouse Ruin on the southeast-facing peninsula near the point (right LDC). Three white circles above the structures give the site an eerie look. Refrain from attempting to gain access into these structures. Use binoculars instead. The confluence of Bullet Canyon and Grand Gulch is 50 minutes down-canyon.

Eat lunch, relax, and rejoice in one of the campsites at the confluence. The pictograph figures at Jailhouse Ruin might have been territorial markings. What do you think they represent? Return the way you came.

Bullet Canyon UTM GPS Coordinates

Bullet Canyon carpark	0,592,928 E; 4,142,941 N	Elevation 6400'	00 min.
SE tributary junction	0,591,299 E; 4,142,405 N	Elevation 6200'	30 min.
Ledge path	0,590,665 E; 4,142,361 N	Elevation 6050'	50 min.
SE tributary junction	0,589,250 E; 4,142,541 N	Elevation 6000'	55 min.
Perfect Kiva Ruin		Elevation 5600'	90 min.
Jailhouse Ruin		Elevation 5600'	100 min.
Grand Gulch confluence	0,584,800 E; 4,144,568 N	Elevation 5300'	150 min.
Bullet Canyon carpark	0,592,928 E; 4,142,941 N	Elevation 6400'	300 min.

■ 38 Government Trail–Big Man Panel

Access: The Government Trail carpark is located west of Utah State Hwy. 261. At mile 18.1, turn west onto San Juan County Route Slickhorn #245, GPS coordinates 0,593,537 E; 4,139,176 N; Elevation 6500'). Drive 0.3 mile to a gated fence with a BLM information board and trail registry. Continue to mile 2.6 and the junction of San Juan County Route Point

Lookout #203 and San Juan County Route Slickhorn #245 (GPS Coordinates 0,590,226 E; 4,140,342 N; Elevation 6350') with a BLM Government Trail sign. Turn northwest (right) and continue to mile 5.4 to the junction of San Juan County Route Slickhorn #245 and San Juan County Route #253A. Turn northwest (right) and drive to mile 6.3 and the high-clearance-vehicle track with a BLM Government Trail sign. The carpark is at mile 8.7, GPS coordinates 0,581,011 E; 4,141,100 N; Elevation 5700'. Parking/camping is limited to several vehicles. Refer to the Grand Gulch map and the Government Trail/Pollys Canyon complex map.

Trail Statistics: The route is 12.2 miles round-trip with an elevation change of 700 feet requiring 5–7 hours to complete. This is a good hike over Class 1–3 terrain requiring moderate effort and moderate route-finding skills.

Attractions: Pollys Canyon arch; Big Man pictograph panel.

Cautions: There is limited midday shade along this route.

Maps: USGS Navajo Mountain (1:100,000), or USGS Pollys Pasture (1:62,500), or Trails Illustrated Grand Gulch Plateau (1:62,500)

Description: Walk the high-clearance-vehicle track from the upper carpark to the lower carpark adjacent to the stock pond if your vehicle was unable to negotiate the rough track. From the trail registry, follow the double track northwest to the rim of Grand Gulch in 60 minutes. Walk in the left track only to avoid further erosion on the other track. Perhaps in time the desert will reclaim that other track, and instead of a road scar, only a hiking trail will remain. From the rim you can see structures with intact doors across the canyon on Pollys Island. Descend the switchbacks to the floor of Grand Gulch in 15 minutes. Turn north (right LUC) and walk up-canyon to the confluence with Pollys Canyon in 5 minutes.

Turn east (right LUC) into Pollys Canyon and walk 5 minutes to the first meander. There is an arch in the east (right LUC) wall. Return to Grand Gulch and walk north (right LDC) for 35 minutes to a bend in the canyon with a thick cottonwood tree bridging the streambed. Stop and look east (right LUC) to locate the steep access trail to the Big Man Pictograph Panel located in the shady overhang above. Return the way you came.

At the junction with Pollys Island and Pollys Canyon, turn west (left LUC) and climb the steep alluvial banks to the sage flats above. Follow the trail around the abandoned meander for 5 minutes to Pollys Island spring in the northwest corner along the north wall. There is a small ruin on a talus slope just east of the spring. Return back to Grand Gulch and exit the canyon by climbing out along the Government Trail.

Government Trail–Big Man Panel UTM GPS Coordinates

Government Trail carpark	0,581,011 E; 4,141,100 N	Elevation 5700'	00 min.
Rim overlook	0,578,753 E; 4,143,909 N	Elevation 5300'	60 min.
Grand Gulch	0,578,285 E; 4,143,909 N	Elevation 5000'	75 min.
Pollys Canyon	0,578,553 E; 4,144,173 N	Elevation 5000'	80 min.
Pollys Canyon arch	0,578,743 E; 4,144,187 N	Elevation 5020'	85 min.
Big Man Pictograph Panel		Elevation 5000'	125 min.
Pollys Island Ruin		Elevation 5000'	165 min.
Government Trail ascent	0,578,285 E; 4,143,909 N	Elevation 5000'	175 min.
Government Trail carpark	0,581,011 E; 4,141,100 N	Elevation 5700'	250 min.

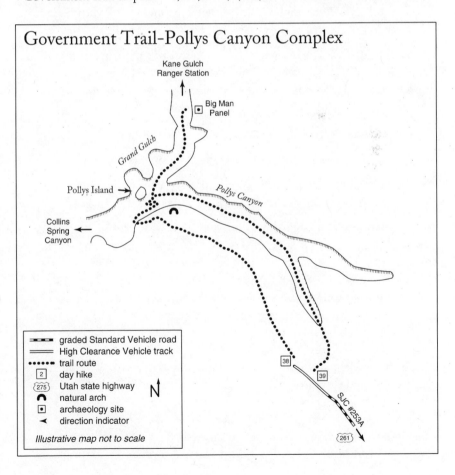

Government Trail-Pollys Canyon Complex

Kane Gulch
Ranger Station

Big Man
Panel

Grand Gulch

Pollys Island →

Pollys Canyon

Collins
Spring ←
Canyon

38

39

- ▰▰▰ graded Standard Vehicle road
- ═══ High Clearance Vehicle track
- •••••• trail route
- [2] day hike
- (275) Utah state highway
- ∩ natural arch
- [□] archaeology site
- ◄ direction indicator

Illustrative map not to scale

N

SJC #253A

(261)

■ **39 Government Trail–Pollys Canyon Loop**

Access: The Government Trail–Pollys Canyon Loop carpark is located
west of Utah State Hwy. 261. At mile 18.1, turn west onto San Juan
County Route Slickhorn #245, GPS coordinates 0,593,537 E; 4,139,176 N;
Elevation 6500'. Go 0.3 mile to a gated fence with a BLM information
board and trail registry. Continue to mile 2.6 and the junction with San
Juan County Route Point Lookout #203 and San Juan County Route
Slickhorn #245 (GPS Coordinates 0,590,226 E; 4,140,342 N; Elevation
6350') with a BLM Government Trail sign. Turn northwest (right) and
continue to mile 5.4 and the junction of San Juan County Route
Slickhorn #245 and San Juan County Route #253A. Go northwest (right)
to mile 6.3 and turn onto the high-clearance track with a BLM
Government Trail sign. The carpark is at mile 8.7 with GPS coordinates
0,581,011 E; 4,141,100 N; Elevation 5700'. Parking/camping is limited to
several vehicles. Refer to the Grand Gulch map and the Government
Trail–Pollys Canyon complex map.

Trail Statistics: The route is 9.6 miles round-trip with an elevation
change of 700 feet requiring 4–6 hours to complete. This is a fair
surface/canyon combination hike over Class 1–4 terrain requiring
moderate effort and difficult route-finding skills.

Attractions: Pollys Canyon arch.

Cautions: There is limited midday shade along this route.

Maps: USGS Navajo Mountain (1:100,000), or USGS Pollys Pasture
(1:62,500), or Trails Illustrated Grand Gulch Plateau (1:62,500)

Description: Follow the high-clearance-vehicle track from the upper
carpark to the lower carpark adjacent to the stock pond if your vehicle
was unable to negotiate the rough track. From the trail registry, follow
the double track northwest to the rim of Grand Gulch in 50 minutes.
Walk in the left track only to avoid further erosion on the other track.
Perhaps in time the desert will reclaim that other track, and instead of a
road scar, only a hiking trail will remain. From the rim you can see
structures with intact doors across the canyon on Pollys Island. Descend
the switchbacks to the floor of Grand Gulch in 15 minutes. Turn north
(right LUC) and walk up-canyon to the confluence with Pollys Canyon in
5 minutes.

Turn east (right LUC) into Pollys Canyon and walk 5 minutes to
the first meander. There is an arch in the east (right LUC) wall. It is 50
minutes to an east-northeast-trending tributary (left LUC). Continue

Grand Gulch

south (right LUC) for 30 minutes to the North Fork of Pollys Canyon
junction (left LUC). Go southeast (right LUC) in the South Fork of Pollys
Canyon for 20 minutes to a 6' dryfall ledge pour-off that is negotiated
using the crossbedding planes on the east wall (right LUC). Continue
another 10 minutes to a double ledge pour-off. There is a cairn route up
the east wall (right LUC) before the pour-off itself. It is 15 minutes to an
east-trending tributary junction (left LUC). Continue south to the canyon
terminus in 20 minutes. Climb up the west wall to the rim (right LUC)
and proceed 5 minutes southwest to the Government Trail access road.
Avoid walking on cryptogamic soils. Turn northwest (right) and walk 20
minutes to the carpark area.

Government Trail–Pollys Canyon Loop UTM GPS Coordinates

Government Trail carpark	0,581,011 E; 4,141,100 N	Elevation 5700'	00 min.
Rim overlook	0,578,753 E; 4,143,909 N	Elevation 5300'	50 min.
Grand Gulch	0,578,285 E; 4,143,909 N	Elevation 5000'	65 min.
Pollys Canyon	0,578,553 E; 4,144,173 N	Elevation 5000'	70 min.
Pollys Canyon arch	0,578,743 E; 4,144,187 N	Elevation 5020'	75 min.
E-NE tributary junction	0,580,411 E; 4,143,744 N	Elevation 5200'	125 min.
North Fork tributary junction	0,580,411 E; 4,143,739 N	Elevation 5240'	155 min.
Pour-off	0,581,884 E; 4,141,743 N	Elevation 5500'	175 min.
East tributary junction	0,582,123 E; 4,141,427 N	Elevation 5540'	190 min.
Rim-top terminus	0,582,138 E; 4,140,749 N	Elevation 5760'	210 min.
Government Trail carpark	0,581,011 E; 4,141,100 N	Elevation 5700'	235 min.

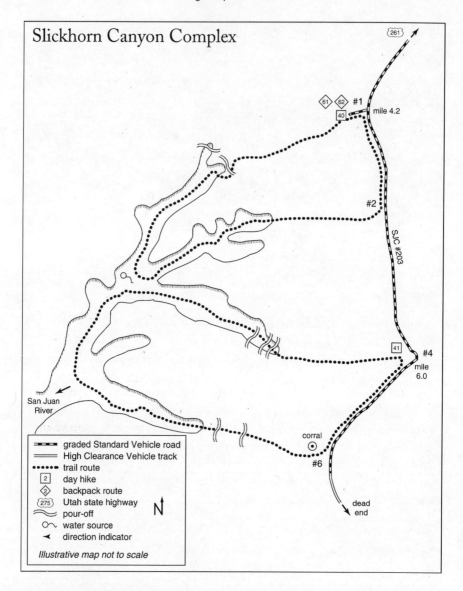

Slickhorn Canyon Complex

graded Standard Vehicle road
High Clearance Vehicle track
trail route
day hike
backpack route
Utah state highway
pour-off
water source
direction indicator

Illustrative map not to scale

N

■ 40 Slickhorn Canyon Access #1–#2 Loop

Access: The Slickhorn Canyon Access #1–Access #2 Loop carpark is located west of Utah State Hwy. 261. At mile 18.1, turn west onto San Juan County Route Slickhorn #245, GPS coordinates 0,593,537 E; 4,139,176 N; Elevation 6500'. Drive 0.3 mile to a gated fence with a BLM information board and trail registry. Continue to mile 2.6 and the junction of San Juan County Route Point Lookout #203 and San Juan County Route Slickhorn #245 (GPS Coordinates 0,590,226 E; 4,140,342 N;

Elevation 6350′). Turn southwest (left) onto Point Lookout #203 and
continue to mile 4.2. Turn west (right) on the standard-vehicle track and
go 0.4 mile to the carpark. There is a rusted blue Ford pickup bed from
the 1950s near the trail registry. Parking/camping is limited to several
vehicles. Refer to Slickhorn Canyon map.

Trail Statistics: The route is 9.8 miles round-trip with an elevation
change of 700 feet requiring 6–7 hours to complete. This is a good
canyon hike over Class 1–3 terrain requiring moderate effort and
moderate route-finding skills.

Attractions: Beautiful contoured sandstone walls with interesting
pinnacle hoodoos.

Cautions: There is limited midday shade along this route. No dogs
are allowed in Slickhorn Canyon or its tributaries. This route has an
extended descent on slickrock surfaces; do not attempt to hike it in
adverse weather conditions.

Maps: USGS Navajo Mountain (1:100,000), or USGS Cedar Mesa North,
Cedar Mesa South, Pollys Pasture, and Slickhorn Canyon East (1:62,500),
or Trails Illustrated Grand Gulch Plateau (1:62,500)

Description: From the trail registry, head west down-canyon in
the shallow drainage. After 15 minutes of easily negotiated stepped

Slickhorn Canyon

pour-offs, there's a northwest-trending tributary junction (right LDC). Go southwest (left LDC) for 30 minutes to a grooved 80' pour-off with an accompanying twin 50' tributary pour-off sharing the same plunge pool. There is a detour route over the "hat rock" knob to the immediate south (left LDC). It follows the high bench for 10 minutes under/over two more dryfalls to a steep descent path. Follow the cairns closely. There is a hoodoo pinnacle on the opposite west canyon wall. The descent traverses slightly left (down-canyon) until a red rock layer is reached, where it switches to the right (up-canyon) before heading straight down to the canyon bottom. Don't try this route if the canyon walls are wet! A cobble section and dense brush section give way shortly to easy alluvial sand trail walking.

The Slickhorn Canyon Access #2 northeast-trending tributary junction is reached in 50 minutes. A balanced rock hoodoo and several rim-top "hat" rocks can be seen in this area. Slickhorn Canyon Access #4 is 10 minutes down-canyon with several good camping sites at its northeast-trending tributary junction (left LDC). Water is intermittent through here with small streambed potholes.

Go northeast (left LDC) into the Slickhorn Canyon Access #2 tributary and walk up-canyon for 35 minutes to a junction with a northeast tributary (right LUC). Go north (left LUC) for 15 minutes to a stepped pour-off and immediate boulder dam. It took me 10 minutes to navigate this series of stepped pour-offs and boulder dams. Once on top, it is 10 minutes to a 10' pour-off with a 20' dryfall immediately above it. A route on the north wall (left LUC) climbs up and follows the ledge ramp up-canyon for 15 minutes to a 6' pour-off. A traverse route up the steep talus slope is on the south wall (right LUC). There is another 6' pour-off, plunge pool and brush thicket immediately up-canyon, with traverse routes on both canyon walls. It is 15 minutes up-canyon walking to Point Lookout #203. Turn north (left) onto the road. It is 25 minutes to the west-trending standard-vehicle track (left) and 10 more minutes along this track to the Slickhorn Canyon Access #1 carpark.

Slickhorn Canyon Access #1–#2 Loop UTM GPS Coordinates

Slickhorn #1 carpark	0,587,878 E; 4,138,506 N	Elevation 6200'	00 min.
80' pour-off	0,585,654 E; 4,137,521 N	Elevation 5800'	45 min.
Descent path top	0,585,610 E; 4,137,101 N	Elevation 5800'	55 min.
Descent path bottom	0,585,532 E; 4,137,160 N	Elevation 5500'	65 min.
Access #2 junction	0,584,295 E; 4,135,680 N	Elevation 5400'	115 min.
NE tributary junction	0,585,807 E; 4,136,158 N	Elevation 5600'	150 min.

Top of boulder dams	0,586,504 E; 4,136,490 N	Elevation 5800'	175 min.
10' pour-off	0,586,880 E; 4,136,665 N	Elevation 5950'	185 min.
6' pour-off	0,587,765 E; 4,136,838 N	Elevation 6090'	200 min.
SJC #203 junction	0,588,831 E; 4,136,442 N	Elevation 6200'	215 min.
Access #1 junction	0,588,414 E; 4,138,574 N	Elevation 6240'	240 min.
Slickhorn #1 carpark	0,587,878 E; 4,138,506 N	Elevation 6200'	250 min.

■ 41 Slickhorn Canyon Access #4–Access #6 Loop

Access: The Slickhorn Canyon Access #4–Access #6 Loop carpark is located west of Utah State Hwy. 261. At mile 18.1, turn west onto San Juan County Route Slickhorn #245, GPS coordinates 0,593,537 E; 4,139,176 N; Elevation 6500'. Drive 0.3 mile to a gated fence with a BLM information board and trail registry. Continue to mile 2.6 to the junction of San Juan County Route Point Lookout #203 and San Juan County Route Slickhorn #245 (GPS Coordinates 0,590,226 E; 4,140,342 N; Elevation 6350'). Turn southwest (left) onto Point Lookout #203 and continue to the carpark at mile 6. There is a subterranean cattlemen's shelter at the carpark. Parking/camping is limited to several vehicles. Refer to the Slickhorn map.

Trail Statistics: The route is 10.8 miles round-trip with an elevation change of 700 feet requiring 6–8 hours to complete. This is a good canyon hike over Class 1–3 terrain requiring moderate effort and moderate route-finding skills.

Attractions: Sandstone walls, hoodoos, dryfalls, and an arch.

Cautions: There is limited midday shade along this route. No dogs are allowed in Slickhorn Canyon or its tributaries.

Maps: USGS Navajo Mountain (1:100,000), or USGS Cedar Mesa South and Slickhorn Canyon East (1:62,500), or Trails Illustrated Grand Gulch Plateau (1:62,500)

Description: Proceed west down-canyon into the drainage from the carpark with its cowboy shelter relic. It is 25 minutes to a northeast-trending tributary junction (right LDC). Go southwest (left LDC) for 5 minutes to a 15' pour-off with a descent route on the east wall (left LDC). There is a boulder bridge immediately down-canyon from the plunge pool area. Negotiate the series of boulder dams and pour-offs to a north-trending tributary junction (right LDC) in 15 minutes. Continue west (left LDC) past an immediate down-canyon 15' pour-off that is negotiated along some boulders on the north wall (right LDC). It is 30 minutes to a north-trending tributary (right LDC) with a "hat-rock" seen directly west on the rim. Go west (left LDC) for 15 minutes to the confluence of Slickhorn Canyon.

Continue southwest (left LDC) for 5 minutes to an arch on the southeast meander (left LDC). It is 35 minutes to an east-northeast–trending tributary junction (left LDC). Proceed west (right LDC) for 5 minutes to a north-northeast tributary junction (left LDC). This is Slickhorn Canyon Access #6. There is a campsite under the cottonwoods in the sand along the alluvial bank that makes a great place for a snack or a nap.

Go north-northeast up-canyon (left LDC) into Slickhorn Canyon Access #6 tributary. It is 25 minutes to a north-trending tributary junction (left LUC). Go east (right LUC) for 5 minutes and locate the ledge traverse route along the south wall. From the ledge traverse, you can see several structures in the opposite north wall along an alcove seam. Continue up-canyon for 30 minutes over several negotiable pour-offs and boulder dams. It is 20 minutes to a north-trending tributary junction (left LUC) among shallow cross-bedded canyon walls. Proceed east (right LUC) and negotiate the immediate pour-off to a south-trending tributary junction (right LUC) in 5 minutes. Continue east (left LUC) for 10 minutes to the head of the drainage.

Head east toward the distant butte along the trail paralleling the drainage for 10 minutes to the corral area. This is the carpark area for Slickhorn Canyon Access #6. Follow Point Lookout #203 road north (left) for 20 minutes to the carpark of Slickhorn Canyon Access #4.

Slickhorn #4–#6 Loop UTM GPS Coordinates

Slickhorn #4 carpark	0,589,074 E; 4,134,364 N	Elevation 6200′	00 min.
NE tributary junction	0,587,670 E; 4,134,344 N	Elevation 6180′	25 min.
15′ pour-off	0,586,704 E; 4,134,505 N	Elevation 6160′	30 min.
North tributary junction	0,586,426 E; 4,134,700 N	Elevation 5800′	45 min.
North tributary junction	0,585,119 E; 4,135,319 N	Elevation 5600′	75 min.
Confluence at Slickhorn	0,584,125 E; 4,135,285 N	Elevation 5500′	90 min.
Arch	0,583,666 E; 4,135,451 N	Elevation 5500′	95 min.
E-NE tributary junction	0,583,364 E; 4,133,968 N	Elevation 5400′	135 min.
Access #6 junction	0,583,047 E; 4,133,500 N	Elevation 5300′	140 min.
North tributary junction	0,583,754 E; 4,133,578 N	Elevation 5400′	165 min.
Ledge traverse	0,584,056 E; 4,133,446 N	Elevation 5400′	170 min.
Top of boulder dams	0,585,271 E; 4,133,003 N	Elevation 5860′	200 min.

North tributary junction	0,585,914 E; 4,133,134 N	Elevation 5900'	220 min.
South tributary junction	0,586,109 E; 4,132,968 N	Elevation 5920'	225 min.
Head of tributary drainage	0,587,104 E; 4,133,159 N	Elevation 6000'	235 min.
Corral & SJC #203 junction	0,587,967 E; 4,132,925 N	Elevation 6200'	245 min.
Slickhorn #4 carpark	0,589,074 E; 4,134,364 N	Elevation 6200'	265 min.

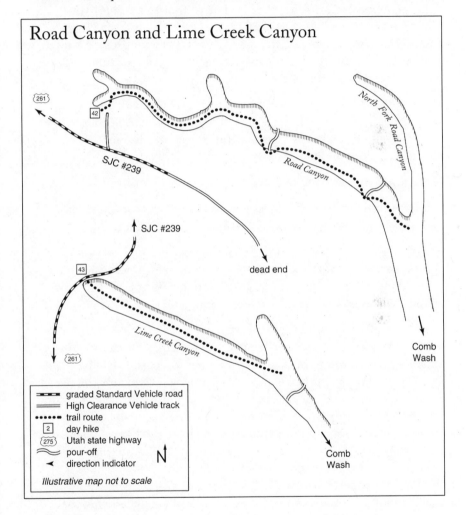

Road Canyon and Lime Creek Canyon

▪▪▪	graded Standard Vehicle road
═══	High Clearance Vehicle track
●●●●●	trail route
2	day hike
275	Utah state highway
∼∼	pour-off
◄	direction indicator

Illustrative map not to scale

■ 42 Road Canyon

Access: The Road Canyon carpark is located east of Utah State Hwy. 261. At mile 18.1, turn east onto the standard-vehicle surface San Juan County Route Cigarette Springs #239, GPS coordinates 0,593,537 E; 4,139,176 N; Elevation 6500'. Zero the mileage at this junction. You will pass a cattle trough at 0.4 mile, a gated fence and BLM trail registry at 0.9 mile, a north spur at 1.2 miles, a south spur at 3.3 miles, a north spur at 3.4 miles, and a second gated fence at 3.5 miles. There is a wash crossing at 5.5 miles, a north camping spur at 5.6 miles, and a high-clearance-vehicle track at mile 5.7 (GPS coordinates 0,602,430 E; 4,137,668 N; Elevation 6100'). Turn north (left) and drive another 0.8 mile to the carpark at mile 6.5 (GPS coordinates 0,602,967 E; 4,138,780 N; Elevation 6000'). Parking/camping is limited to several vehicles. There are good camping sites and vistas farther east along the Cigarette Springs #239 before it ends at a promontory at mile 8.5.

Trail Statistics: The route is 14.2 miles round-trip with an elevation change of 1000 feet requiring 8–10 hours to complete. This is a good canyon hike over Class 1–3 terrain requiring moderate effort and moderate route-finding skills.

Attractions: Seven Kiva Ruin.

Cautions: Most water sources were small and medium streambed potholes and plunge pools. There is limited midday shade along this route.

Maps: USGS Bluff (1:100,000), or USGS Cedar Mesa North, Snow Flat Spring Cave, Cedar Mesa South, and Cigarette Spring Cave (1:62,500), or Trails Illustrated Grand Gulch Plateau (1:62,500)

Description: Head north to the tributary rim and follow the cairns marking the descent route. Descend to the bottom of the canyon in 15 minutes. Walk east (right LDC) for 25 minutes to a north-trending tributary with a large alcove surprisingly devoid of structures. However, proceed south (right LDC) around the bend to Seven Kiva Ruin. Refrain from entering any of the structures.

For the curious, proceed 10 minutes down-canyon to a 12' pour-off and plunge pool. A ledge traverse route on the south wall (right LDC) starts near some big boulders. Immediately above these boulders is a petroglyph panel on a large black-stained rock with a dozen figures facing south. It is 20 minutes of careful walking along this occasionally cairn-marked ledge route to reach the canyon bottom again. Continue east (right LDC) down-canyon to a north-trending tributary junction (left LDC) in 10 minutes. Proceed southeast (right LDC) to a west-trending tributary junction (right LDC) in 5 minutes. Go east (left LDC) for 20 minutes to a north-northeast-trending tributary junction (left LDC). Continue southeast (right LDC) for 30 minutes to a southwest-trending tributary junction (right LDC). Head south (left LDC) for 15 minutes to a west-trending tributary junction (right LDC) along a high bank trail that avoids the 15' pour-off in the canyon bottom. Continue down-canyon for 20 minutes to a small campsite and spring in a northeast-trending tributary (left LDC). Continue south (right LDC) to the North Fork of Road Canyon tributary junction immediately down-canyon. Enjoy a snack and return the way you came.

Road Canyon UTM GPS Coordinates

Road Canyon carpark	0,602,967 E; 4,138,780 N	Elevation 6000'	00 min.
Bottom of descent path	0,603,425 E; 4,138,853 N	Elevation 5650'	15 min.
North tributary junction		Elevation 5600'	40 min.
Seven Kiva ruin		Elevation 5600'	40 min.
Top of ledge traverse		Elevation 5580'	50 min.
Bottom of ledge traverse	0,605,463 E; 4,138,649 N	Elevation 5400'	70 min.
North tributary junction	0,605,990 E; 4,138,639 N	Elevation 5350'	80 min.
West tributary junction	0,606,102 E; 4,138,273 N	Elevation 5200'	85 min.
N-NE tributary junction	0,607,599 E; 4,138,380 N	Elevation 5100'	105 min.
SW tributary junction	0,608,560 E; 4,137,541 N	Elevation 5050'	135 min.
West tributary junction	0,609,671 E; 4,136,884 N	Elevation 5000'	150 min.
North Fork junction	0,610,149 E; 4,136,811 N	Elevation 5000'	170 min.
Road Canyon carpark	0,602,967 E; 4,138,780 N	Elevation 6000'	340 min.

■ 43 Lime Creek Canyon

Access: The Lime Creek Canyon carpark is located east of Utah State Hwy. 261. At mile 18.1, turn east onto San Juan County Route Cigarette Springs #239, GPS coordinates 0,593,537 E; 4,139,176 N; Elevation 6500'). Zero the mileage at this junction. You will pass a cattle trough at 0.4 mile, a gated fence and BLM trail registry at 0.9 mile, and a north spur at 1.2 miles. Turn south (right) onto the high-clearance-vehicle track at 3.3 miles and go another 1.8 miles to a wash crossing with GPS coordinates 0,596,995 E; 4,137,108 N; Elevation 6400'. There is a small carpark to the north and another one to the south of the wash crossing. Parking/camping is limited to several vehicles. Refer to the Road and Lime Creek Canyons map.

Trail Statistics: The route is 15.4 miles round-trip with an elevation change of 1100 feet requiring 8–10 hours to complete. This is a good canyon hike over Class 1–3 terrain requiring moderate effort and moderate route-finding skills.

Attractions: A beautiful sandstone canyon complex.

Cautions: There is limited midday shade along this route.

Maps: USGS Bluff (1:100,000), or USGS Cedar Mesa North, Cedar Mesa South, and Cigarette Spring Cave (1:62,500), or Trails Illustrated Grand Gulch Plateau (1:62,500)

Description: Head east into the drainage for 45 minutes over several easily negotiated pour-offs to a north-trending tributary junction (left LDC). Continue southeast (right LDC) for another 40 minutes to an intersection with a north-trending tributary junction with double hoodoo pinnacles (left LDC) opposite a south-trending tributary amphitheater (right LDC). Notice the interesting erosion patterns and red hues decorating the canyon walls here. Proceed southeast (straight LDC) for another 5 minutes and check out the alcoves around you. There are four different alcoves with structures high up on the inaccessible walls. I call this site Ruin Cluster Amphitheater. Use binoculars to see details of the structures.

Continue down-canyon for 40 minutes to a spring flowing out of a resistance ledge on the northeast wall (left LDC). It is another 35 minutes through some brushy sections to a southeast-facing alcove (left LDC) containing a pictograph of a white bird headdress on an anthropo-morphic figure. Use binoculars to see the details because the rock art is inaccessible. A north-trending tributary junction (left LDC) is reached in 20 minutes and an impassable 30' terminus pour-off in another 45 minutes. Return the way you came.

Lime Creek Canyon UTM GPS Coordinates

Lime Creek Canyon carpark	0,596,995 E; 4,137,108 N	Elevation 6400'	00 min.
North tributary junction	0,598,619 E; 4,137,182 N	Elevation 6000'	45 min.
Double hoodoo pinnacle	0,599,486 E; 4,136,793 N	Elevation 5900'	85 min.
Ruin Cluster Amphitheater	0,599,907 E; 4,136,802 N	Elevation 5900'	90 min.
Ledge spring	0,600,170 E; 4,136,012 N	Elevation 5800'	130 min.
North tributary junction	0,604,760 E; 4,133,661 N	Elevation 5400'	185 min.
Pour-off terminus	0,606,905 E; 4,132,334 N	Elevation 5200'	230 min.
Lime Creek Canyon carpark	0,596,995 E; 4,137,108 N	Elevation 6400'	460 min.

■ 44 Upper Johns Canyon Loop

Access: The Upper Johns Canyon Loop carpark is located west of Utah State Hwy. 261 at mile 17.3, GPS coordinates 0,594,112 E; 4,136,339 N; Elevation 6520'. The carpark is on the shoulder on the southwest side of the highway and is limited to several vehicles.

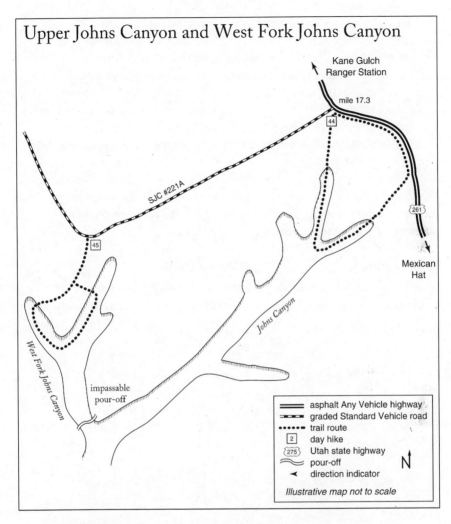

Upper Johns Canyon and West Fork Johns Canyon

Kane Gulch
Ranger Station

mile 17.3

44

SJC #221A

45

261

Mexican
Hat

Johns Canyon

West Fork Johns Canyon

impassable
pour-off

	asphalt Any Vehicle highway
	graded Standard Vehicle road
	trail route
2	day hike
275	Utah state highway
	pour-off
◄	direction indicator

N

Illustrative map not to scale

Trail Statistics: The route is 6.7 miles round-trip with an elevation change of 600 feet requiring 4–6 hours to complete. This is a fair hike over Class 1–4 terrain requiring moderate effort and moderate route-finding skills.

Attractions: Canyoneering-style hiking.

Cautions: There is limited midday shade along this route. Do not attempt this hike in adverse weather conditions.

Maps: USGS Bluff (1:100,000), or USGS Cedar Mesa South (1:62,500), or Trails Illustrated Grand Gulch Plateau (1:62,500)

Description: Head west to the BLM information board and trail registry. Turn south here (left) and follow the drainage down-canyon for 5 minutes to a northeast tributary junction Continue down-canyon for 5 minutes to an overhanging 15' pour-off with a difficult descent route on the west wall (right LDC). Walk 40 more minutes to a northeast-trending tributary junction (left LDC). Continue down-canyon for 15 minutes to a north-northwest–trending tributary junction and turn north (right LDC) into this tributary. Walk 20 minutes to a 15' pour-off with a traverse route on the east wall (right LUC). It is 10 minutes farther up-canyon to reach the mesa surface. Find the double track across the slickrock to the northeast and follow these sandy tracks north for 25 minutes to San Juan County Route #221A. Turn east (right) and follow the roadbed 20 minutes back to the carpark.

Upper Johns Canyon Loop UTM GPS Coordinates

Upper Johns Canyon carpark	0,594,117 E; 4,136,325 N	Elevation 6500'	00 min.
NE tributary junction	0,594,161 E; 4,135,813 N	Elevation 6450'	05 min.
Scrambling descent route	0,594,132 E; 4,134,993 N	Elevation 6300'	20 min.
NE tributary junction	0,594,297 E; 4,133,321 N	Elevation 6100'	60 min.
N-NW tributary junction	0,593,834 E; 4,132,570 N	Elevation 5900'	75 min.
15' pour-off	0,593,337 E; 4,134,096 N	Elevation 6100'	105 min.
Rim top	0,593,390 E; 4,134,525 N	Elevation 6400	115 min.
SJC #221A junction	0,593,386 E; 4,135,842 N	Elevation 6450'	140 min.
Upper Johns Canyon carpark	0,594,117 E; 4,136,325 N	Elevation 6500'	200 min.

■ 45 West Fork Johns Canyon Loop

Access: The West Fork Johns Canyon Loop carpark is located west of Utah State Hwy. 261 on San Juan County Route #221A. Take Hwy. 261 to mile 17.3, GPS coordinates 0,594,112 E; 4,136,339 N; Elevation 6520'. Turn west onto Route #221A, a standard-vehicle road surface, and go through an immediate cattle gate adjacent to the BLM bulletin board. It is 8.6 miles to the carpark area on the south side of road (left) where the road turns northwest at GPS coordinates 0,590,781 E; 4,134,106 N; Elevation 6500'. Parking/camping is limited to several vehicles. Refer to the Upper Johns Canyon map.

Trail Statistics: The route is 5.2 miles round-trip with an elevation change of 600 feet requiring 3–4 hours to complete. This is a fair hike over Class 1–4 terrain requiring moderate effort and difficult route-finding skills.

Attractions: Canyoneering style hiking.

Cautions: There is limited midday shade along this route and a scrambling section to exit the canyon. Do not attempt this hike in adverse weather conditions.

Maps: USGS Bluff (1:100,000), or USGS Cedar Mesa South (1:62,500), or Trails Illustrated Grand Gulch Plateau (1:62,500)

Description: Follow the 4WD track south to the slickrock section in 20 minutes. Go west across the slickrock surface to the canyon rim. Find an access route down into the drainage. It is 40 minutes of difficult walking to a 6-inch natural bridge in the cross-bedding of the sandstone streambed. Continue down-canyon 15 minutes to a junction with a northeast-trending tributary (left LDC). For the curious, the terminus pour-off at the bottom of the West Fork of Johns Canyon is 45 minutes farther down-canyon.

Turn into the northeast-trending tributary and traverse over several smaller pour-offs to the inaccessible Black-Striped Ruin (AN) facing southeast (left LUC) in 25 minutes. It is located in a buff-colored alcove below the prominent black-striped desert varnish stains. In 5 more minutes of up-canyon walking, a junction with a northeast-trending tributary is encountered (right LUC). Continue north (left LUC) for 25 minutes to a west-trending tributary junction (left LUC). There is a Class 4 scrambling exit (left LUC) near the 20' pour-off at the west-trending tributary's head in 10 minutes. Follow the drainage north for 15 minutes to the San Juan County Route #221A intersection. Follow the road west (left) back to the carpark in 10 minutes.

West Fork Johns Canyon Loop UTM GPS Coordinates

West Fork Johns carpark	0,590,781 E; 4,134,106 N	Elevation 6400'	00 min.
Slickrock section	0,590,694 E; 4,132,779 N	Elevation 6320'	20 min.
6" streambed bridge	0,590,742 E; 4,132,277 N	Elevation 5900'	65 min.
NE tributary junction	0,591,152 E; 4,131,424 N	Elevation 5600'	80 min.
NE tributary junction	0,591,508 E; 4,132,560 N	Elevation 6000'	110 min.
Pour-off top	0,591,835 E; 4,134,228 N	Elevation 6320'	135 min.
SJC #221A road junction	0,591,679 E; 4,134,672 N	Elevation 6380'	150 min.
West Fork Johns carpark	0,590,781 E; 4,134,106 N	Elevation 6400'	160 min.

● 46 Muley Point Overlook

Access: The Muley Point Overlook carpark is located west of Utah State Hwy. 261. At mile 9.6, GPS coordinates 0,593,761 E; 4,125,991 N; Elevation 6400', there is a "Muley Viewpoint" sign where the pavement

changes to gravel. Turn west onto standard-vehicle Muley Point #241
and go 4 miles to the carpark area. Parking/camping is limited to
several dozen vehicles.

Muley Point overlook of the Goosenecks of the San Juan River and Monument
Valley

Trail Statistics: The route is ¼-mile round-trip with a nominal elevation change requiring 10–30 minutes to complete. This is a good surface walk over Class 1–2 terrain requiring easy effort and easy route-finding skills.

Attractions: Vistas of Monument Valley, Valley of the Gods, and the Goosenecks of the San Juan River.

6

Utah State Highway 261
South Section

THE NORTH-SOUTH UTAH STATE HWY. 261 IS PAVED, WITH NARROW LANES
and no shoulders for most of its 32.5 miles and no passing lanes. The
3-mile Moqui Dugway section of graded gravel road surface, with a
10% grade descending 1100 feet, connects Cedar Mesa to the lower
tablelands. The northern section of highway rolls over the rather blank
juniper highlands and sage flats with little indication of the marvelous
surrounding sandstone canyons until you reach the Moqui Dugway. The
southern section crosses the red-rock tablelands of Halgaito Shale. The
access roads to the carpark areas are either maintained standard-vehicle
or high-clearance-vehicle clay surfaces that get exceedingly slick when
wet. There are pit toilets but no potable water or garbage collection at
Goosenecks State Park. The hikes are organized from north to south
(Valley of the Gods Overlook to the Goosenecks of the San Juan) with
numbered circles representing car walks and numbered squares
representing day hikes.

E. L. Goodridge opened up the Mexican Hat oil field on March 4,
1908. A road was hastily built from Bluff to Goodridge (now named
Mexican Hat) to haul in drilling equipment to the oil field, but no
economical reserves were discovered. Nevertheless, Goodridge built a
primitive road to the mouth of Slickhorn Canyon and drilled an
exploratory well in what is now the river-runner camping area. The
steam engine necessary for the drilling operation was hauled by mules
from Gallup, New Mexico, but was lost on the last cliffs before reaching
the drilling site. The debris from the wreck remains scattered about the
cliffs. Goodridge then abandoned the Slickhorn Canyon site. Don
Danvers drilled two more wells in 1952–53, but no oil has ever been
shipped from Slickhorn. The Mexican Hat synclinal fields have
produced viable oil around the Aneth area, but the deposits nearest
the river have already been leached out by the San Juan itself.

Cowpuncher and stagecoach owner Henry Honaker superintended
the Honaker Trail construction from 1893 until its completion in June
1894. The trail was intended to service the gold placer claims on the
river's edge. However, the first horse to attempt the descent fell off the

trail near Horn Point and was killed. No pack animal has ever made the round-trip. The placer mines along the San Juan River were also a bust.

The Goosenecks of the San Juan River, formerly known as "The Twist," are one of the best examples of incised meanders in the world. The river takes 5 miles to travel one linear mile. Incised meanders occur when a slow-moving river flowing over a flat landscape is suddenly captured in its course by quickly rising landforms. Since the river is captured and can't escape its banks, it continues to cut down through the rising landform. There are great views of the Rapplee anticline, Monument Valley, and the Valley of the Gods from the Moqui Dugway sign pullout.

Note: The yellow paint markers do not designate trails but were left by University of New Mexico geologists as stratigraphic identifiers when they studied the Honaker Trail Formation. Also, the campsites along the river's edge at the foot of the Honaker Trail are reserved for river-runners.

Access Points along Highway 261

Moqui Dugway sign	mile 9.3	0,594,049 E; 4,125,615 N	Elevation 6100′
Valley of the Gods Loop	mile 5.4	0,594,717 E; 4,124,508 N	Elevation 5300′
Hwy. 261 & Hwy. 316	mile 0.9	0,599,529 E; 4,117,333 N	Elevation 4680′
Hwy. 261 & Hwy. 163	mile 0.0	0,600,764 E; 4,116,920 N	Elevation 4500′

Car Walks	Quality	Skill	Effort	Time	Vehicle
● 52 Valley of the Gods Driving Loop					
	fair	easy	easy	2 hr.	All
● 51 Goosenecks Overlook	good	easy	easy	15 min.	All

Day Hikes	Quality	Skill	Class	Effort	Time	Miles (r-t)
■ 47 Honaker Trail	good	moderate	2	strenuous	3–4 hr.	3.8
■ 48 Johns Canyon Rim	fair	easy	1	easy	5–7 hr.	10.4
■ 49 Middle Johns Canyon	fair	easy	1	easy	5–7 hr.	9.5
■ 50 Lower Johns Canyon	fair	moderate	3	moderate	8–10 hr.	14.6

■ 47 Honaker Trail

Access: The Honaker Trail carpark is located northwest of Utah State Hwy. 316 on San Juan County Route Johns Canyon #244. Take Utah State Hwy. 261 to mile 0.9, GPS coordinates 0,599,529 E; 4,117,333 N; Elevation 4680′. Turn west onto Utah State Hwy. 316 and continue 0.5 mile to

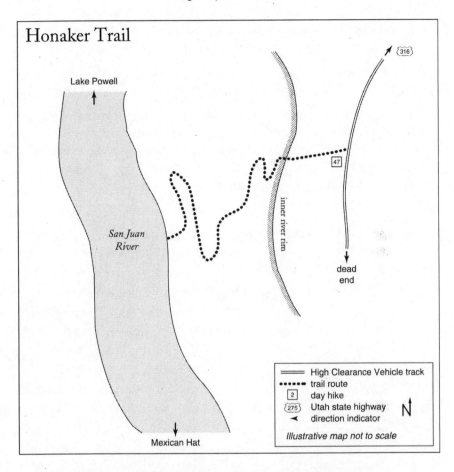

Honaker Trail

Lake Powell

San Juan River

inner river rim

47

dead end

316

High Clearance Vehicle track
trail route
2   day hike
275 Utah state highway
◄   direction indicator

N

Illustrative map not to scale

Mexican Hat

San Juan County Route Johns Canyon #244 to the north. Follow this standard-vehicle road surface to mile 2.5 and turn southwest (left) onto a high-clearance-vehicle track near a mobile water tank and metal Honaker sign (GPS coordinates 0,564,697 E; 4,117,693 N; Elevation 5120'). Continue to a north-south axis T intersection at mile 4.1. Turn south (left) and go 0.2 mile to the carpark. You will be able to see a tall stacked cairn on the canyon rim to the west. Parking is limited to two vehicles. There are campsites along the north-south canyon rim track.

Trail Statistics: The route is 3.8 miles round-trip with an elevation change of 1300 feet requiring 3–4 hours to complete. This is a good hike over Class 1–2 terrain requiring strenuous effort and moderate route-finding skills.

Attractions: Fossil specimens exposed in the various rock layers.

Cautions: There is limited midday shade along this route, but in the early morning the canyon wall creates good shade. Avoid taking dogs because limestone quickly abrades their paws.

Maps: USGS Bluff (1:100,000), or USGS The Goosenecks (1:62,500), or Trails Illustrated Grand Gulch Plateau (1:62,500)

Description: Head west on the double track from the carpark to the large cairn on the rim of the canyon in 5 minutes. A moderately steep footpath descends through the various cliff levels along rough ledges to the San Juan River near some popular river-runner camps. It is 30 minutes to Horn Point and 45 minutes more to the San Juan River. Return the way you came.

Honaker Trail UTM GPS Coordinates

Honaker Trail carpark	0,593,121 E; 4,116,089 N	Elevation 5200'	00 min.
Rim overlook	0,592,868 E; 4,116,104 N	Elevation 5100'	05 min.
Horn Point	0,592,126 E; 4,115,562 N	Elevation 4600'	35 min.
San Juan River	0,592,019 E; 4,115,645 N	Elevation 3900'	80 min.
Honaker Trail carpark	0,593,121 E; 4,116,089 N	Elevation 5200'	160 min.

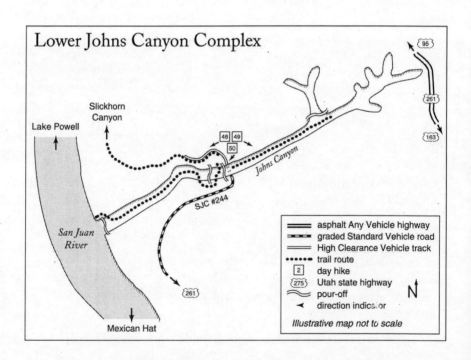

Lower Johns Canyon Complex

■ 48 Johns Canyon Rim

Access: The Johns Canyon Rim carpark is located northwest of Utah State Hwy. 316. Take Utah State Hwy. 261 to mile 0.9, GPS coordinates 0,599,529 E; 4,117,333 N; Elevation 4680'. Turn west onto Utah State Hwy. 316 and continue 0.5 mile to San Juan County Route Johns Canyon #244 to the north. Follow this standard-vehicle road surface past a metal Honaker sign at mile 2.5, a metal gate at mile 6.5, to the water crossing of Johns Canyon at mile 13.9. Parking is limited to several vehicles. There are several camping spots along the rim access road and near the carpark.

Trail Statistics: This route is 10.4 miles round-trip with an elevation change of 50 feet requiring 5–7 hours to complete. It is a fair hike along Class 1–2 terrain requiring easy effort and easy route-finding skills.

Attractions: Ancestral Puebloan rock art panels on boulder surfaces.

Cautions: There is limited midday shade along this route.

Maps: USGS Bluff and Navajo Mountain (1:100,000), or USGS Cedar Mesa South and Slickhorn Canyon East (1:62,500), or Trails Illustrated Grand Gulch Plateau (1:62,500)

Description: It is 70 minutes from the carpark to a panel with a dozen figures, mostly deer. It is another 20 minutes to a panel with several dozen assorted figures. The Glen Canyon NRA sign is reached in 10 minutes. Immediately west of the sign are three boulders close together containing six dozen assorted figures on their east-, west-, and south-facing surfaces. Continue west for another 20 minutes to a small panel with three sheep and a bird procession near the ground. In another 15 minutes two dozen figures can be seen on a white boulder. Why the change in mediums? It is 20 minutes to a vista near the rim of the San Juan River below a prominent pinnacle knob. All the petroglyph panels are on the north side of the track or the right side as you walk toward the San Juan River. The roadway continues for another 11 miles to the confluence with Slickhorn Canyon with no water sources on the rim ledges. The campsites at the mouth of Slickhorn Canyon are reserved for river-runners. Explore at your own initiative, but I turned around here. Return the way you came.

Johns Canyon Rim UTM GPS Coordinates

Johns Canyon Rim carpark   0,588,797 E; 4,125,653 N   Elevation 5200'   00 min.
Glen Canyon NRA sign   0,585,207 E; 4,124,590 N   Elevation 5200' 100 min.

Vista below pinnacle knob　0,582,988 E; 4,123,942 N　Elevation 5200'　155 min.
Johns Canyon Rim carpark　0,588,797 E; 4,125,653 N　Elevation 5200'　310 min.

■ 49 Middle Johns Canyon

Access: The carpark for the middle section of Johns Canyon is located northwest of Utah State Hwy. 316. Take Utah State Hwy. 261 to mile 0.9, GPS coordinates 0,599,529 E; 4,117,333 N; Elevation 4680'. Turn west onto Utah State Hwy. 316 and continue 0.5 mile to San Juan County Route Johns Canyon #244 to the north. Follow this standard-vehicle road surface past a metal Honaker sign at mile 2.5 and a metal gate at mile 6.5, to the water crossing of Johns Canyon at mile 13.9. Parking is limited to several vehicles. There are several camping spots along the rim access road and near the carpark. Refer to the Johns Canyon map.

Trail Statistics: This route is 9.5 miles round-trip with an elevation change of 400 feet requiring 5–7 hours to complete. This is a fair hike over Class 1 terrain requiring easy effort and easy route-finding skills.

Attractions: Ranching structures.

Cautions: There is limited midday shade along this route. This is a multiple-use corridor.

San Juan River in flood at Johns Canyon

Maps: USGS Bluff and Navajo Mountain (1:100,000), or USGS Cedar Mesa South and Slickhorn Canyon East (1:62,500), or Trails Illustrated Grand Gulch Plateau (1:62,500)

Description: From the limestone ledge carpark, follow the wash up-canyon for 5 minutes to a waist-high wall with a small-diameter pipe in its center along the north wall (right LUC). This is probably a relic from the cattle-grazing days. At the second limestone ledge crossing of the Johns Canyon streambed, turn northeast (right LUC) onto the double track and walk 30 minutes to a small corral and fence posts. On a small knoll northeast of the track is a decaying cowboy dugout with an intact rock hearth. Return to the double track and continue up-canyon. It is 35 minutes to the confluence with the West Fork of Johns Canyon through Russian thistle and tall grasses. The West Fork of Johns Canyon has a series of impassable pour-offs immediately up-canyon from this junction. Go northeast instead (right LUC) into the main stem of Johns Canyon along the double track.

It is 10 minutes following the double track up-canyon to where it ends at the rocky streambed underneath a series of east-southeast-facing alcoves in the west wall (left LUC). Bring binoculars because there are no access routes up to the Triple Alcove Ruin (AN) or the Triangle Overhang Ruin (AN), which you can see in another 5 minutes of up-canyon walking (left LUC). Return the way you came.

Middle Johns Canyon UTM GPS Coordinates

Middle Johns Canyon carpark	0,588,797 E; 4,125,653 N	Elevation 5200'	00 min.
Cowboy well	0,589,016 E; 4,126,049 N	Elevation 5200'	05 min.
Cowboy dugout	0,590,196 E; 4,126,688 N	Elevation 5300'	35 min.
WF Johns Canyon confluence	0,591,298 E; 4,128,907 N	Elevation 5400'	70 min.
Middle Johns Canyon carpark	0,588,797 E; 4,125,653 N	Elevation 5200'	170 min.

■ 50 Lower Johns Canyon

Access: The carpark for the lower section of Johns Canyon is located northwest of Utah State Hwy. 316. Take Utah State Hwy. 261 to mile 0.9, GPS coordinates 0,599,529 E; 4,117,333 N; Elevation 4680'. Turn west onto Utah State Hwy. 316 and continue 0.5 mile to San Juan County Route Johns Canyon #244 to the north. Follow this standard-vehicle road surface past a metal Honaker sign at mile 2.5 and a metal gate at mile 6.5, to the water crossing of Johns Canyon at mile 13.9. Parking is limited to several vehicles. There are several campsites along the rim access road and near the carpark. Refer to the Johns Canyon map.

Trail Statistics: This route is 14.6 miles round-trip with an elevation change of 800 feet requiring 8–10 hours to complete. It is a fair hike along Class 1–3 terrain requiring moderate effort and moderate route-finding skills.

Attractions: Fossils and chert fragments embedded in the streambed.

Cautions: There is limited midday shade along this route.

Maps: USGS Bluff and Navajo Mountain (1:100,000), or USGS Cedar Mesa South, Goulding Northeast and Slickhorn Canyon East (1:62,500), or Trails Illustrated Grand Gulch Plateau (1:62,500)

Description: Head west down-canyon from the limestone ledge crossing to the immediate pour-off. There are easy routes down each side. Continue westerly down-canyon for 15 minutes to an 80′ pour-off at the junction with a southeast-trending tributary (left LDC). Traverse west along the south wall (left LDC) and descend the steep talus slope. The faint descent trail has only a few cairns marking its route. Follow them carefully through here! Once in the bottom of Johns Canyon, continue west down-canyon (left LDC) to a north-trending tributary (right LDC) in 20 minutes. Continue west (left LDC) for 35 minutes to a 4′ pour-off, which is easily negotiated. It is 25 minutes to a series of constriction plunge pools and an immediate 4′ pour-off below them. There is a traverse path around these obstacles along the north wall (right LDC). Go down-canyon for 20 more minutes to a north-trending tributary dryfall with hanging garden seeps along the north wall (right LDC). There are several easily negotiated pour-offs and plunge pools with rough cobbles throughout this section. Continue down-canyon for 35 minutes to a gray layer of limestone and a 60′ pour-off.

From here the San Juan River canyon walls are within sight. A faint descent trail can be seen traversing a ledge on the south wall (left LDC). It is 15 minutes to the bottom of this talus slope. Cross the canyon bottom to the good trail above the immediate north canyon wall (right LDC) starting at the small pour-off. The canyon bottom will take you to the top of an impassable pour-off and sculptured plunge pools. There are two more impassable pour-offs before water reaches the San Juan River. Instead, it is 5 minutes of walking along the ledge to the overlook area above the confluence of Johns Canyon and the San Juan River.

I hiked this canyon after three steady days of rain and was amazed at the high water volume flowing down the San Juan River. The sandy beach normally below the bottom pour-off at the confluence of Johns Canyon had chocolate-colored river water running over it with a strong eddy current. The recent rains made most of the side canyons run, and the San Juan River was swollen with their inputs. Enjoy a snack, check the weather conditions, and return the way you came.

Lower Johns Canyon UTM GPS Coordinates

Carpark	0,588,797 E; 4,125,653 N	Elevation 5200'	00 min.
80' pour-off	0,588,284 E; 4,125,478 N	Elevation 5200'	15 min.
North tributary junction	0,587,402 E; 4,125,677 N	Elevation 5000'	35 min.
4' pour-off	0,585,744 E; 4,124,322 N	Elevation 4800'	70 min.
Constriction plunge pools	0,584,768 E; 4,123,639 N	Elevation 4700'	95 min.
North tributary garden seeps	0,583,954 E; 4,123,820 N	Elevation 4600'	115 min.
60' pour-off	0,582,641 E; 4,122,481 N	Elevation 4500'	150 min.
Bottom ledge descent	0,582,348 E; 4,122,159 N	Elevation 4400'	165 min.
San Juan River overlook	0,582,090 E; 4,122,291 N	Elevation 4400'	170 min.
Carpark	0,588,797 E; 4,125,653 N	Elevation 5200'	340 min.

Goosenecks of the San Juan River

● 51 Goosenecks Overlook State Park

Access: The Goosenecks of the San Juan River State Park is located at the end of Utah State Hwy. 316. Take Utah State Hwy. 261 mile 0.9, GPS coordinates 0,599,529 E; 4,117,333 N; Elevation 4680'. Turn west onto Utah State Hwy. 316 and continue 3.5 miles along the paved all-vehicle road surface to the carpark. There are a dozen camping spaces, six picnic tables, two pit toilets, several Native American vendors, and two informative plaques in the view kiosk area.

Trail Statistics: The route is ¼-mile round-trip with a nominal elevation change requiring 10–30 minutes to complete. This is a good surface walk over Class 1 terrain requiring easy effort and easy route-finding skills.

Attractions: Magnificent views of the entrenched meanders of the San Juan River, the Alhambra Rock diatreme, and Monument Valley.

● 52 Valley of the Gods Driving Loop

Access: The Valley of the Gods Driving Loop is located east of Utah State Hwy. 261 and north of Utah State Hwy. 163. It has two highway entrances. From Utah State Hwy. 261, turn east onto San Juan County Route Valley of the Gods #242 at mile 5.4 with GPS coordinates 0,594,717 E; 4,124,508 N; Elevation 5300'. Or from Utah State Hwy. 163, turn north onto San Juan County Route Valley of the Gods #242 at mile 29 with GPS coordinates 0,605,245 E; 4,121,388 N; Elevation 4500'. There is a Valley of the Gods sign at each entrance. There are several dozen camping spots along Valley of the Gods #242.

Trail Statistics: The 17 miles of clay-based all-vehicle road surface takes 1–2 hours to drive. There are a dozen wash crossings along this route and a few sharp turns.

Attractions: Beautiful buttes, keyholes, natural arches, monoliths, pinnacles, ramparts, and other geological erosion features.

Valley of the Gods from Moqui Dugway

7

Utah State Highway 276 Section

THE NORTH-SOUTH UTAH STATE HWY. 276 IS PAVED, WITH NARROW LANES and no shoulders. The road rolls over the rather blank sage flats between the Red House Cliffs and Cedar Mesa. The access roads from Utah State Hwy. 276 are composed of sand and clay, which are slippery when wet. Even 4WD vehicles will have problems with traction on these roads during and after stormy weather. However, the lower elevation and eastern tilt of the terrain allows the access roads to dry out more quickly than most others in Cedar Mesa do. The Red House Cliffs have a great deal of petrified wood. Utah State Hwy. 276 is part of the Mormon Trail.

Access Points along Highway 276

| Cow Tank Canyon | mile 86.4 | 0,580,611 E; 4,152,489 N | Elevation 5665' |
| Collins Spring | mile 83.8 | 0,586,727 E; 4,157,522 N | Elevation 5600' |

Day Hikes	Quality	Skill	Class	Effort	Time	Miles (r-t)
■ 53 Cow Tank Canyon	fair	easy	2	easy	5–7 hr.	10
■ 54 Collins Spring–Banister Ruin						
	good	easy	2	easy	6–8 hr.	10.1

■ 53 Cow Tank Canyon

Access: Cow Tank Canyon carpark is located east of Utah State Hwy. 276. Take Utah State Hwy. 95 to mile 83.8, GPS coordinates 0,586,727 E; 4,157,522 N; Elevation 6200'. Turn south onto Hwy. 276 and drive 4.9 miles to mile 86.4, GPS coordinates 0,580,611 E; 4,152,489 N; Elevation 5665'. This is just north of a metal cattle guard across the highway. Park on the slickrock section immediately east of the highway. Parking/camping is limited to several vehicles.

Trail Statistics: The route is 10 miles round-trip with an elevation change of 350 feet requiring 5–7 hours to complete. This is a fair hike over Class 1–2 terrain requiring easy effort and easy route-finding skills.

Attractions: Exotic petrified wood, agate, metamorphic, and volcanic fragments.

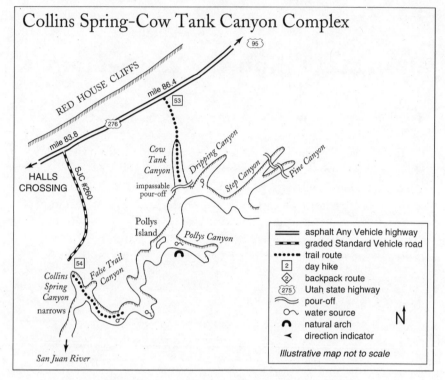

Collins Spring–Cow Tank Canyon Complex

Cautions: There is limited midday shade along this route.

Maps: USGS Hite Crossing and Navajo Mountain (1:100,000), or USGS Moss Back Butte, Red House Spring and Pollys Pasture (1:62,500), or Trails Illustrated Grand Gulch Plateau (1:62,500)

Description: Head southeast from the carpark and descend into the drainage. In 15 minutes, a barbed-wire cattle fence blocks the wash. Use the sandstone bedding planes along the north wall to step over the fence (left LDC). Continue down-canyon for 5 minutes to a junction with a northeast-trending tributary (left LDC). Go south (right LDC) for 40 minutes to a shallow junction with another northeast-trending tributary (left LDC). Continue south (right LDC) for 15 minutes to a junction with a north-trending tributary (right LDC). Head south (left LDC) for 20 minutes to a narrowed section that contained flood debris blocking the streambed near a cottonwood tree in May 1998. The obstacle can be avoided by walking on the east rim (left LDC).

Continue down-canyon 5 minutes to a 40′ pour-off with deep potholes carved into the sandstone ledge. Walk along the east rim ledge (left LDC), passing a house-size boulder resting precariously on the ledge, for 10 minutes to a south-trending rib spur. Descend the rib to the south-facing amphitheater and streambed bottom. There is a 25' impassable pour-off at the confluence of Grand Gulch in 15 minutes. Return the way you came.

Cow Tank Canyon UTM GPS Coordinates

Carpark	0,580,641 E; 4,152,426 N	Elevation 5665'	00 min.
Cattle fence	0,580,704 E; 4,151,738 N	Elevation 5650'	15 min.
NE tributary junction	0,580,670 E; 4,151,465 N	Elevation 5600'	20 min.
NE tributary junction	0,579,719 E; 4,149,405 N	Elevation 5500'	60 min.
North tributary junction	0,579,275 E; 4,148,459 N	Elevation 5400'	75 min.
Flood debris obstacle	0,578,963 E; 4,148,177 N	Elevation 5350'	95 min.
40' pour-off	0,579,143 E; 4,147,694 N	Elevation 5200'	100 min.
Grand Gulch confluence	0,579,470 E; 4,146,577 N	Elevation 5300'	125 min.
Carpark	0,580,641 E; 4,152,426 N	Elevation 5665'	200 min.

Arch in Collins Spring Canyon

■ 54 Collins Spring–Banister Ruin

Access: Collins Spring–Banister Ruin carpark is located east of Utah State Hwy. 276. Take Utah State Hwy. 95 to mile 83.8, GPS coordinates 0,586,727 E; 4,157,522 N; Elevation 6200'. Turn south on Utah State Hwy. 276 and drive to mile 84.7, GPS coordinates 0,578,134 E; 4,151,431 N; Elevation 5600'. Turn east onto San Juan County Route Gulch Creek #260 and drive 6.3 miles on a standard-vehicle road surface to the Collins Spring Canyon carpark. There is a BLM information board with a trail registry at the carpark. There is limited camping space in the carpark area, but there are several good sites along the access road. Parking is limited to a dozen vehicles. Refer to the Cow Tank Canyon map.

Trail Statistics: The route is 10.1 miles round-trip with an elevation change of 200 feet requiring 6–8 hours to complete. This is a good hike over Class 1–2 terrain requiring easy effort and easy route-finding skills.

Attractions: Banister Ruin.

Cautions: There is limited midday shade along this route. Don't touch or climb on the historic structures. Pack animals and pets are not allowed in Grand Gulch down-canyon of the narrows.

Maps: USGS Navajo Mountain (1:100,000), or USGS Red House Spring (1:62,500), or Trails Illustrated Grand Gulch Plateau (1:62,500)

Description: The trail leads southeast from the BLM information sign by descending the slickrock ledges to the bottom of Collins Spring Canyon in 5 minutes. Either walk in the canyon bottom to minimize erosion or follow the entrenched footpath over the sandy alluvial bend flats. In 5 minutes, you'll see a west-facing alcove in the east wall containing a large abandoned cowboy encampment (left LDC). This encampment is immediately down-canyon from an old wooden fence gate blocking the blasted out pathway in the east wall. There is a 40' pour-off immediately down-canyon with a traverse route blasted out on the southwest ledges (right LDC).

Continue down-canyon for 20 minutes to a 20' pour-off with a traverse route on the east wall (left LDC). There is a trail-level arch along this traverse. It is 5 minutes of walking down-canyon to a north-trending tributary junction (left LDC). Turn south (right LDC) and walk another 10 minutes to the confluence with Grand Gulch. Note the prominent pinnacle totem rock down-canyon on the rim as a marker for your return.

Turn south (right LDC) and head through the brief, muddy narrows section. There is a west-trending tributary junction (right LDC) immediately below the narrows with an alluvial bank. Head back through the narrows and continue up-canyon northeast (left LUC) across the streambed onto the next sand flat past a jumbled but steeply sloped north-trending tributary named False Trail Canyon (left LUC). It is 10 minutes from the Collins Spring Canyon confluence to the abandoned

meander and rincon rock art panel. It takes 15 minutes to walk around
the rincon. Continue up-canyon for another 45 minutes to Banister Ruin,
located in a high south-facing alcove across from a big sandy camp
under mature cottonwood trees. Take binoculars to enjoy the details of
the inaccessible site. Return the way you came.

Collins Spring–Banister Ruin UTM GPS Coordinates

Collins Spring carpark	0,573,113 E; 4,143,548 N	Elevation 5000'	00 min.
Cowboy encampment	0,573,381 E; 4,143,089 N	Elevation 4800'	10 min.
North tributary junction	0,574,147 E; 4,142,182 N	Elevation 4800'	35 min.
Narrows	0,574,201 E; 4,141,368 N	Elevation 4780'	50 min.
Collins rincon panel		Elevation 4780'	60 min.
Banister Ruin		Elevation 4780'	110 min.
Collins Spring carpark	0,573,113 E; 4,143,548 N	Elevation 5000'	220 min.

8

Backpack Routes

ALL ROUTES (EXCEPT ARCH CANYON, AT TIME OF PUBLICATION) REQUIRE
an advance reservation and special-use permit from the BLM. Do not
request a permit for Step Canyon or Slickhorn Canyon–Johns Canyon
unless your party is competent and committed.

The San Juan River–Kane Gulch route necessitates floating down the
San Juan River and hiking up Grand Gulch to the Kane Gulch Ranger
Station carpark. Trip logistics can be formidable. Private permits and
information on commercial outfitters for floating the river and hiking
the canyon are available from the Monticello BLM field office at (435) 587-
1500.

Cedar Mesa contains a wealth of well-preserved signs of an ancient
civilization. Please review the site visitation protocols in the
introduction.

Cautions

— Take your preferred means of drinking water purification and wear
sturdy footwear.
— Stay on the major paths to avoid increasing erosion.
— All typical water hazards can be avoided.
— Slickrock gets slippery when wet. There are slickrock surfaces around
the pour-off areas.

Itineraries

I've listed a popular itinerary for each backpack, but deviations are
expected and encouraged. Many of these side trips are described in the
day hike descriptions. Given typical travel and organizational/logistical
complications, the first and last days are assumed to include only a half
day of walking. Side trips for finding spring water and archaeological
sites could easily add another 10 miles to your trip.

Backpack Route	Quality	Skill	Class	Effort	Days	Miles (r-t)
◆ 55 Step Canyon	good	difficult	4	moderate	2–4	12.6
◆ 56 Arch–Texas–Butts Canyons						
	excellent	easy	1	easy	3–5	15.4
◆ 57 Kane Gulch–Bullet Canyon						
	excellent	moderate	3	moderate	3–5	22.8
◆ 58 Kane Gulch–Government Trail						
	excellent	easy	2	easy	4–6	28
◆ 59 Kane Gulch–Collins Spring						
	excellent	easy	2	easy	5–8	38
◆ 60 Owl-McCloyd–Fish Canyons Loop						
	excellent	moderate	3	strenuous	3–5	17
◆ 61 Slickhorn #1–#6 Loop						
	good	moderate	3	moderate	2–4	15.5
◆ 62 Slickhorn #1–Johns Canyon Loop						
	fair	moderate	4	moderate	6–8	51
◆ 63 Collins Spring–San Juan River						
	good	moderate	3	moderate	5–8	35.4
◆ 64 San Juan River–Kane Gulch						
	excellent	moderate	3	moderate	8–10	51.7

◆ 55 Step Canyon

Access: The Step Canyon complex is located south of Utah State Hwy. 95 between Fry Canyon and Natural Bridges National Monument. Take Utah State Hwy. 95 to the Mormon Trail road, signed as San Juan County Route Mormon Trail #230A, at mile 87.2 on the south side of the highway, GPS coordinates 0,591,455 E; 4,155,116 N; Elevation 6620'. Follow the standard-vehicle road surface for 3 miles to the dead-end slickrock rim carpark. Parking/camping is limited to several vehicles.

Trail Statistics: The route is 12.6 miles round-trip with an elevation change of 950 feet requiring 2–4 days to complete. This is a good canyon hike over Class 1–4 terrain requiring moderate effort and difficult route-finding skills.

Attractions: Canyoneering and Quail Pictograph Panel.

Cautions: Camping sites are limited to the cowboy encampment cache and the three sites around the Grand Gulch confluence. Water sources are limited in Step Canyon. Two pour-offs in Step Canyon require a stacked rock booster step or limb ladder to circumnavigate.

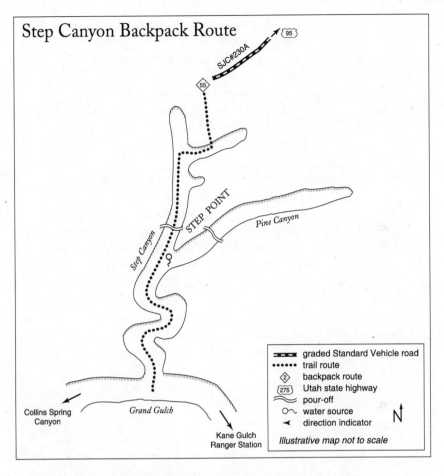

Step Canyon Backpack Route

Legend:
- graded Standard Vehicle road
- trail route
- ② backpack route
- ⑵⁷⁵ Utah state highway
- pour-off
- ∘∿ water source
- ◄ direction indicator
- N
- *Illustrative map not to scale*

These helpers are occasionally removed by humans or weather phenomena. Their absence will make the route impassable. Check in with the Kane Gulch Ranger Station for the current status of these canyons and their helper stations.

Maps: USGS Blanding, Navajo Mountain and Hite Crossing (1:100,000), or USGS Moss Back Butte and Pollys Pasture (1:62,500), or Trails Illustrated Grand Gulch Plateau (1:62,500)

Description: Day 1, Step Point to Cowboy Encampment; Day 2, Cowboy Encampment to Grand Gulch confluence; Day 3, return to Step Point carpark. This pace averages 4 backpacking miles a day. However, the cottonwood limb ladder in the middle of Step Canyon is crucial. Without it, it is impossible to scramble down the 8′ pour-off. A better alternative for exploring the middle Grand Gulch areas is to walk in from the Government Trail access.

From the carpark, traverse east-southeast to a small cleft and follow the slickrock runoff rivulets south (straight LDC) for 10 minutes to a drainage. Go west (right LDC) and follow the streambed down-canyon for 10 minutes to a 10' pour-off. Avoid this pour-off by traversing 5 minutes south (left LDC) into the next adjacent drainage and descending its 2' pour-off instead. Continue down-canyon for 10 minutes to a north-trending tributary junction (right LDC). Proceed south (left LDC) for 25 minutes, until reaching a junction with a northeast-trending tributary (left LDC) with two deep plunge pools. Continue south (right LDC) for 10 minutes to an east-trending tributary junction (left LDC). Keep going south (right LDC), past a square benchmark cairn on the west rim against the skyline, for 35 minutes to a junction with an east-trending tributary (left LDC). Persist in a southerly direction (right LDC) for 5 more minutes to an old cowboy encampment along a low southeast-facing alcove in the western wall (right LDC) surrounded by barb-wire fence remnants.

Continue down-canyon 30 minutes to an 8' pour-off, but traverse along the eastern wall (left LDC) to a down-climb route. You will need either a stacked rock step or a limb ladder at the bottom to overcome this obstacle. Otherwise, return the way you came!

It is 20 minutes to the T junction with Pine Canyon (left LDC) near a solitary hoodoo on the south rim. There is a small spring here in the streambed. Head west (right LDC) to a developing arch within a riverside boulder (left LDC) in 25 minutes. This is quite a rare geological feature. It is 5 minutes to an east-trending tributary junction (left LDC) and a mushroom cap rock garden along the rim (right LUC). Continue down-canyon 10 minutes to a north-northwest-trending tributary cleft junction (right LDC) and another 10 minutes to the confluence with Grand Gulch.

Two-Story Ruin is visible immediately up-canyon in Grand Gulch (left LUC). Quail Pictograph Panel is on the down-canyon side and has handprints, anthropomorphs, birds, and sheep painted in red, white, green, brown, and yellow. This is one of my favorite rock art panels. Notice the abundance of rockfall debris along this sand ledge. Don't touch the wall, shout, or stay too long. Several campsites exist at the confluence. Return the way you came and sign out on the trail registry.

Step Canyon UTM GPS Coordinates

Step Point carpark	0,588,092 E; 4,152,489 N	Elevation 6200'	00 min.
Streambed path	0,587,956 E; 4,151,899 N	Elevation 6100'	10 min.
Pour-off traverse bottom	0,587,419 E; 4,151,894 N	Elevation 6000'	25 min.
North tributary junction	0,586,815 E; 4,151,757 N	Elevation 5900'	35 min.

NE tributary junction	0,586,195 E; 4,150,675 N	Elevation 5800'	60 min.
East tributary junction	0,585,981 E; 4,150,454 N	Elevation 5700'	70 min.
East tributary junction	0,584,913 E; 4,150,000 N	Elevation 5600'	105 min.
Cowboy encampment	0,584,347 E; 4,149,976 N	Elevation 5600'	110 min.
Pour-off traverse	0,583,924 E; 4,148,955 N	Elevation 5550'	140 min.
Pine Canyon junction	0,583,732 E; 4,148,443 N	Elevation 5300'	160 min.
East tributary junction	0,583,020 E; 4,147,806 N	Elevation 5280'	210 min.
N-NW tributary junction	0,582,459 E; 4,147,049 N	Elevation 5260'	230 min.
Grand Gulch confluence	0,582,089 E; 4,146,674 N	Elevation 5240'	240 min.
Step Point carpark	0,588,092 E; 4,152,489 N	Elevation 6200'	480 min.

◆ 56 Arch-Texas-Butts Canyons

Access: Arch Canyon is located northwest of San Juan County Route Comb Wash #235. Take Utah State Hwy. 95 to mile 107.4, GPS coordinates 0,618,870 E; 4,152,180 N; Elevation 4900'. There are pit toilets but no potable water in the south-side camping area. Turn north on San Juan County Route Comb Wash #235 and drive to a gated fence on a hill at mile 2.0. Go through the gate to an immediate junction at mile 2.1. Take the east branch (right) and turn north (left) at mile 2.3, before crossing Comb Wash, and drive past the BLM information sign on Arch Canyon Trail #002. The trail registry is at the cattle guard at mile 2.4.

Trail Statistics: The route is 15.4 miles round-trip (not counting side trips) from the mouth of Arch Canyon to the end of the road with an elevation change of 600 feet requiring 3–5 days to complete. Additionally, Arch Canyon is 6.9 miles, Texas Canyon is 6.1 miles, and Butts Canyon is 3.9 miles to their headwalls, respectively, from the end of the road and require another 1–3 days to explore. This is an excellent hike over Class 1 terrain requiring easy effort and easy route-finding skills. The upper tributaries are much more difficult, with Class 1–3 terrain.

Attractions: Four natural arches framed with alpine vegetation.

Cautions: This is a multiple-use trail.

Maps: USGS Blanding (1:100,000), or USGS Hotel Rock, Kigalia Point and South Long Point (1:62,500), or Trails Illustrated Grand Gulch Plateau (1:62,500)

Description: Day 1, Arch Canyon carpark to Texas Canyon junction; Day 2, day hike in Texas and Butts Canyons; Day 3, day hike in upper

Arch Canyon Backpack Route

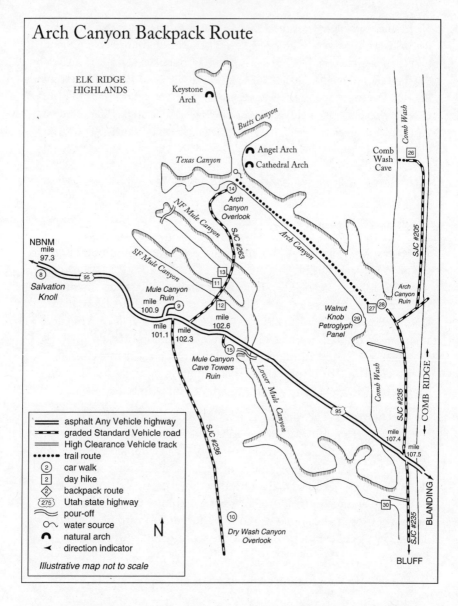

ELK RIDGE
HIGHLANDS

Keystone
Arch

Butts Canyon

Texas Canyon

Angel Arch

Cathedral Arch

Comb
Wash
Cave

Comb Wash

26

14

Arch
Canyon
Overlook

NF Mule Canyon

SJC #263

Arch Canyon

SJC #205

NBNM
mile
97.3

SF Mule Canyon

8

95

Salvation
Knoll

Mule Canyon
Ruin

mile
100.9

9

13

11

12

mile
102.6

Walnut
Knob
Petroglyph
Panel

28

27

29

Arch
Canyon
Ruin

mile
101.1

mile
102.3

15

Mule Canyon
Cave Towers
Ruin

Lower Mule Canyon

95

mile
107.4

Comb Wash

SJC #235

COMB RIDGE

mile
107.5

SJC #236

30

BLANDING

10

Dry Wash Canyon
Overlook

SJC #235

BLUFF

	asphalt Any Vehicle highway
	graded Standard Vehicle road
	High Clearance Vehicle track
	trail route
2	car walk
2	day hike
2	backpack route
275	Utah state highway
	pour-off
	water source
	natural arch
	direction indicator

N

Illustrative map not to scale

Arch Canyon; Day 4, return to Arch Canyon carpark. This pace averages
8 backpacking miles a day. The Arch Canyon complex is a rare gem of
red-hued sandstone walls soaring up to blazing blue skies with conifer
green in the streambed bottoms. Fall and spring seasons add their
blossoms to the color continuum.

Arch Canyon Trail #002 is a 4WD track that crosses the perennial
stream and its steep banks repeatedly. Explore the ruin behind the

fenced turnstile and the old BLM information sign at the mouth of the canyon. There are structures, pictographs, petroglyphs, and cowboy glyphs along the wall. Notice the many circular wall indentations from the supports of the upper-level structures, now missing. Walk west up-canyon 5 minutes to a cobbled section of the road. Look to your north (right LUC) and across the streambed to Arch Cobble Ruin (AN) under the alcove facing southeast. Continue up-canyon for 45 minutes to a junction with a north-trending tributary (right LUC) that leads to Hotel Rock.

It is 30 minutes to Dream Speaker Spire (left LUC) at the junction of a west-trending tributary. Continue up-canyon for another 40 minutes, passing a prominent ruin in an inaccessible alcove high along the north wall (right LUC), to a north-trending tributary junction (right LUC) in 20 minutes. Notice that ponderosa pines are now thriving in the streambed bottoms.

A small arch on the north wall (right LUC) is reached in 15 minutes. It is another 30 minutes to the junction with Texas Canyon (left LUC) and the end of the road. Cathedral Arch is seen from this point along the northeast wall (right LUC). Angel Arch is another 10 minutes up-canyon, along the northeast wall (right LUC).

There are several camps within 10 minutes of the National Forest boundary in Texas and upper Arch Canyons in addition to the obvious ones around the road terminus. Use an existing campsite to prevent pioneering new sites. I found moderate streambed springs and potholes nearby in both Texas and Arch Canyons. Texas Canyon is a narrow cobbled channel with brushy sections. In October 1999, there were brilliant fall colors in Texas Canyon with red maples, yellow cottonwoods, golden scrub oak, and green conifers. I walked to the junction of its tributary forks and returned. Upper Arch Canyon squeezes down to a narrow streambed filled with boulder dams and pour-offs. I hiked only to Keystone Arch. Weather forced a hasty retreat from the Arch Canyon complex, and I never explored Butts Canyon. Return the way you came and sign out on the trail registry.

Arch-Texas-Butts Canyons UTM GPS Coordinates

Arch Canyon carpark	0,617,563 E; 4,156,120 N	Elevation 5000'	00 min.
Arch Cobbled Ruin		Elevation 5000'	05 min.
North tributary junction	0,614,378 E; 4,157,320 N	Elevation 5180'	50 min.
Dream Speaker Spire	0,612,047 E; 4,158,720 N	Elevation 5250'	80 min.
North tributary junction	0,610,964 E; 4,160,943 N	Elevation 5450'	120 min.
Small arch	0,610,297 E; 4,161,564 N	Elevation 5500'	135 min.

Texas Canyon junction	0,609,273 E; 4,162,279 N	Elevation 5600'	165 min.
Cathedral Arch	0,609,551 E; 4,163,109 N	Elevation 5700'	170 min.
Angel Arch	0,609,420 E; 4,163,914 N	Elevation 5720'	180 min.
Butts Canyon junction	0,608,951 E; 4,164,499 N	Elevation 5700'	200 min.
Keystone Arch	0,606,197 E; 4,166,269 N	Elevation 6000'	270 min.
Texas Canyon junction	0,609,273 E; 4,162,279 N	Elevation 5600'	375 min.
Arch Canyon carpark	0,617,563 E; 4,156,120 N	Elevation 5000'	540 min.

◆ 57 Kane Gulch–Bullet Canyon

Access: The Kane Gulch carpark is located east of Utah State Hwy. 261 between Utah State Hwy. 95 and Utah State Hwy. 163. From the north, take Utah State Hwy. 95 and turn south on Utah State Hwy. 261 at mile 93.2, GPS coordinates 0,598,414 E; 4,159,525 N; Elevation 6800'. Drive south 3.8 miles to the Kane Gulch Ranger Station carpark with pit toilet and information sign at mile 28.7, GPS coordinates 0,597,584 E; 4,153,458 N; Elevation 6400'. Parking is available for several dozen vehicles.

From the south, take Utah State Hwy. 163 to mile 24.9 and GPS coordinates 0,600,764 E; 4,116,920 N; Elevation 4500'. Turn north on Utah State Hwy. 261 and continue to mile 28.7 at the Kane Gulch Ranger Station carpark.

The Bullet Canyon carpark is located west of Utah State Hwy. 261, 7 miles south of the Kane Gulch Ranger Station on San Juan County Route South Road #251 at mile 21.7, GPS coordinates 0,594,317 E; 4,143,029 N; Elevation 6425'. It is 1.2 miles on a standard-vehicle road surface to the carpark, where there is limited camping space and parking for a dozen vehicles.

Trail Statistics: The route is 22.8 miles (not counting side trips or shuttle) with an elevation change of 1100 feet requiring 3–5 days to complete. This is an excellent canyon backpack route over Class 1–3 terrain requiring moderate effort and moderate route-finding skills. Arrange your own shuttle.

Attractions: Ancestral Puebloan sites and rock art panels.

Maps: USGS Blanding (1:100,000), or Cedar Mesa North and Kane Gulch (1:62,500), or Trails Illustrated Grand Gulch Plateau (1:62,500)

Description: Day 1, Kane Gulch carpark to Junction Ruin; Day 2, Junction Ruin to Sheiks Canyon; Day 3, Sheiks Canyon to Jail House Ruin; Day 4, Jail House Ruin to Bullet Canyon carpark. This pace averages 8 backpacking miles a day. Side hikes are enticing enterprises,

Kane Gulch-Bullet Canyon Backpack Route

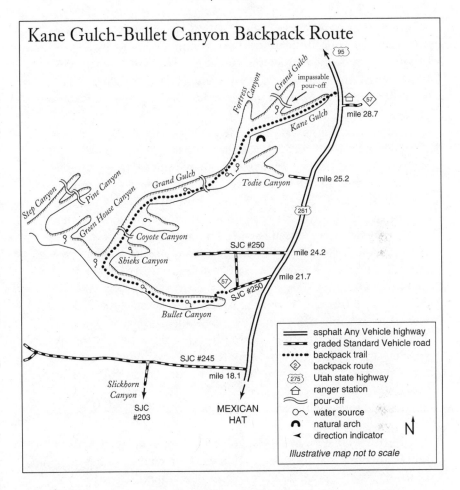

═══════	asphalt Any Vehicle highway
═▬═▬═	graded Standard Vehicle road
••••••	backpack trail
◇②◇	backpack route
⬡275⬡	Utah state highway
⌂	ranger station
≈	pour-off
◯⌣	water source
⌒	natural arch
◄	direction indicator

Illustrative map not to scale

but just finding a sunny slickrock knoll to soak up the ambience of this wonderful canyon system and its prehistory is enough for me. Listen to the sounds of nature surrounding you and the flow of blood through your vessels. There is silence, tranquility, and resilience in everything.

The trail starts on the western side of the highway. Sign in on the trail registry. Look both ways TWICE for oncoming traffic before crossing the pavement. Head in a southwesterly direction down the wash. It is 50 minutes to a steep slickrock boulder section. Luckily, there is a north traverse route (right LDC) that passes the Wilderness Study Area BLM sign before crossing the streambed and continuing down the south side of the canyon (left LDC).

It is 30 more minutes to the confluence with Grand Gulch and its sandy alluvial banks shaded by mature cottonwood trees. Junction Ruin is through the camping area (right LDC) and up-canyon against the southeast-facing alcove bend (left LDC). Yellow, red, and white handprints and some petroglyphs can be found near the structures. Walk down-canyon for 20 minutes to Turkey Pen Ruin in the south-facing alcove (right LDC). Stay off the midden areas at both Junction and Turkey Pen Ruin sites.

Stimper Arch is around the bend another 5 minutes down-canyon along the south wall (left LDC) near the rim. The confluence with north-trending Fortress Canyon (right LDC) is 10 minutes away. A 5-minute hike up Fortress Canyon will take you to the terminal 80' pour-off.

From the Fortress Canyon confluence, continue down-canyon 50 minutes to Todie Canyon (left LDC). Hike down-canyon for 35 minutes to the open meander amphitheater containing Pour-Off Pool and its traverse route on the south wall (left LDC). Continue for another 15 minutes to Lion Track Ruin in a southeast-facing alcove (right LDC). Split-Level Ruin is 15 more minutes, located in a south-facing alcove (right LDC). The midden areas are chained off with stanchions to keep people and pets out of this sensitive archaeological area. Shelf Ruin is another 35 minutes, underneath a south-facing alcove along three levels (right LDC). It is 30 minutes to the confluence with Coyote Canyon (left LDC). Continue another 15 minutes to the rincon called the Thumb and its two structures. The confluence with Sheiks Canyon is 25 more minutes. The Green Mask Ruin is 5 minutes up Sheiks Canyon (left LUC), just before the terminal dryfall.

The confluence with Bullet Canyon is 75 minutes away. Head into Bullet Canyon. It is 50 minutes to Jailhouse Ruin on the southeast-facing peninsula near the point (left LUC). Three white circles above the structures give an eerie look to the site. There is an abundance of good camping sites between Jailhouse Ruin and Perfect Kiva Ruin, which is another 10 minutes up-canyon, in the north amphitheater along a southeast-facing alcove (left LUC). These are incredible sites, so treat them with the utmost respect.

Continue up-canyon for 35 minutes to a southwest-trending tributary junction (left LUC). Walk 5 minutes to a traverse path along a ledge that avoids some of the worst boulder dams (left LUC). It is 20 minutes to a southeast-trending tributary junction (left LUC). Continue east for 20 minutes to the ascent trail on the north wall (left LUC). Follow the stacked cairns closely. Head east on the path for 10 minutes to the carpark. Don't forget to sign out on the trail registry.

Kane Gulch–Bullet Canyon UTM GPS Coordinates

Kane Gulch Ranger Station	0,597,584 E; 4,153,458 N	Elevation 6400'	00 min.
Junction Ruin		Elevation 6060'	95 min.
Turkey Pen Ruin		Elevation 6040'	115 min.
Stimper Arch	0,593,342 E; 4,151,678 N	Elevation 6040'	120 min.
Fortress Canyon confluence	0,592,707 E; 4,151,274 N	Elevation 6040'	130 min.
Todie Canyon confluence	0,592,200 E; 4,149,364 N	Elevation 6040'	180 min.
Pour-Off Pool traverse	0,591,133 E; 4,148,732 N	Elevation 6040'	215 min.
Lion Track Ruin		Elevation 6040'	230 min.
Split-Level Ruin		Elevation 6040'	245 min.
Shelf Ruin		Elevation 6040'	280 min.
Coyote Canyon confluence	0,587,243 E; 4,146,809 N	Elevation 6040'	310 min.
The Thumb Ruin		Elevation 6040'	325 min.
Sheiks Canyon confluence	0,586,252 E; 4,145,362 N	Elevation 5600'	350 min.
Green Mask Ruin		Elevation 5600'	355 min.
Sheiks Canyon confluence	0,586,252 E; 4,145,362 N	Elevation 5600'	360 min.
Bullet Canyon confluence	0,584,800 E; 4,144,568 N	Elevation 5600'	435 min.
Jailhouse Ruin		Elevation 5600'	485 min.
Perfect Kiva Ruin		Elevation 5600'	495 min.
SE tributary junction	0,589,250 E; 4,142,541 N	Elevation 6000'	530 min.
Ledge path	0,590,665 E; 4,142,361 N	Elevation 6050'	535 min.
SE tributary junction	0,591,299 E; 4,142,405 N	Elevation 6200'	555 min.
Bullet Canyon carpark	0,592,928 E; 4,142,941 N	Elevation 6400'	585 min.

◆ 58 Kane Gulch–Government Trail

Access: The Kane Gulch carpark is located east of Utah State Hwy. 261 between Utah State Hwy. 95 and Utah State Hwy. 163. From the north, take Utah State Hwy. 95 and turn south on Utah State Hwy. 261 at mile 93.2, GPS coordinates 0,598,414 E; 4,159,525 N; Elevation 6800'. Drive south 3.8 miles to the Kane Gulch Ranger Station carpark with pit toilet and information sign at mile 28.7, GPS coordinates 0,597,584 E; 4,153,458 N; Elevation 6400'. Parking is limited to several dozen vehicles.

From the south, take Utah State Hwy. 163 to mile 24.9 and GPS coordinates 0,600,764 E; 4,116,920 N; Elevation 4500'. Turn north on Utah State Hwy. 261 and continue to mile 28.7 at the Kane Gulch Ranger Station carpark.

The Government Trail carpark is located west of Utah State Hwy. 261, 10.6 miles south of the Kane Gulch Ranger Station, at mile 18.1, GPS coordinates 0,593,537 E; 4,139,176 N; Elevation 6500'. Turn west onto San

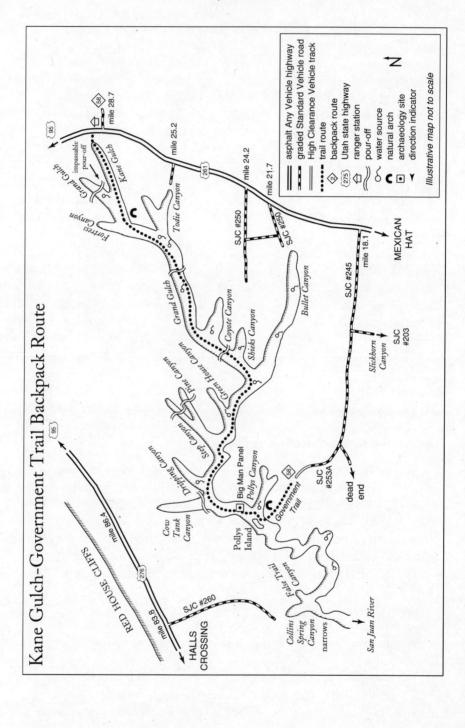

Kane Gulch-Government Trail Backpack Route

Juan County Route Slickhorn #245 and go 0.3 mile to a gated fence with a BLM information board and trail registry. Continue to mile 2.6 and the junction of San Juan County Route Point Lookout #203 and San Juan County Route Slickhorn #245 (GPS Coordinates 0,590,226 E; 4,140,342 N; Elevation 6350') with a BLM Government Trail sign. Turn northwest (right) and continue to mile 5.4 to the junction of San Juan County Route Slickhorn #245 and San Juan County Route #253A. Turn northwest (right) and drive to mile 6.3 and the Government Trail high-clearance-vehicle track. The carpark is at mile 8.7 with GPS coordinates 0,581,011 E; 4,141,100 N; Elevation 5700'. Parking/camping is limited to several vehicles. You must have a permit from the BLM to walk this route.

Trail Statistics: The route is 28 miles (not counting side trips), with an elevation change of 1200 feet requiring 4–6 days to complete. This is an excellent canyon backpack route over Class 1–2 terrain requiring easy effort and easy route-finding skills.

Attractions: Ancestral Puebloan sites and rock art panels.

Maps: USGS Blanding (1:100,000), or Cedar Mesa North, Kane Gulch, Pollys Pasture and Red House Spring (1:62,500), or Trails Illustrated Grand Gulch Plateau (1:62,500)

Description: Day 1, Kane Gulch carpark to Junction Ruin; Day 2, Junction Ruin to Sheiks Canyon; Day 3, Sheiks Canyon to Bullet Canyon; Day 4, Bullet Canyon to Pollys Island; Day 5, Pollys Island to Government Trail carpark. This pace averages 8 backpacking miles a day. Side hikes are enticing enterprises, but listening for the voices of prehistoric humans whispering at night is eerie. I swear their ghosts still walk these canyons.

The trail starts on the western side of the highway. Sign in on the trail registry. Look both ways TWICE for oncoming traffic before crossing the pavement. Head in a southwesterly direction down the wash. It is 50 minutes to a steep slickrock boulder section. Luckily, there is a north traverse route (right LDC) that passes the Wilderness Study Area BLM sign before crossing the streambed and continuing down the south side of the canyon (left LDC). It is 30 more minutes to the confluence with Grand Gulch and its sandy alluvial banks shaded by mature cottonwood trees. Junction Ruin is through the camping area (right LDC) and up-canyon against the southeast-facing alcove bend (left LDC). There are yellow, red, and white handprints and some petroglyphs near the structures. Walk down-canyon for 20 minutes to Turkey Pen Ruin in the south-facing alcove (right LDC). Stay off the midden areas at both

Junction and Turkey Pen Ruin sites. Stimper Arch is around the bend another 5 minutes down-canyon along the south wall (left LDC) near the rim. The confluence with north-trending Fortress Canyon (right LDC) is 10 minutes away. A 5-minute hike up Fortress Canyon will take you to the terminal 80' pour-off.

From Fortress Canyon, continue down-canyon 50 minutes to Todie Canyon (left LDC). Hike down-canyon for 35 minutes to the open meander amphitheater containing Pour-Off Pool and its traverse route on the south wall (left LDC). Continue for another 15 minutes to Lion Track Ruin in a southeast-facing alcove (right LDC). Split-Level Ruin is 15 more minutes and it's located in a south-facing alcove (right LDC). The midden areas are chained off with stanchions to keep people and pets out of this sensitive archaeological area. Shelf Ruin is 35 minutes, underneath a south-facing alcove along three levels (right LDC). It is 30 minutes to the confluence with Coyote Canyon (left LDC). Two structures are seen immediately up-canyon of the rincon called the Thumb in 15 minutes. The confluence with Sheiks Canyon is 25 more minutes. The Green Mask Ruin is 5 minutes up Sheiks Canyon (left LUC), just before the terminal dryfall.

The confluence with Bullet Canyon is 75 minutes away. Head into Bullet Canyon. It is 50 minutes to Jailhouse Ruin on the southeast-facing peninsula near the point (left LUC). Three white circles above the four structures give an eerie look to the site. There is an abundance of good camping sites between Perfect Kiva Ruin and Jailhouse Ruin. Walk up-canyon another 10 minutes to Perfect Kiva Ruin, in the north amphitheater along a southeast-facing alcove (left LUC). These are incredible sites, so treat them with the utmost respect. Return to Grand Gulch.

The confluence with Green House Canyon is 30 minutes down-canyon in Grand Gulch with its adjacent Totem Pole Ruin. Two-Story Ruin is 50 minutes farther down-canyon (right LDC) in an east-southeast facing alcove. Step Canyon confluence (right LDC) is reached in 5 minutes. There are several campsites here. It is 30 minutes to a southeast-trending tributary junction (left LDC) followed by a northeast-trending tributary junction (right LDC) in another 25 minutes. The confluence with Dripping Canyon (right LDC) is 15 minutes farther and has several good campsites nearby. A south-trending tributary junction (left LDC) is passed in 15 minutes, and the confluence with Cow Tank Canyon (right LDC) is reached in another 5 minutes. Dead Spar Knoll (AN) rock art panel is 10 minutes up Cow Tank Canyon. Return to Grand Gulch.

The Bird Parade Panel is 10 minutes down-canyon from the Cow Tank Canyon confluence in a southeast-facing alcove (right LDC) in a sharp S bend. Longhouse Ruin is 15 minutes farther under a southeast-facing alcove (right LDC) across from a big campsite under some mature cottonwood trees. The Big Man Panel is 25 minutes down-canyon in a northwest-facing overhang high above the streambed (left LDC). There was a cottonwood tree bridge crossing the streambed here in March 1999. The confluence with Pollys Canyon (left LDC) and the Pollys Island rincon (right LDC) are 35 minutes farther down-canyon.

Turn east (left LDC) and walk 5 minutes to an arch (right LUC). Return to Grand Gulch and walk 5 minutes west of Grand Gulch to visit the Pollys Spring Ruin. There are several camps around the Pollys Island area. Return to Grand Gulch at the Pollys Canyon confluence. Government Trail is intercepted in 10 minutes (left LDC) and takes 15 minutes to ascend. It is 50 minutes to the lower carpark. Walk only in the right track so the other track can be reclaimed by the desert. Don't forget to sign out on the trail registry.

Kane Gulch–Government Trail UTM GPS Coordinates

Kane Gulch Ranger Station	0,597,584 E; 4,153,458 N	Elevation 6400'	00 min.
Junction Ruin		Elevation 6060'	95 min.
Turkey Pen Ruin		Elevation 6040'	115 min.
Stimper Arch	0,593,342 E; 4,151,678 N	Elevation 6040'	120 min.
Fortress Canyon confluence	0,592,707 E; 4,151,274 N	Elevation 6040'	130 min.
Todie Canyon confluence	0,592,200 E; 4,149,364 N	Elevation 6040'	180 min.
Pour-Off Pool traverse	0,591,133 E; 4,148,732 N	Elevation 6040'	215 min.
Lion Track Ruin		Elevation 6040'	230 min.
Split-Level Ruin		Elevation 6040'	245 min.
Shelf Ruin		Elevation 6040'	280 min.
Coyote Canyon confluence	0,587,243 E; 4,146,809 N	Elevation 6040'	310 min.
The Thumb Ruin		Elevation 6040'	325 min.
Sheiks Canyon confluence	0,586,252 E; 4,145,362 N	Elevation 5600'	350 min.
Green Mask Ruin		Elevation 5600'	355 min.
Sheiks Canyon confluence	0,586,252 E; 4,145,362 N	Elevation 5600'	350 min.
Bullet Canyon confluence	0,584,800 E; 4,144,568 N	Elevation 5600'	435 min.
Jailhouse Ruin		Elevation 5600'	485 min.
Perfect Kiva Ruin		Elevation 5600'	495 min.
Grand Gulch confluence	0,584,800 E; 4,144,568 N	Elevation 5600'	555 min.
Green House Canyon confluence	0,583,597 E; 4,145,793 N	Elevation 5600'	585 min.
Two-Story Ruin		Elevation 5600'	635 min.

Step Canyon confluence	0,582,089 E; 4,146,674 N	Elevation 5600'	640 min.
SE tributary junction	0,581,323 E; 4,146,177 N	Elevation 5600'	670 min.
NE tributary junction	0,580,690 E; 4,146,902 N	Elevation 5600'	695 min.
Dripping Canyon confluence	0,580,171 E; 4,146,909 N	Elevation 5600'	710 min.
E-NE tributary junction	0,579,546 E; 4,146,651 N	Elevation 5600'	725 min.
Cow Tank Canyon confluence	0,579,470 E; 4,146,577 N	Elevation 5600'	730 min.
Dead Spar Knoll panel		Elevation 5600'	740 min.
Grand Gulch confluence	0,579,470 E; 4,146,577 N	Elevation 5600'	750 min.
Bird Parade Panel		Elevation 5600'	760 min.
Longhouse Ruin		Elevation 5600'	775 min.
Big Man Panel		Elevation 5600'	800 min.
Pollys Canyon confluence	0,578,553 E; 4,144,173 N	Elevation 5600'	835 min.
Pollys Canyon arch	0,578,553 E; 4,144,173 N	Elevation 5000'	840 min.
Grand Gulch confluence	0,578,553 E; 4,144,173 N	Elevation 5600'	855 min.
Government Trail junction	0,578,285 E; 4,143,909 N	Elevation 5600'	865 min.
Government Trail carpark	0,581,011 E; 4,141,100 N	Elevation 5700'	930 min.

◆ 59 Kane Gulch–Collins Spring

Access: The Kane Gulch carpark is located east of Utah State Hwy. 261 between Utah State Hwy. 95 and Utah State Hwy. 163. From the north, take Utah State Hwy. 95 and turn south on Utah State Hwy. 261 at mile 93.2, GPS coordinates 0,598,414 E; 4,159,525 N; Elevation 6800'. Drive south 3.8 miles to the Kane Gulch Ranger Station carpark with pit toilet and information sign at mile 28.7, GPS coordinates 0,597,584 E; 4,153,458 N; Elevation 6400'. Parking is limited to several dozen vehicles.

From the south, take Utah State Hwy. 163 to mile 24.9 and GPS coordinates 0,600,764 E; 4,116,920 N; Elevation 4500'. Turn north on Utah State Hwy. 261 and continue to mile 28.7 at the Kane Gulch Ranger Station carpark.

Collins Spring Canyon carpark is located east of Utah State Hwy. 276 between Utah State Hwy. 95 and Hall's Crossing on Lake Powell. Take Utah State Hwy. 95 to mile 83.8, GPS coordinates 0,586,727 E; 4,157,522 N; Elevation 6200'. Turn south onto Hwy. 276 and drive to mile 84.7. Turn east (left) onto San Juan County Route Gulch Creek #260, GPS coordinates 0,578,134 E; 4,151,431 N; Elevation 5600'. Go 6.3 miles on a standard-vehicle road surface to the Collins Spring Canyon carpark. Parking is limited to a dozen vehicles.

Trail Statistics: The route is 38 miles (not counting side trips), with an elevation change of 2000 feet requiring 5–8 days to complete. This is an

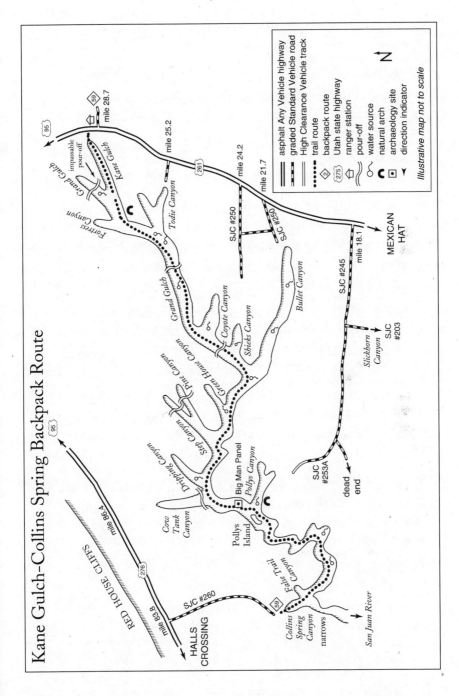

Kane Gulch-Collins Spring Backpack Route

excellent canyon backpack route over Class 1–2 terrain requiring easy effort and easy route-finding skills.

Attractions: Ancestral Puebloan sites, rock art panels and arches.

Maps: USGS Blanding (1:100,000), or Cedar Mesa North, Kane Gulch, Pollys Pasture and Red House Spring (1:62,500), or Trails Illustrated Grand Gulch Plateau (1:62,500)

Description: Day 1, Kane Gulch carpark to Junction Ruin; Day 2, Junction Ruin to Sheiks Canyon; Day 3, Sheiks Canyon to Bullet Canyon; Day 4, Bullet Canyon to Cow Tank Canyon; Day 5, Cow Tank Canyon to Banister Ruin; Day 6, Banister Ruin to Collins Spring Canyon carpark. This pace averages 8 backpacking miles a day. Take the time to listen to the ambience of the sounds of nature surrounding you. You are a mere cog in the wheel of chaotic coincidences that drive evolution.

The trail starts on the western side of the highway. Sign in on the trail registry. Look both ways TWICE for oncoming traffic before crossing the pavement. Head in a southwesterly direction down the wash. It is 50 minutes to a steep slickrock boulder section. Luckily, there is a north traverse route (right LDC) that passes the Wilderness Study Area BLM sign before crossing the streambed and continuing down the south side of the canyon (left LDC).

It is 30 more minutes to the confluence with Grand Gulch and its sandy alluvial banks shaded by mature cottonwood trees. Junction Ruin is through the camping area (right LDC) and up-canyon against the southeast-facing alcove bend (left LDC). There are yellow, red and white handprints and some petroglyphs near the structures. Walk down-canyon for 20 minutes to Turkey Pen Ruin in the south-facing alcove (right LDC). Stay off the midden areas at both Junction and Turkey Pen Ruin sites. Stimper Arch is around the bend another 5 minutes down-canyon along the south wall (left LDC) near the rim. The confluence with north-trending Fortress Canyon (right LDC) is 10 minutes away. A 5-minute hike up Fortress Canyon will take you to the terminal 80' pour-off.

From Fortress Canyon, continue down-canyon 50 minutes to Todie Canyon (left LDC). Hike down-canyon for 35 minutes to the open meander amphitheater containing Pour-Off Pool and its traverse route on the south wall (left LDC). Continue for another 15 minutes to Lion Track Ruin in a southeast-facing alcove (right LDC). Split-Level Ruin is 15 more minutes and is located in a south-facing alcove (right LDC). The midden areas are chained off with stanchions to keep people and pets out of this sensitive archaeological area. Shelf Ruin is another 35 minutes, underneath a south-facing alcove along three levels (right LDC). It is 30 minutes to the confluence with Coyote Canyon (left LDC). Continue another 15 minutes to the rincon called the Thumb and its two structures. The confluence with Sheiks Canyon is 25 more minutes. The Green Mask Ruin is 5 minutes up Sheiks Canyon (left LUC), just before the terminal dryfall.

The confluence with Bullet Canyon is 75 minutes away. Head into Bullet Canyon. It is 50 minutes to Jailhouse Ruin on the southeast-facing peninsula near the point (left LUC). Three white circles above the structures give an eerie look to the site. There is an abundance of good camping sites between Perfect Kiva Ruin and Jailhouse Ruin. Walk up-canyon another 10 minutes to Perfect Kiva Ruin. It is in the north amphitheater along a southeast-facing alcove (left LUC). These are incredible sites, so treat them with the utmost respect. Return to Grand Gulch.

The confluence with Green House Canyon is 30 minutes down-canyon in Grand Gulch with its adjacent Totem Pole Ruin. Two-Story Ruin is 50 minutes farther down-canyon (right LDC) in an east-southeast facing alcove. Step Canyon confluence (right LDC) is reached in 5 minutes. There are several campsites here. It is 30 minutes to a southeast-trending tributary junction (left LDC) followed by a northeast-trending tributary junction (right LDC) in another 25 minutes. The confluence with Dripping Canyon (right LDC) is 15 minutes farther and has several good campsites nearby. A south-trending tributary junction (left LDC) is passed in 15 minutes, and the confluence with Cow Tank Canyon (right LDC) is reached in another 5 minutes. Dead Spar Knoll (AN) rock art panel is 10 minutes up Cow Tank Canyon. Return to Grand Gulch.

The Bird Parade Panel is 10 minutes down-canyon from the Cow Tank Canyon confluence in a southeast-facing alcove (right LDC) in a sharp S bend. Longhouse Ruin is 15 minutes farther under a southeast-facing alcove (right LDC) across from a big campsite under some mature cottonwood trees. The Big Man Panel is 25 minutes down-canyon in a northwest-facing overhang high above the streambed (left LDC). There was a cottonwood tree bridge crossing the streambed here in March 1999. The confluence with Pollys Canyon (left LDC) and the Pollys Island rincon (right LDC) are 35 minutes farther down-canyon.

The arch up Pollys Canyon is seen in 5 minutes. Visiting Pollys Island Spring Ruin takes 30 minutes. The bottom junction to Government Trail is passed in 10 minutes (left LDC), and the down-canyon junction of the rincon is intersected in another 5 minutes. There are several camps around this rincon area. Big Pour-Off traverse is 80 minutes down-canyon with the traverse route on the western side (right LDC). The confluence with Deer Canyon (left LDC) is reached in 35 minutes. Deer Spring access trail (left LDC) is reached in 15 more minutes. Banister Ruin, under a southeast-facing overhang (right LDC), is another 30 minutes down-canyon with an ideal large campsite under mature cottonwood trees opposite. It is 45 minutes to a rincon (left LDC). The confluence with Collins Spring Canyon (right LDC) is another 5 minutes. A prominent rim-top totem rock is seen down-canyon from the Collins Spring Canyon confluence. There are several camps in the confluence area.

It is 75 minutes to the Collins Spring Canyon carpark passing a north-trending tributary junction (right LUC) at minute 10 and a trailside arch (right LUC) at minute 20. The cowboy encampment (right LUC) is above the dryfall traverse route (left LUC) at minute 55. Don't forget to sign out on the trail registry.

Kane Gulch–Collins Spring UTM GPS Coordinates

Kane Gulch Ranger Station	0,597,584 E; 4,153,458 N	Elevation 6400'	00 min.
Junction Ruin		Elevation 6060'	95 min.
Turkey Pen Ruin		Elevation 6040'	115 min.
Stimper Arch	0,593,342 E; 4,151,678 N	Elevation 6040'	120 min.
Fortress Canyon confluence	0,592,707 E; 4,151,274 N	Elevation 6040'	130 min.
Todie Canyon confluence	0,592,200 E; 4,149,364 N	Elevation 6040'	180 min.
Pour-Off Pool traverse	0,591,133 E; 4,148,732 N	Elevation 6040'	215 min.
Lion Track Ruin		Elevation 6040'	230 min.
Split-Level Ruin		Elevation 6040'	245 min.
Shelf Ruin		Elevation 6040'	280 min.
Coyote Canyon confluence	0,587,243 E; 4,146,809 N	Elevation 6040'	310 min.
The Thumb Ruin		Elevation 6040'	325 min.
Sheiks Canyon confluence	0,586,252 E; 4,145,362 N	Elevation 5600'	350 min.
Green Mask Ruin		Elevation 5600'	355 min.
Bullet Canyon confluence	0,584,800 E; 4,144,568 N	Elevation 5600'	425 min.
Jailhouse Ruin		Elevation 5600'	50 min.
Perfect Kiva Ruin		Elevation 5600'	60 min.
Green House Canyon jct.	0,583,597 E; 4,145,793 N	Elevation 5600'	455 min.
Two-Story Ruin		Elevation 5600'	510 min.
Step Canyon confluence	0,582,089 E; 4,146,674 N	Elevation 5600'	515 min.
SE tributary junction	0,581,323 E; 4,146,177 N	Elevation 5600'	545 min.
NE tributary junction	0,580,690 E; 4,146,902 N	Elevation 5600'	570 min.
Dripping Canyon confluence	0,580,171 E; 4,146,909 N	Elevation 5600'	585 min.

E-NE tributary junction	0,579,546 E; 4,146,651 N	Elevation 5600'	600 min.
Cow Tank Canyon junction	0,579,470 E; 4,146,577 N	Elevation 5600'	605 min.
Dead Spar Knoll panel		Elevation 5600'	10 min.
Bird Parade Panel		Elevation 5600'	605 min.
Longhouse Ruin		Elevation 5600'	620 min.
Big Man Panel		Elevation 5600'	645 min.
NE tributary junction	0,579,025 E; 4,145,136 N	Elevation 5600'	650 min.
Pollys Canyon confluence	0,578,553 E; 4,144,173 N	Elevation 5600'	680 min.
Government Trail junction	0,578,285 E; 4,143,909 N	Elevation 5600'	690 min.
Pollys Island D-C junction	0,578,049 E; 4,143,916 N	Elevation 5600'	695 min.
Big Pour-Off traverse	0,576,762 E; 4,142,380 N	Elevation 5600'	765 min.
Deer Canyon confluence	0,577,181 E; 4,141,487 N	Elevation 4740'	800 min.
Deer Spring access	0,576,644 E; 4,141,220 N	Elevation 4740'	815 min.
Banister Ruin		Elevation 4780'	845 min.
Collins Rincon Panel		Elevation 4780'	905 min.
Collins Spring confluence	0,574,395 E; 4,141,759 N	Elevation 4780'	915 min.
North tributary junction	0,574,147 E; 4,142,182 N	Elevation 4800'	925 min.
Cowboy encampment	0,573,381 E; 4,143,089 N	Elevation 4800'	950 min.
Collins Spring carpark	0,573,113 E; 4,143,548 N	Elevation 5000'	1000 min.

◆ 60 Owl-McCloyd-Fish Canyons Loop

Access: The Owl-McCloyd-Fish Canyons Loop carpark is located east of Utah State Hwy. 261 between Utah State Hwy. 95 and Utah State Hwy. 163. Take Utah State Hwy. 95 to mile 93.2, GPS coordinates 0,598,414 E; 4,159,525 N; Elevation 6800'. Turn south on Hwy. 261 and drive to mile 27.7 and the San Juan County Route Long Spike #253 on the east side of the highway, GPS coordinates 0,596,551 E; 4,148,042 N; Elevation 6600 feet. Turn east onto a standard-vehicle road surface with an "Owl Creek 5" BLM sign. It is 5.1 miles to the carpark. Parking/camping is limited to a dozen vehicles. The trailhead, information board, and register are directly north of the carpark.

Trail Statistics: The route is 17 miles round-trip with a brutal 600 feet climb out of Fish Canyon. The route requires 3–5 days to complete. This is an excellent canyon hike over Class 1–3 terrain requiring strenuous effort and moderate route-finding skills.

Attractions: Natural arches and desert canyon ambience.

Cautions: There is a lot of slickrock scrambling along the route. At several spots during the descent and ascent paths, backpackers may want to haul their packs and/or set up a safety hand-line. Never try to

Owl-McCloyd-Fish Canyons Backpack Route

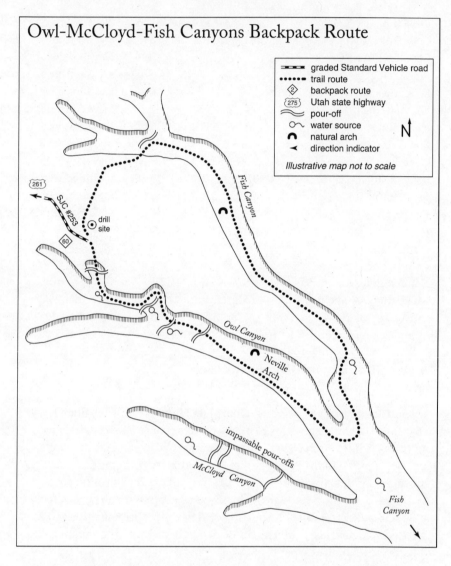

▭▬▭▬	graded Standard Vehicle road
••••••	trail route
◇2	backpack route
(275)	Utah state highway
≈	pour-off
⌒~	water source
∩	natural arch
◄	direction indicator

Illustrative map not to scale

descend either route if the slickrock is wet! Take 30′ of line with you in case you want to haul backpacks over some of the obstacles along the ascent and descent routes. Fatalities have occurred in this canyon complex when people have fallen while trying to reach inaccessible cliff sites. There is moderate midday shade in Owl Canyon and limited midday shade in Fish Canyon. The plunge pools in the middle of both canyons usually have water in them, but check with the Kane Gulch Ranger Station for additional information. Leave your pets behind for this walk.

Upper section of Fish Canyon

Maps: USGS Bluff and Blanding (1:100,000), or USGS Snow Flat Spring Cave, Bluff Northwest and Cedar Mesa North (1:62,500), or Trails Illustrated Grand Gulch Plateau (1:62,500). Note that McCloyd Canyon is not marked on these maps.

Description: Day 1, Fish and Owl carpark to Fish and Owl Canyons junction; Day 2, an 11-mile round-trip day hike to McCloyd Canyon; Day 3, Fish and Owl Canyons junction to upper Fish Canyon; Day 4, return to Fish and Owl carpark. This pace averages 8 backpacking miles a day.

The trail down Owl Canyon starts behind the BLM information board and follows the shallow drainage to the descent path in 5 minutes. Follow the cairns carefully as you descend the steep slickrock surfaces. It is 15 minutes to a northwest-trending tributary junction (right LDC). Continue another 10 minutes to a west-trending tributary junction (right LDC). Proceed southeast (left LDC) for 25 minutes to a dished out pour-off and plunge pool. It is 10 minutes walking up-canyon north (left LDC) into the tributary to detour around the pour-off. Notice the small bridge on the south side of the dished-out pour-off from the bottom. It is 10 minutes to the main stem junction of Owl Canyon and its west-trending south fork tributary (right LDC). The pour-off and plunge pool are traversed on the north wall (left LDC). Proceed east down-canyon for 20 minutes to a spring and pour-off, with a south wall (right LDC) traverse route. In 10 minutes, the canyon begins to widen. Neville Arch is seen in an additional 10 minutes. The large arch is on the north wall near the rim top (left LDC). It is another 45 minutes across grassy sand flats to the junction with Fish Canyon. There are several good camps in this confluence area with beaver pond water about an hour down-canyon, and streambed water 20 minutes up-canyon in Fish.

(Side hike: To explore McCloyd Canyon as an 11-mile round-trip side trip, head down-canyon following an entrenched trail running perpendicular to the winding streambed course for 70 minutes to McCloyd Canyon. Turn northwest (right LDC) and follow the path up into the canyon as it gets narrower and steeper for 50 minutes to a west-trending tributary (left LUC). The impassable pour-off is 30 minutes up-canyon from this junction. Return the way you came.)

Walk up-canyon in Fish Canyon for 45 minutes to a pool with a prominent hoodoo on the north wall. I didn't see any fish in the murky water in April 1998, but killifish, shiners, suckers, chubs, toads, and frogs inhabit these waters. Nearby is an arch in the east wall seen from a row of moderate-sized cottonwood trees beside a pool. A good campsite is 10 minutes up-canyon and near water. It is 35 minutes to a high alcove ruin, best viewed with binoculars, in the east wall but facing south (right LUC) and in another 5 minutes, a small vertical arch in the west wall (left LUC) is glimpsed.

It is 10 minutes to the junction of Fish Canyon and the West Fork of Fish Canyon. There are structures in a south-facing high alcove up-canyon in Fish Canyon along the east wall (right LUC). You need binoculars to see any details. There is a small campsite here. The upper tributaries are enticing side hikes but get progressively more difficult to navigate the farther you go.

Go west (left LUC) into the West Fork of Fish Canyon for 10 minutes, following the cairns carefully around several pour-offs. Just upstream from a weeping wall with Gambel oaks and a series of seeps (left LUC) is the ascent path (left LUC). It is 20 minutes of steep, tight switchbacks. Follow the cairns closely to a scrambling move at the top to gain the rim. While Owl Canyon's descent was mainly slickrock surface, the ascent path out of Fish Canyon is mainly soil, with some slickrock. Once on top, follow the trail as it winds its way through several small drainages to the carpark in 30 minutes. Don't forget to sign out at the trail registry.

Owl-McCloyd-Fish Canyons UTM GPS Coordinates

Fish & Owl carpark	0,604,483 E; 4,147,880 N	Elevation 6200′	00 min.
Descent path	0,604,776 E; 4,147,602 N	Elevation 6180′	05 min.

West tributary	0,604,883 E; 4,146,715 N	Elevation 5400'	30 min.
Dished pour-off	0,606,210 E; 4,146,398 N	Elevation 5300'	55 min.
West tributary	0,606,312 E; 4,146,008 N	Elevation 5000'	75 min.
Neville Arch	0,608,077 E; 4,145,249 N	Elevation 4900'	115 min.
Owl & Fish confluence	0,610,584 E; 4,143,150 N	Elevation 4850'	160 min.
East wall arch	0,610,223 E; 4,145,930 N	Elevation 4900'	205 min.
West wall arch	0,608,053 E; 4,148,456 N	Elevation 5200'	270 min.
WF Fish & Fish junction	0,606,210 E; 4,150,265 N	Elevation 5400'	280 min.
Ascent path	0,605,400 E; 4,150,382 N	Elevation 5500'	290 min.
Rim top	0,605,293 E; 4,150,021 N	Elevation 6100'	310 min.
Fish & Owl carpark	0,604,483 E; 4,147,880 N	Elevation 6200'	340 min.

McCloyd Canyon Side Trip UTM GPS Coordinates

Owl & Fish confluence	0,610,584 E; 4,143,150 N	Elevation 4850'	00 min.
McCloyd Canyon	0,611,494 E; 4,141,066 N	Elevation 4800'	70 min.
West tributary junction	0,608,707 E; 4,142,423 N	Elevation 5000'	120 min.
Tributary ruin	0,608,107 E; 4,142,350 N	Elevation 5050'	130 min.
Terminus pour-off	0,608,282 E; 4,142,984 N	Elevation 5100'	150 min.
Owl & Fish confluence	0,610,584 E; 4,143,150 N	Elevation 4850'	300 min.

◆ 61 Slickhorn Canyon Access #1–Access #6 Loop

Access: The Slickhorn Canyon Access #1–Access #6 Loop carpark is located west of Utah State Hwy. 261 between Utah State Hwy. 95 and Utah State Hwy. 163. Take Utah State Hwy. 95 to mile 93.2, GPS coordinates 0,598,414 E; 4,159,525 N; Elevation 6800'. Turn south on Hwy. 261 and drive to mile 18.1, GPS coordinates 0,593,537 E; 4,139,176 N; Elevation 6500'. Turn west onto San Juan County Route Slickhorn #245 and go 0.3 mile to a gated fence with a BLM information board and trail registry. Continue to mile 2.6 to the junction between San Juan County Point Lookout #203 and San Juan County Slickhorn #245 road at GPS Coordinates 0,590,226 E; 4,140,342 N; Elevation 6350'. Turn southwest (left) onto San Juan County #203 and continue to mile 4.2. Turn west (right) on the standard-vehicle track and go 0.4 mile to the carpark. There is a rusted blue Ford pickup bed from the 1950s near the trail registry. Parking/camping is limited to several vehicles.

Trail Statistics: The route is 15.5 miles round-trip with an elevation change of 800 feet requiring 2–4 days to complete. This is a good canyon hike over Class 1–3 terrain requiring moderate effort and moderate route-finding skills.

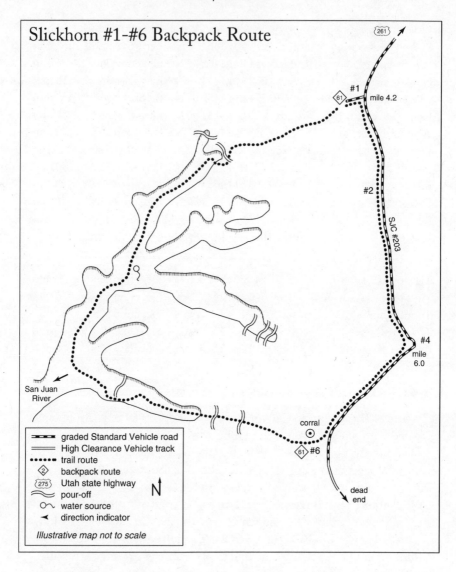

Slickhorn #1–#6 Backpack Route

Legend:

- ▰▰▰ graded Standard Vehicle road
- ═══ High Clearance Vehicle track
- •••••• trail route
- ◇ backpack route
- (275) Utah state highway
- ⁓ pour-off
- ᴏ⌒ water source
- ◄ direction indicator

Illustrative map not to scale

Attractions: An isolated sandstone canyon complex.

Cautions: No dogs are allowed in Slickhorn Canyon or its tributaries. A haul line for backpacks is recommended. There is a steep section on slickrock surfaces in Access #1 that should not be attempted if wet.

Maps: USGS Navajo Mountain (1:100,000), or USGS Pollys Pasture and Slickhorn Canyon East (1:62,500), or Trails Illustrated Grand Gulch Plateau (1:62,500)

Description: Day 1, Slickhorn Canyon Access #1 carpark to Slickhorn Canyon Access #4 junction; Day 2, Slickhorn Canyon Access #4 junction to Slickhorn Canyon Access #6 junction; Day 3, Slickhorn Canyon Access #6 junction to Slickhorn Canyon Access #1 carpark. This pace averages 8 backpacking miles a day. Take the time to study the evidence of complex geological erosion processes surrounding you.

Go southwest past the trail registry and head west down-canyon into the shallow drainage. It is 15 minutes of easily negotiated pour-offs to a northwest-trending tributary junction (left LDC). Continue southwest (right LDC) for 30 minutes to a grooved 80' pour-off. It has a twin 50' pour-off from a tributary sharing the same plunge pool below. There is a detour route over the "hat rock" knob to the immediate south (left LDC). It follows the high bench for 10 minutes under/over two more dryfalls to a steep descent path. Follow the cairns closely. There is a hoodoo pinnacle on the opposite west canyon wall. The descent traverses slightly left (down-canyon) until a red rock layer is reached, where it switches to the right (up-canyon) before heading straight down into the streambed. Don't try this route if the canyon walls are wet! A cobble streambed section and dense brush section give way shortly to easy alluvial sand trail walking.

The Slickhorn Canyon Access #2 northeast-trending tributary is reached in 50 minutes with a good campsite at its junction. A balanced rock hoodoo and several rim-top "hat" rocks can be seen in this area. Slickhorn Canyon Access #4 is 10 minutes down-canyon with several good campsites at its northeast-trending tributary junction. Water is intermittent through here, with small streambed potholes. It is 5 minutes to an arch on the southeast meander. It is 35 minutes to an east-trending tributary junction (left LDC). Proceed down-canyon (right LDC) for 5 minutes to a north-northeast tributary junction (left LDC). This is Access #6 confluence with Slickhorn. There is a camp under the cottonwoods in the sand along the alluvial bank.

Go north-northeast up-canyon (left LDC) into Slickhorn Canyon Access #6 drainage, sometimes referred to as Trail Fork Canyon. It is 20 minutes to a north tributary (left LUC). Go east (right LUC) and locate the ledge traverse route along the south wall in 5 minutes. From the ledge traverse you can use binoculars to view several structures in the opposite north wall along an alcove seam. Continue up-canyon for 30 minutes over several negotiable pour-offs and boulder dams. It is 20 more minutes to a north-trending tributary junction (left LUC) among shallow cross-bedded canyon walls. Go east (right LUC) and negotiate the immediate over-hanging pour-off on either side. At the south-trending tributary junction above the pour-off, go east (left LUC) for 10 minutes to the top of the drainage. Head east toward the butte along the trail paralleling the drainage to a corral area. This is the carpark area for Slickhorn Canyon Access #6. Follow Point Lookout #203 north (left) for 90 minutes to the carpark of Slickhorn Canyon Access #1. Don't forget to sign out at the trail registry.

Slickhorn Canyon Access #1–Access #6 Loop UTM GPS Coordinates

Slickhorn #1 carpark	0,587,878 E; 4,138,506 N	Elevation 6200'	00 min.
80' pour-off	0,585,654 E; 4,137,521 N	Elevation 5800'	45 min.
Descent path top	0,585,610 E; 4,137,101 N	Elevation 5800'	55 min.
Descent path bottom	0,585,532 E; 4,137,160 N	Elevation 5500'	65 min.
Access #2 tributary junction	0,584,295 E; 4,135,680 N	Elevation 5400'	115 min.
Access #4 tributary junction	0,584,125 E; 4,135,285 N	Elevation 5500'	125 min.
Arch	0,583,666 E; 4,135,451 N	Elevation 5500'	130 min.
East tributary junction	0,583,364 E; 4,133,968 N	Elevation 5400'	165 min.
Access #6 tributary junction	0,583,047 E; 4,133,500 N	Elevation 5300'	170 min.
North tributary junction	0,583,754 E; 4,133,578 N	Elevation 5400'	200 min.
Ledge traverse	0,584,056 E; 4,133,446 N	Elevation 5400'	205 min.
Top of boulder dams	0,585,271 E; 4,133,003 N	Elevation 5860'	235 min.
North tributary junction	0,585,914 E; 4,133,134 N	Elevation 5900'	255 min.
South tributary junction	0,586,109 E; 4,132,968 N	Elevation 5920'	260 min.
Head of tributary drainage	0,587,104 E; 4,133,159 N	Elevation 6000'	270 min.
Corral & SJC #203 junction	0,587,967 E; 4,132,925 N	Elevation 6200'	280 min.
Access #1 junction	0,588,414 E; 4,138,574 N	Elevation 6240'	360 min.
Slickhorn #1 carpark	0,587,878 E; 4,138,506 N	Elevation 6200'	370 min.

◆ 62 Slickhorn Canyon Access #1–Johns Canyon Loop

Access: The Slickhorn Canyon Access #1 carpark is located west of Utah State Hwy. 261 between Utah State Hwy. 95 and Utah State Hwy. 163. Take Utah State Hwy. 95 to mile 93.2, GPS coordinates 0,598,414 E; 4,159,525 N; Elevation 6800'. Turn south on Hwy. 261 and drive to mile 18.1, GPS coordinates 0,593,537 E; 4,139,176 N; Elevation 6500'. Turn west onto San Juan County Route Slickhorn #245 and go 0.3 mile to a gated fence with a BLM information board and trail registry. Continue to mile 2.6 to the junction between San Juan County Point Lookout #203 and San Juan County Slickhorn #245 road at GPS Coordinates 0,590,226 E; 4,140,342 N; Elevation 6350'. Turn southwest (left) onto San Juan County #203 and continue to mile 4.2. Turn west (right) on the standard-vehicle track and go 0.4 mile to the carpark. There is a rusted blue Ford pickup

Slickhorn #1-Johns Canyon Backpack Route

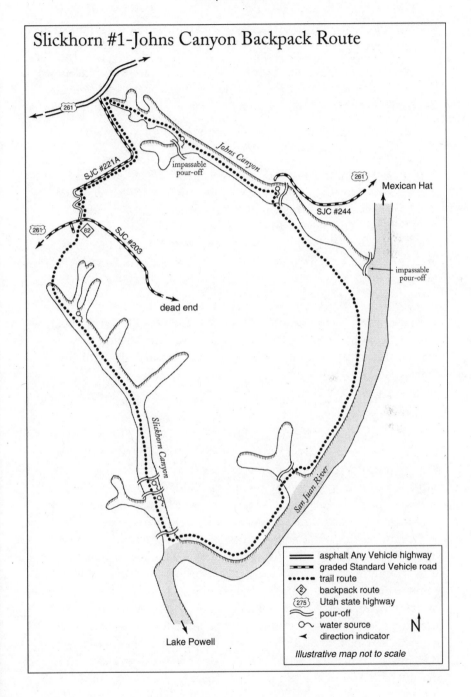

Legend:
- asphalt Any Vehicle highway
- graded Standard Vehicle road
- trail route
- ② backpack route
- (275) Utah state highway
- pour-off
- water source
- direction indicator

N

Illustrative map not to scale

bed from the 1950s near the trail registry. Parking/camping is limited to
several vehicles.

Trail Statistics: The route is 51 miles with an elevation change of 1300
feet requiring 6–8 days to complete. This is a fair canyon hike over Class
1–4 terrain requiring moderate effort and moderate route-finding skills.

Attractions: Isolation in two varied canyon complexes.

Cautions: No dogs are allowed in Slickhorn Canyon or its tributaries.
Camping at the confluence of Slickhorn Canyon and the San Juan River
is reserved for river-runners. The 15.8-mile San Juan River rim section
and the 8-mile mesa-top road section have no shade and usually no
water sources. There are steep slickrock scrambling sections where the
use of a 30′ haul line is advisable. Never attempt this route in adverse
weather conditions. This route is rarely walked, and generally only by
people searching for solitude. Ancestral Puebloan sites are few, and
water sources rare. It is for the experienced only.

Maps: USGS Navajo Mountain (1:100,000) and USGS Bluff (1:100,000),
or USGS Cedar Mesa North, Cedar Mesa South, Pollys Pasture and
Slickhorn Canyon East (1:62,500), or Trails Illustrated Grand Gulch
Plateau (1:62,500)

Description: Day 1, Slickhorn Canyon Access #1 to Slickhorn Canyon
Access #4 junction; Day 2, Slickhorn Canyon Access #4 junction to Inner
River Rim Trail; Day 3, Inner River Rim Trail to Johns Canyon carpark;
Day 4, Johns Canyon carpark to West Fork of Johns Canyon confluence;
Day 5, West Fork of Johns Canyon confluence to Upper Johns Canyon
carpark; Day 6, Upper Johns Canyon carpark to Slickhorn Canyon
Access #1 carpark. This pace averages 8 backpacking miles a day except
for a long day hiking the waterless Inner River Rim Trail.

Starting at Slickhorn Canyon Access #1 carpark, go southwest of the
trail registry and head west down-canyon into the shallow drainage.
It is 15 minutes of easily negotiated pour-offs to a northwest-trending
tributary junction (left LDC). Continue southwest (right LDC) for 30
minutes to a grooved 80′ pour-off. There is a 50′ pour-off from a twin
tributary sharing the same plunge pool below. Follow the detour route
over the "hat rock" knob to the immediate south (left LDC). It traces the
high bench for 10 minutes under and over two more dryfalls to a steep
descent path. Follow the cairns closely. There is a hoodoo pinnacle on
the opposite west canyon wall. The descent traverses slightly left (down-
canyon) until a red rock layer is reached, where it switches to the right
(up-canyon) before heading straight down into the streambed. Don't try

this route if the canyon walls are wet! A cobble streambed section and dense brush section give way shortly to easy alluvial sand trail walking. The Slickhorn Canyon Access #2 northeast-trending tributary is reached in 50 minutes with a good campsite at its junction. A balanced rock hoodoo and several rim-top "hat" rocks can be seen in this area. The northeast-trending tributary of Slickhorn Canyon Access #4 junction is 10 minutes farther down-canyon with several good campsites at its confluence (left LDC). Water is intermittent through here with small streambed potholes.

From Slickhorn Canyon Access #4 junction, it is 5 minutes to an arch on the southeast meander. It is 35 minutes to an east-trending tributary (left LDC). Proceed west (right LDC) for 5 minutes to a north-northeast tributary junction (left LDC). This is Slickhorn Canyon Access #6. There is a camp under the cottonwoods in the sand along the alluvial bank where I found a dozen pieces of trash. Remember to leave any campsite or lunch stop cleaner than you found it.

Continue down-canyon for 20 minutes to a north-trending tributary junction (right LDC) followed by 30 minutes to an east-trending tributary junction (left LDC) and a large pothole. In 10 more minutes there is another east-northeast-trending tributary junction (left LDC). In the next 45 minutes you'll encounter several boulder dam obstacles, which would be very interesting if the streambed depressions were filled with water, until a northeast-trending tributary junction is reached (left LDC). Most of the traverse routes around the boulder obstacles were on the eastern side (left LDC). It is 85 minutes of increasingly strenuous walking to a 10' pour-off with an east wall traverse route (left LDC). A limestone ledge second pour-off is encountered in 30 minutes with an exposed traverse route on the east wall (left LDC) that required lowering backpacks to one another and some scrambling. You don't want an injury here: you are much too far away from assistance. Another pour-off is immediately down-canyon, with the traverse route on the west wall (right LDC). The last pour-off is encountered in 25 minutes, with a traverse route on the east wall (left LDC). This pour-off and plunge pool are a popular swimming area for river-runners walking up from the San Juan River, a mere 35 minutes down-canyon.

Near the mouth of Slickhorn Canyon at the San Juan River is a traverse route that connects to the canyon rim road climbing up past some abandoned drilling equipment (left LDC). This is the E. L. Goodridge road, created to get drilling equipment down into the canyon. However, after two dreadful years hacking out the road and lugging the drilling equipment by mules to the rim, the equipment fell down the slope and was destroyed. The oil reserves were never commercially exploited, but the capped pipes in the test drill sites can still be seen near the river-runner camps.

The plunge pools at the bottom of the road and the San Juan River itself are the last reliable spots to get water for the next 16 miles, so fill your water bottles and lug them up the switchbacks. There is some old drilling debris near the top of the ascent trail that's worth some exploration. Head up the river canyon, passing two southwest-facing dryfalls to an east-trending tributary junction crossing along limestone ledges in 130 minutes. Keep your eyes open for boulder petroglyph panels. It is 120 minutes to an east-trending tributary junction and 15 more minutes to a crossing of another east-trending tributary dryfall. Another 40 minutes of steady walking brings you around a prominent point and into Johns Canyon.

In 15 minutes, look for two dozen figures on a white boulder. The Glen Canyon NRA sign is reached in 35 minutes more. It is 100 more minutes of walking to the limestone plunge pools of Johns Canyon. Water can be found between the two road crossings of the streambed. There are several camps in this area, too.

From the southwestern crossing of Johns Canyon, follow the wash up-canyon for 5 minutes to a waist-high wall with a small-diameter pipe in its center along the north wall (right LUC). This is probably a relic from the cattle-ranching days of yesteryear. At the second limestone ledge crossing of the Johns Canyon streambed, turn northeast (right LUC) onto the double track and walk 30 minutes to a small corral and fence posts. On a small knoll about 5 minutes northeast of the track is a decaying cowboy dugout with an intact rock hearth. Return to the double track and continue up-canyon. It is 35 minutes to the confluence with the West Fork of Johns Canyon. The West Fork of Johns Canyon has a series of impassable pour-offs immediately up-canyon from this junction.

Instead, go northeast (right LUC) into the main stem of Johns Canyon along the double track. There are numerous petroglyph panels on black desert varnish–stained boulders on the alluvial slopes below the dividing wall between the West Fork and main stem of Johns Canyon, but they are off the beaten path of the double track. It is 10 more minutes following the double track up-canyon to where it ends at the rocky streambed underneath a series of east-southeast-facing high alcoves in the west wall (left LUC). There is a long wall with vertical wood posts connecting the wall with the alcove ceiling in one of the three alcoves. Bring binoculars because there are no access routes up to these alcoves. It is another 5 minutes of up-canyon walking to two more structures on a high ledge underneath an overhanging triangular rock facing south-southeast in the northwest wall (left LUC). Again, you will need binoculars to see any details of this structure. It is 15 more minutes hiking over cobbles to a junction with an east-northeast-trending tributary (right LUC). Turn north (left LUC) and walk 25 minutes up the main canyon to a north-northwest-trending tributary junction (left LUC). Continue northeast (right LUC) up the main canyon for 20 more minutes to a shared plunge pool with a north-northwest-trending tributary (left LUC).

Go northeast (right LUC) and traverse the pour-off and plunge pool along the north wall (left LUC). There are wall remnants in a black-striped, buff-colored southeast-facing alcove (left LUC) immediately up-canyon from the traverse route. Continue north up-canyon through cottonwood trees for 15 minutes to a junction between north and northeast tributaries. Go north (left LUC) for 15 minutes to a traverse route on the east wall (right LUC) around a 15' pour-off. Continue up-canyon for 20 minutes to the rim top just east of the BLM bulletin board and cattle fence. Turn west (left LUC) and walk 65 minutes along San Juan County Route #221A for 2.2 miles to the West Fork of Johns Canyon carpark area. Follow the road north-northwest around the curve for 75 minutes and 2.6 miles over rolling mesa-top terrain to the double track descent route. The road bed changes to a track here. The 0.5-mile descent takes 15 minutes and intersects San Juan County Route #203. Turn north and hike along the graded surface for 1.1 miles to Slickhorn Canyon Access #1 junction. Turn west (left) and finish the last 0.4 mile back to your vehicle.

Slickhorn Canyon Access #1–Johns Canyon Loop UTM GPS Coordinates

Access #1 carpark	0,587,878 E; 4,138,506 N	Elevation 6200'	00 min.
80' pour-off	0,585,654 E; 4,137,521 N	Elevation 5800'	45 min.
Descent path top	0,585,610 E; 4,137,101 N	Elevation 5800'	55 min.
Descent path bottom	0,585,532 E; 4,137,160 N	Elevation 5500'	65 min.
Access #2 tributary junction	0,584,295 E; 4,135,680 N	Elevation 5400'	115 min.
Access #4 tributary junction	0,584,125 E; 4,135,285 N	Elevation 5500'	125 min.
Arch	0,583,666 E; 4,135,451 N	Elevation 5500'	130 min.
East tributary junction	0,583,364 E; 4,133,968 N	Elevation 5400'	165 min.
Access #6 tributary junction	0,583,047 E; 4,133,500 N	Elevation 5300'	170 min.
North tributary junction	0,582,481 E; 4,133,368 N	Elevation 5200'	190 min.
E-NE tributary junction	0,582,164 E; 4,132,520 N	Elevation 5100'	220 min.
E-NE tributary & pour-off	0,581,735 E; 4,132,169 N	Elevation 5100'	230 min.
NE tributary junction	0,580,555 E; 4,131,052 N	Elevation 5000'	295 min.

10′ pour-off traverse	0,578,482 E; 4,130,998 N	Elevation 4900′	380 min.
30′ pour-off traverse	0,577,248 E; 4,130,919 N	Elevation 4400′	410 min.
15′ north tributary pour-off	0,576,872 E; 4,130,754 N	Elevation 4200′	440 min.
San Juan River	0,575,521 E; 4,130,207 N	Elevation 3800′	500 min.
Old drilling debris site	0,575,746 E; 4,130,120 N	Elevation 4000′	510 min.
NE tributary junction	0,579,721 E; 4,127,633 N	Elevation 4500′	630 min.
E-NE tributary junction	0,581,433 E; 4,125,219 N	Elevation 4800′	750 min.
Pinnacle knob point	0,582,988 E; 4,123,942 N	Elevation 5000′	790 min.
Glen Canyon NRA sign	0,585,207 E; 4,124,590 N	Elevation 5100′	850 min.
Limestone crossing carpark	0,588,797 E; 4,125,653 N	Elevation 5200′	960 min.
Cowboy well	0,589,016 E; 4,126,049 N	Elevation 5200′	965 min.
Cowboy dugout	0,590,196 E; 4,126,688 N	Elevation 5300′	995 min.
WF Johns confluence	0,591,298 E; 4,128,907 N	Elevation 5400′	1030 min.
E-NE tributary junction	0,592,649 E; 4,130,799 N	Elevation 5600′	1070 min.
N-NW tributary junction	0,593,824 E; 4,132,545 N	Elevation 5900′	1135 min.
15′ pour-off	0,593,317 E; 4,134,072 N	Elevation 6100′	1205 min.
Ruin overlook		Elevation 6220′	1215 min.
Upper Johns carpark	0,593,308 E; 4,134,540 N	Elevation 6500′	1240 min.
SJC #221A junction	0,593,381 E; 4,135,837 N	Elevation 6560′	1310 min.
West Fork Johns carpark	0,590,923 E; 4,134,281 N	Elevation 6380′	1375 min.
SJC #203 junction	0,588,685 E; 4,136,884 N	Elevation 6220′	1465 min.
Slickhorn #1 carpark	0,587,878 E; 4,138,506 N	Elevation 6200′	1480 min.

◆ 63 Collins Spring Canyon–San Juan River

Access: Collins Spring Canyon carpark is located east of Utah State Hwy. 276 between Utah State Hwy. 95 and Hall's Crossing on Lake Powell. Take Utah State Hwy. 95 to mile 83.8, GPS coordinates 0,586,727 E; 4,157,522 N; Elevation 6200′. Turn south on Hwy. 276 and drive to mile 84.7 and the San Juan County Route Gulch Creek #260 on the east side of the highway, GPS coordinates 0,578,134 E; 4,151,431 N; Elevation 5600′. Turn east and go 6.3 miles on a standard-vehicle road surface to the Collins Spring Canyon carpark. There is a BLM information board with trail registry at the carpark. Parking is limited to a dozen vehicles.

Trail Statistics: The route is 35.4 miles round-trip (not counting side trips), with a 1200-foot change in elevation that takes 5–8 days to complete. This is a good hike over Class 1–3 terrain requiring moderate effort and moderate route-finding skills.

Attractions: Ancestral Puebloan rock art panels and Shaw Arch.

Cautions: Camping at the confluence with the San Juan River is

Collins Spring-San Juan River Backpack Route

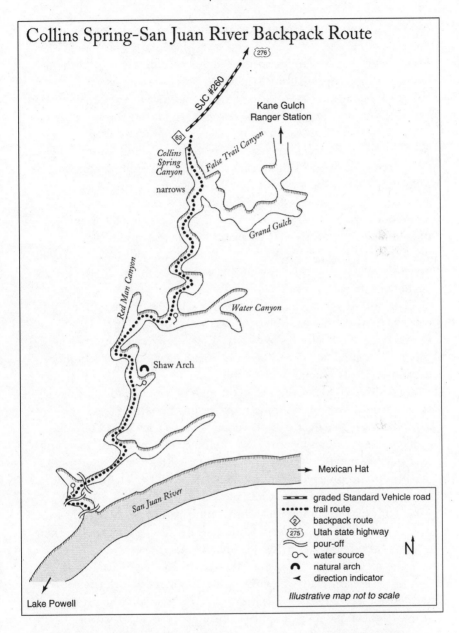

reserved for river-runners. No pets allowed down-canyon of Collins Spring Canyon in Grand Gulch.

Maps: usgs Navajo Mountain (1:100,000), or usgs Red House Spring and Slickhorn Canyon West (1:62,500), or Trails Illustrated Grand Gulch Plateau (1:62,500)

Description: Day 1, Collins Spring Canyon carpark to Water Canyon; Day 2, Water Canyon to Shaw Arch; Day 3, day hike to San Juan River; Day 4, Shaw Arch to Collins Spring Canyon confluence; Day 5, Grand Gulch to Collins Spring Canyon carpark. This pace averages 8 backpacking miles a day. Take the time to study the lessons in the rock art panels created by a culture just as capable and complex as our own.

The trail leads southeast from the BLM information sign by descending the slickrock ledges to the bottom of Collins Spring Canyon in 5 minutes. Either walk in the canyon bottom to minimize erosion or follow the entrenched footpath over the sandy alluvial bend flats. In 5 minutes, you'll see a west-facing alcove in the east wall containing a large abandoned cowboy encampment (left LDC). This encampment is immediately down-canyon from an old wooden fence gate blocking the blasted out pathway in the east wall. There is a 40' pour-off immediately down-canyon with a traverse route blasted out on the southwest ledges (right LDC).

Continue down-canyon for 20 minutes to a 20' pour-off with a traverse route on the east wall (left LDC). There is a trail-level arch along this traverse. It is 5 minutes of walking down-canyon to a north-trending tributary junction (left LDC). Turn south (right LDC) and walk another 10 minutes to the confluence with Grand Gulch.

Turn south (right LDC) and head through the brief, muddy narrows section. There is a west-trending tributary junction (right LDC) immediately below the narrows with an alluvial bank. Head down-canyon for 60 minutes to a panel with a hundred handprints on a south-facing alcove and ledge (right LDC). It is 90 minutes to a 100' long panel of anthropomorphic pictographs of red, white, and green hues (right LDC). Save some film, because it is another 10 minutes to the ghostly panel with 100 pictographs of anthropomorphs and animals (right LDC) of gray, red, white, and yellow. Around the bend is Water Canyon. There is usually running water in the streambed in this area.

Red Man Canyon is another 20 minutes down-canyon (right LDC), with an east-facing alcove 5 minutes farther down-canyon. There is a narrow slot tributary entering Grand Gulch immediately below this alcove (right LDC). It is 45 minutes to the junction with a northeast-trending tributary (left LDC) and 15 minutes farther to Shaw Arch (left LDC). There are red, white, green and yellow handprint pictographs on the abutment walls, with several dozen petroglyphs inscribed into the sandstone boulders. Sometimes there is water flowing out of a small spring in the down-canyon tributary drainage. Don't camp underneath the arch since rockfall is frequent. Choose the grassy meadow on the up-canyon side instead.

It is best to day hike down to the San Juan River from the Shaw Arch campsite since camping is not permitted near the river. It is 120 minutes to a west-trending amphitheater (right LDC) with a slickrock knoll for enjoying the view and sunshine. It is another 15 minutes to an east-trending tributary amphitheater (left LDC) and 45 minutes farther to a north-trending tributary junction (right LDC). Continue through some flash flood debris dams and boulder obstacles to a northwest-trending tributary junction and pour-off (right LDC) in 20 minutes. There is usually running water in this area. This tributary can be followed to reach the mesa top and its extensive views of the surrounding landscape. However, the San Juan River is only 30 minutes and a mile farther down-canyon. Continue down-canyon from the junction pour-off and follow the streambed down-canyon to a 30' pour-off. There is a traverse trail on the west wall (right LDC) over the red sandbanks. Follow the trail to the terminal pour-off at the river. Return the way you came and sign out on the trail registry.

Collins Spring–San Juan River UTM GPS Coordinates

Collins Spring carpark	0,573,113 E; 4,143,548 N	Elevation 5000'	00 min.
Cowboy encampment	0,573,381 E; 4,143,089 N	Elevation 4800'	10 min.
North tributary junction	0,574,147 E; 4,142,182 N	Elevation 4800'	35 min.
Grand Gulch	0,574,395 E; 4,141,759 N	Elevation 4800'	45 min.
Narrows & tributary junction	0,574,201 E; 4,141,368 N	Elevation 4800'	50 min.
100 handprints panel		Elevation 4800'	110 min.
100' anthropomorphic panel		Elevation 4700'	200 min.
100 anthropomorphs panel		Elevation 4700'	210 min.
Water Canyon	0,572,850 E; 4,138,022 N	Elevation 4600'	215 min.
Red Man Canyon	0,571,948 E; 4,137,988 N	Elevation 4600'	235 min.
NE tributary junction	0,572,038 E; 4,136,232 N	Elevation 4500'	285 min.
Shaw Arch	0,571,864 E; 4,135,591 N	Elevation 4550'	300 min.
Amphitheater junction	0,570,869 E; 4,132,309 N	Elevation 4300'	420 min.
East tributary junction	0,570,810 E; 4,131,875 N	Elevation 4300'	435 min.
North tributary junction	0,569,742 E; 4,131,266 N	Elevation 4200'	480 min.
Pour-off tributary junction	0,569,045 E; 4,130,807 N	Elevation 4000'	520 min.
San Juan River confluence	0,569,928 E; 4,130,807 N	Elevation 3800'	530 min.
Collins Spring carpark	0,573,113 E; 4,143,548 N	Elevation 5000'	1060 min.

◆ 64 San Juan River–Kane Gulch

Access: This route necessitates floating down the San Juan River and hiking up Grand Gulch to the Kane Gulch Ranger Station carpark. Trip logistics can be formidable. Private permits and information on commercial outfitters for floating the river and hiking the canyon are available from the Monticello BLM field office at (435) 587-1500.

Trail Statistics: The route is 51.7 miles (not counting side trips), with an elevation change of 3000 feet requiring 8–10 days to complete. This is an excellent canyon backpack route over Class 1–3 terrain requiring moderate effort and moderate route-finding skills. Arrange your own shuttle. You must have a permit from the BLM to walk this route.

Attractions: Ancestral Puebloan sites, rock art panels, rincons, and natural arches, plus a river float trip.

Cautions: No pets are allowed from the river to Collins Spring Canyon in Grand Culch. There is limited midday shade along this route.

Maps: USGS Blanding (1:100,000), or Cedar Mesa North, Kane Gulch, Pollys Pasture, Red House Spring and Slickhorn Canyon West (1:62,500), or Trails Illustrated Grand Gulch Plateau (1:62,500)

Description: This route is described, in reverse order, under the Kane Gulch–Collins Spring Canyon, page 168, and the Collins Spring Canyon–San Juan River, page 186, route headings.

Suggested Reading

All Topo Maps: Utah (!Gage, 1998).

The Amateur Archaeologist's Handbook, by Maurice Robbins with Mary B. Irving (Harper and Row, 1981).

Anasazi and Pueblo Painting, by J. J. Brody (University of New Mexico Press, 1991).

The Anasazi of Mesa Verde and the Four Corners, by William M. Ferguson (University Press of Colorado, 1996).

Anasazi Ruins of the Southwest in Color, by William M. Ferguson and Arthur H. Rohn (University of New Mexico Press, 1987).

Ancient Ruins of the Southwest: An Archaeological Guide, by David Grant Noble (Northland Press, 1981).

An Archaeologist's Guide to Chert and Flint, by Barbara E. Wedtke (University of California, Los Angeles, 1992).

"Archaeology Fact Sheet on Utah Wilderness," by Southern Utah Wilderness Alliance (1998).

The Backpacker's Handbook, by Hugh McManners (Dorling Kindersley Book, 1995).

Best Easy Day Hikes: Grand Staircase-Escalante and the Glen Canyon Region, by Ron Adkison (Falcon Publishing, 1998).

"Blanding, Utah-Colorado." U.S. Geological Survey map (1982).

"Bluff, Utah-Colorado." U.S. Geological Survey map (1983).

The Camper's Companion: The Pack-Along Guide for Better Outdoor Trips, by Rick Greenspan and Hal Kahn (Foghorn Press, 1991).

Canyon Country Geology for the Layman and Rockhound, by F. A. Barnes (Wasatch Publishers, 1978).

Canyon Country Prehistoric Rock Art, by F. A. Barnes (Wasatch Publishers, 1995).

Canyon Hiking to the Colorado Plateau, by Michael Kelsey (Kelsey Publishing, 1991).

Canyoneering: The San Rafael Swell, by Steve Allen (University of Utah Press, 1992).

Canyoneering 2: Technical Loop Hikes in Southern Utah, by Steve Allen (University of Utah Press, 1995).

Canyoneering 3: Loop Hikes in Utah's Escalante, by Steve Allen (University of Utah Press, 1997).

Canyonlands Country: Geology of Canyonlands and Arches National Parks, by Donald Baars (Cañon Publishers and Canyonlands Natural History Association, 1989).

Cowboys and Cave Dwellers: Basket Maker Archaeology in Utah's Grand Gulch, by Fred M. Blackburn and Ray A. Williamson (School of American Research Press, 1997).

Down Canyon, by Ann Haymond Zwinger (University of Arizona Press, 1995).

Dynamics of Southwest Prehistory, edited by Linda S. Cordell and George J. Gumerman (Smithsonian Institution Press, 1989).

Enemy Ancestors: The Anasazi World with a Guide to Sites, by Gary Matlock (Northland Publishing, 1988).

Everett Ruess: A Vagabond for Beauty, by W. L. Rusho (Peregrine Smith, 1983).

A Field Guide to Rock Art Symbols of the Greater Southwest, by Alex Patterson (Johnson Books, 1992).

Geologic History of Utah, by Lehi F. Hintze (Brigham Young University, 1988).

Geology of Utah, by William Lee Stokes (Utah Museum of Natural History and Utah Geological and Mineral Survey, 1986).

Glen Canyon and the San Juan County, by Gary Topping (University of Idaho Press, 1997).

Grand Gulch Plateau Cultural and Recreational Area Management Plan, by Bureau of Land Management (Department of the Interior, 1993).

"Grand Gulch Plateau BLM–San Juan Resource Area, Utah" (National Geographic Maps Trails Illustrated, 1991).

The Great Southwest Nature Factbook, by Susan J. Tweit (Alaska Northwest Books, 1992).

Handbook of North American Indians, by William C. Sturtevant (Smithsonian Institution, 1983).

High in Utah, by Michael R. Weibel and Dan Miller (University of Utah Press, 1999).

Hiking Grand Staircase-Escalante and the Glen Canyon Region, by Ron Adkison (Falcon Publishing, 1998).

A History of San Juan County in the Palm of Time, by Robert S. McPherson (Utah State Historical Society, 1995).

In Search of the Old Ones: Exploring the Anasazi World of the Southwest, by David Roberts (Simon and Schuster, 1996).

The Indian Heritage of America, by Alvin M. Josephy Jr. (Houghton Mifflin, 1991).

The Monkey Wrench Gang, by Edward Abbey (Lippincott, 1975).

My Canyonlands, by Kent Frost (Canyon Country, 1997).

"Navajo Mountain Utah-Arizona," U.S. Geological Survey (1981).

PCT Hiker's Handbook, by Ray Jardine (AdventureLore Press, 1996).

Pages of Stone, by Halka Chronic (The Mountaineers, 1988).

"Pain, Reality, and Romance in the Desert," by Ron Penner, (*Wasatch*

Canyon Reporter, April 1995).

Petroglyphs and Pictographs of Utah, vol. 2, *The South, Central, West and Northwest*, by Kenneth B. Castleton (Utah Museum of Natural History, 1987).

The Prehistory of the Southwest, by Linda S. Cordell (Academic Press, 1984).

The Quiet Crisis and the Next Generation, by Stewart Udall (Peregrine Smith, 1988).

Roadside Geology of Utah, by Halka Chronic (Mountain Press Publishing, 1990).

"Ron Penner reached the NOLS semester group at midnight," by Liane Owen, the leader (NOLS, 1995).

San Juan Canyons: A River Runner's Guide, by Don Baars and Gene Stevenson (Cañon Publishers, 1986).

Sand County Almanac, by Aldo Leopold (Oxford University Press, 1987).

Silent Spring, by Rachel Carson (Fawcett Crest, 1964).

"Southeastern Utah Map #5," Utah Multipurpose Maps (Utah Travel Council, 1987).

"The Southwest," by William D. Lipe, in *Ancient Native Americans*, edited by Jesse D. Jennings (W. H. Freeman and Company, 1978).

Time, Space, and Transition in Anasazi History, by Michael S. Berry (University of Utah Press, 1982).

Using GPS, by Conrad Dixon (Sheridan House, 1994).

Utah Atlas and Gazetteer, 3rd edition (DeLorme, 2000).

Utah Hiking: The Complete Guide to More Than 300 of the Best Hikes in Utah, by Buck Tilton (Foghorn Press, 1999).

Utah History Encyclopedia, edited by Allan Kent Powell (University of Utah Press, 1994).

Utah Place Names, edited by John W. Van Cott (University of Utah Press, 1990).

Utah Wilderness Inventory U.S. Department of the Interior, Bureau of Land Management (1999).

Walden, by Henry David Thoreau (AMS Press, 1982).

"When Bad Water Goes Good," by Buck Tilton, *Paddler Magazine* (November/December 1998).

Wild Utah: A Guide to 45 Roadless Recreation Areas, by Bill Cunningham and Polly Burke (Falcon Publishing, 1998).

"Wilderness at the Edge: A Citizen Proposal to Protect Utah's Canyons and Deserts," by the Utah Wilderness Coalition (1990).

Wind in the Rock, by Ann Zwinger (Harper and Row, 1978).

About the Author

PETER FRANCIS TASSONI WAS BORN IN THE MIDWEST IN 1966 AND RAISED in western Washington. A graduate of the University of Washington, he has climbed the volcanic peaks of the Cascades, floated many of the rivers in the western United States, and explored the deserts of the Southwest in a vain attempt to avoid responsibility and its trappings. He is an amateur geologist, pontificating poet, and dedicated desert river rat. He would rather sleep safely among the coyotes than tempt fate in a four-star hotel. His articles on adventure and the environment have appeared in local, regional, and national publications. Speaking of himself, he says, "I work like I don't need money, dance like nobody is watching, and live like tomorrow is a faded memory."

Acknowledgments

I WOULD LIKE TO ACKNOWLEDGE THE FOLLOWING PEOPLE FOR THEIR
direct and indirect assistance in developing this guidebook: Jamie
Baucum, for spending a few rainy October days tending the coffeepot
and passing out chocolate cookies; Mark Bennett, for his camera
equipment and enthusiasm to "test" several routes; Dennis McGrane
and his three sons, who loaned me their Optimus stove when mine
failed along the Kane Gulch–Collins Spring Canyon route; Dave Shearer,
for the navigation tools; Cliff and Becky Soderberg, for shuttling me
back from Collins Spring Canyon to Kane Gulch Ranger Station after
a miserable snowy trip during which I was suffering from a viral
infection; and all the folks with the National Park Service, Bureau of
Land Management, and Utah State Archaeology offices for their
assistance in providing corrections to this manuscript.

I also want to thank the folks at Bio-Foods Inc. for their generous
donation of Balance Bars in support of this endeavor. I especially liked
the almond brownie ones.

Scott DuBois at All Topo Maps in Salt Lake City introduced me to
digitized USGS map technology.

I'd like to thank my partner, Wendy Lagerquist, and her yellow
Labrador retriever, Reese, for their hiking companionship; the Hallz
family, for hosting me in their home while I revised the manuscript; and
finally, Jeff Grathwohl, for having the courage to nurture this guide and
its author through the arduous publishing process.